T0168358

Of Men and Monsters

Of Men and Monsters

*Jeffrey Dahmer and the Construction
of the Serial Killer*

Richard Tithecott

Foreword by James R. Kincaid

THE UNIVERSITY OF WISCONSIN PRESS

The University of Wisconsin Press
1930 Monroe Street
Madison, Wisconsin 53711

3 Henrietta Street
London WC2E 8LU, England

Copyright © 1997
The Board of Regents of the University of Wisconsin System
All rights reserved

3   5   7   6   4

Printed in the United States of America

Library of Congress Cataloging-in-Publication Data

Tithecott, Richard.
Of men and monsters: Jeffrey Dahmer and the construction of the
serial killer / Richard Tithecott; foreword by James R. Kincaid.
206 pp.   cm.
Includes bibliographical references and index.
ISBN 0-299-15680-X (cloth: alk. paper)
ISBN 0-299-15684-2 (paperback: alk. paper)
1. Serial murderers.   2. Dahmer, Jeffrey.   I. Title.
HV6515.T57   1997
a364.15'23'092—dc21
[B]   97-15170

To the memory of my mother,

Margaret Tithecott

Contents

Contents

Foreword

Recent surveys of the store of general knowledge possessed by Americans reveal that 11 percent have a firm grasp of evaporation; 23 percent know pretty much where the equator is; 63 percent can identify Jimmy Carter and 34 percent Gerald Ford; over 8 percent can do long division; Edgar Alan Poe is correctly linked to "writer" by 19 percent; as for the larynx, almost as many people regard it as "a body part" as feel it is "some kind of animal"; and one person (0.002 percent) can locate Lake Huron on a map. Yet a solid 100 percent, every single adult and child, knows Jeffrey Dahmer, identifies him as serial killer, homosexual, cannibal, ghoul—now dead, killed by a righteous man, albeit a prison inmate, who had had enough.

Why is Jeffrey Dahmer number one? Why should that be? Why should Jeffrey Dahmer mean so much to us, figure so prominently in our cultural geography? Even if I haven't got the survey results quite right—though I heard about them from Mother, who got them from her friend Bess—I'm sure the point is still valid and the questions just as stinging. What are we doing with Jeffrey Dahmer and all other serial killers? Why do we construct them as we do? What do they represent for us? What stories do they allow us to circulate? What conditions of "knowing" do they generate? What needs do they bring into being and then serve? What cultural itches do they scratch?

It's clear enough that we have a not very clandestine affair going with these monster-hunks, these white male superhero fiends, these Hannibal Lecters. We build them up as Others so we can fear and despise them, while we long for them and admire them. They are projections not only of nightmare but of some dark wish fulfillment we want to play with but not acknowledge. We keep our relations with the serial killer under cover, where all the fun is.

But it's not just fun, as Richard Tithecott shows—certainly not harmless fun. In this barrel-house brilliant study, Tithecott uncovers grisly point after grisly point, not about the serial killer but about us and our needs. It's like taking a tour through Jeffrey Dahmer's freezer, only to find out we are the ones who've done the shopping and stocked it. Less metaphorically, this is a book not about what makes the serial killer tick but about those of us, all of us, who have wound the clock and need to keep it running. Less metaphorically still, Tithecott asserts at the start that serial killers are not simply an assault on our cultural center, totally outside our moral circumference, but continuous with it, necessary to it. The "perversion" of the serial killer, he says, is a "fulfillment" of our civilization.

To make good on this radical and deeply unwelcome claim, Tithecott leads us briskly and with unwavering acuity through a labyrinthine set of interconnecting links in the makeup of this seductive and indispensable serial killer. He probes, for instance, why this figure is seen as mysterious but sane, beyond the reach of psychiatrists and philosophers, but somehow within the ken of the psychic/intuitive and, most centrally, of the police, the FBI. These serial killers, always "evil" as well as sane, extend the boundaries of the police enormously, extend them specifically into moral territory. The FBI becomes an agency of good, of God, as it tracks down, as only it can, these inhuman monsters. Thus, as the police becomes scientized, they also become sanctified. This promotion of police omnipotence is a deeply conservative move, suggesting the fascist attractions of this serial killer construction.

The serial killer, Tithecott points out, is "motiveless," which means there's nothing to do with him but hunt him down; he exists in an isolated Gothic world where all that counts is eradicating the horror. Any attempt to "explain" the serial killer is always seen as weak, unmanly; it is really to be in league with them, sympathizing with them in a feminine or queer way. The motiveless serial killer serves not only a patriarchal myth but a brutally misogynistic and homophobic one too.

Tithecott's serial killers also serve the culture's need to avoid systemic problems by isolating and individualizing. These inexplicable and motiveless monsters are seen as freaks of nature, never as a social problem. Insofar as they can be comprehended, they need to be comprehended in reference to catastrophe, to extreme trauma. The myth of origins, rooted in the same comforting belief in individualism, allows us to see these serial killers, though never with sympathy, as results of "bad families," unlike the good families we have everywhere else.

Jeffrey Dahmer stands at the center of this study both because he is such a spectacular instance of our culture's employment of the serial killer and because he also challenges it. For instance, what exactly is the importance of his cannibalism and why do we make so much of it?

Tithecott suggests that Dahmer's munching on his victims—if indeed he actually did so—is so important to us for a host of reasons connected to needs almost unimaginably deep—needs, too, that recently have been hungering, the demand for cannibals so greatly exceeding the supply.

Dahmer is the white savage, Tithecott shows, a contradiction in terms. He is also the nice boy, the son of everybody in Ohio, who somehow went wrong. Did he come from a bad family, an abusive one? Were they poor, sexually twisted, black, non-Christian? Nope. Dahmer is a challenge to us, partly because, if we look closely, he seems so little a product of a particular family, so much a manufacture of a general cultural need. Lionel Dahmer's *A Father's Story* tries desperately to establish a focused family-centered explanation: Where did I go wrong?

Lionel Dahmer, a decent and responsible middle-class guy with a Ph.D. in chemistry and equal credentials in good parenting, provides an account so intelligent and so bent on self-blame and on skewing the record that it broadcasts its own despair at finding a spot for the parent as sufficient grounds for understanding. He often tries simply to announce that he's on to Jeffrey's perversions, having located "their distant origins within myself" (212), that "the only difference . . . was that I had awakened out of a nightmare, and my son had awakened into one" (215). But what *was* Lionel's nightmare, and in what way was he like Jeffrey? Lionel was often overly concerned with details, could have spent more time with the boy (though he seems to have been pretty attentive, all things considered), lacked sparkling social skills, had trouble expressing feelings. Recognize yourself here? Your kid a cannibal? Lionel ends wistfully, "I have come to believe that some of the compulsions that overwhelmed my son may have had their origins in me" (253), a sentence that flaps so feebly in the breeze ("I have come to believe . . . some . . . may have?) it testifies only to the senior Dahmer's willingness to try hard. "Fatherhood remains," he says, "a grave enigma," so grave (and enigmatic) that he warns "every father after me, 'Take care, take care, take care!' " (255). Take care of what?

If we look too long at Jeffrey Dahmer, Jeffrey Dahmer begins to look back at us. The serial killer is not just what we need, but what we need, before too long, to kill. We win both ways: we project our darkest urges outward, play with them, and then, in a fit of righteous denial, squash and deny them.

Richard Tithecott sees all this and shows us, with wonderful clarity, just how the process works. No study I know goes more deeply and shrewdly into our alliance with serial killers. This is not, however, a smash-mouth book, content to pulverize us with our own complicity. Tithecott's wit can be devastating, but it is always generous; and this book is written not as a satiric exposé but as a kind of prescription, a cultural analysis that offers not just insight but new possibilities. It is, finally, a gracious book, allowing us the opening to shape our needs in new forms, forms more open and lithe. This great book lets light into the darkest dungeons we built and asks us to turn them into dance halls.

JAMES R. KINCAID

Acknowledgments

For their wonderful support and encouragement, I would like to thank my family: Terry, Margaret, Michael, Adèle, William, and Alice. I am deeply grateful to my wife and best friend, Sheila, both for her love and for her invaluable help in writing the book. Among my friends and colleagues, Nancy J. Vickers and Vincent Cheng deserve special mention for their creativity, energy and humor. Many thanks also to the following: Andrew Harley, Raphael Kadushin, Sheila Leary, and Colleen Heinkel.

Of Men and Monsters

Introduction

Geraldo:	Jack, in the old days were there many of these guys—many Jack the Rippers out there? Or is this a modern-day phenomenon?
Jack Olsen:	There was Jack the Ripper and hardly anybody else. It is a modern phenomenon and it's an American phenomenon for the most part. The FBI feel there's more than three hundred of them going at any given time.
Geraldo:	Right now?
Jack Olsen:	Yes, caught and uncaught.
Sondra London:	I think it depends on your definition. If we look back in history we had the gunslingers who would be called serial killers today. Dan Rolling likes to go back to the knights of old when a man was revered for his prowess with a double-sided sword.
Geraldo:	Danny was quite a chivalrous fellow.

(*Geraldo*, 29 March 1993: "Inside the Mind of Serial Killers and the Women Who Love Them." Jack Olsen is the author of a book on Arthur J. Shawcross, convicted of killing ten prostitutes. Sondra London has written on—and, at the time of the show's airing, was the fiancée of—Dan Rolling, "The Gainesville Killer.")

Although society has always produced for itself a plentiful supply of monsters to choose from, it seems to me that contemporary monstrosity assumes its most compelling form for us as the serial killer. Whether or not the number of people who kill repeatedly has risen in recent years, the *idea* of the serial killer seems to be increasingly important to the way we perceive our world. Whether or not our contemporary construction of the serial killer is a new way to represent an old phenomenon, or whether it represents a new reality, it is one with which we seem particularly fascinated, one which seems to require continual rewriting or—in a period which has seen the release of *The Silence of the Lambs, Jennifer Eight, Henry: Portrait of a Serial Killer, Sliver, Natural Born Killers, Seven*, and numerous other serial killer epics—rescreening. Our construction of the serial killer, the construction of ourselves as audience to that spectacle, and the relationship between spectacle and audi-

3

ence are the subjects of this book. The figure of the serial killer I draw is blurred: a figure conflated with an image of its representer.

Several commentators support Jack Olsen's claim that serial killing is all-American. For Robert Ressler, it "has become something as American as apple pie" (in Davis 1991, 166). For Deborah Cameron and Elizabeth Frazer, serial killing is "the (as yet) specifically American phenomenon" (Cameron and Frazer 27). Jack Levin and James Alan Fox use "America's Growing Menace" as the sub-title for their book *Mass Murder* (1985). However, while we may begin with an idea of serial killing as being specifically a part of American or American-influenced culture,[1] or even, in moments of deepest cynicism, as being an American Dream come true, the more we talk about it, the more we want to universalize it, to describe it in ways which imply that the mysterious, conveniently indescribable thing we call "nature" is really what's behind it all. Noting that "in the last twenty years the United States, with only five percent of the world's population, has produced seventy-five percent of the world's serial murderers", Joel Norris suggests that "as the influence of American culture spreads to less developed countries, the fear is that, unless checked somehow, the *disease* of serial murder will spread as well" (my italics; Norris 1988, 19). While Norris can hear Bundy, Berkowitz, and Gacy humming "The Star-Spangled Banner" as they work, fears that our value-system might be connected to what they do are assuaged by putting such behavior on a par with a viral infection. With other diseases we're quick to provide a social context, but here we're quite happy to allow nature free play. We'd rather not ask why the "disease" seems to infect only the dominant, or once-dominant, social nexus, white men. While we may accept figures from the FBI telling us that "over the years, it's become clear that most [serial killer] offenders are white males" (*Newsweek*, 5 August 1991:41), we fail to explore correspondence between the meanings we give to serial killing and the meaning of masculinity and of whiteness in modern America. In his book on Dahmer, Norris remarks that serial killers "represent an attack on the entire moral structure of a community" (Norris 1992, 264). My project is in part to make the point that they are *represented* as such and that this representation has a his-

1. Philip Jenkins, among others, questions the idea that "there is a peculiarly American vulnerability to this sort of crime" (Jenkins 1994, 41). He suggests that statistics indicating a high frequency of serial killing in the United States might be attributable to "a greater awareness of the offense than in other countries, and a greater willingness by law enforcement agencies to recognize linkages between murders" (41). Moreover, he argues, speculation about serial murder activity on the scale that occurs in the United States is less likely in other countries, especially British-influenced ones, owing to stricter libel laws.

tory. In the process I hope to give room to the possibility that a part of that moral structure might be continuous with, not opposed to, the phenomenon.

The construction of the serial killer is, I suggest, built on the denial of such a possibility. When it is stated that "some researchers estimate that since 1980 murders with unknown motives have increased by 270 percent," and that "official statistics" confirm that "in 1988 as many as 4,859 murders were committed in the United States by someone with an unclear or unknown reason" (Sears, x),[2] to what extent do the terms *unknown motive* or *unknown reason* indicate a refusal to make sense of such violence in a way which would associate serial killing with some of society's dominant values? Jeffrey Dahmer, the killer of mostly blacks, of mostly gays, is sometimes perceived as a "hate killer," as a homophobe, as a racist, but he is represented more often as something else and something more, a fully fledged serial killer, a figure imbued with mystery and power. The serial killer has hate within his soul, but it is hate whose source is perceived as asocial, not of the world we know.

Sometimes denial takes the form of distancing ourselves from the killer by exaggerating the macabre nature of his acts. Sometimes it takes the form of silence, of figuring him as inhabiting a world of the ineffable, beyond language, beyond culture. When the latter occurs, the killer who emerges is one endowed with power, for power is something we like to imagine belonging above and beyond our worlds and our words. And with the Gothic identified as a space ruled by the power beyond, we find it natural to place our heroes within familiar Gothic narratives. Among Hollywood's favorite ways to tell a story, such narratives are, S. L. Vernado suggests, propelled by "the numinous": "the non-rational factor in the idea of the divine and its relation to the rational" which informs "man's underlying sense of supernatural fear, wonder, and delight when he is confronted by the divine" (Vernado 58). Hearing about Jeffrey Dahmer building a temple of self-worship out of body parts, experimenting in divinity, regarding himself as a numen, we're not slow in dreaming him up as the embodiment of the irrational to our boring rationality. If it is estrangement, it is estrangement accompanied by wonder and delight. The serial killer, both repulsive and attractive, verges on the sacred.

Like all sacred beings, one of his greatest assets is his invisibility. For the serial killer "on the loose," this is what separates him from the average murderer. Invisibility gives him the status of being "lost," of

2. Eric W. Hickey mentions Holmes and DeBurger (19–21) and Ressler, Burgess, and Douglas (2) as also documenting a "dramatic rise of stranger-to-stranger homicides, or murders with no apparent motive" (Hickey 3).

being threateningly "free." In an age in which the value of images perhaps exceeds the value of words, the search for the serial killer is the search for visual identification rather than explication. However, when he is caught, we cannot look at him for long. We feel the need to turn away. He is taboo. His image says everything and nothing, for it is "normality" which stares back at us. The brief glimpse we allow ourselves is enough to tell us what we want to know, enough to frighten and delight us. It is ourselves we see. The serial killer is inscribed with the power of unspeakableness, of meaning suspended, unheeded. Refusing to read the signs, we return them. The serial killer construction is polysemous, and shines brightly with meaning returned to its source.

Here I wish to write a history of the serial killer's empowerment. It is a history which has correspondence with the histories of gender, race, and class. Our failure to disempower the serial killer can depend upon our failure to question what power means to us. Discussing *The Silence of the Lambs'* Hannibal Lecter, Dennis Nilsen (convicted British serial killer) says, "He is shown as a potent figure, which is pure myth. It is his power and manipulation which please the public. But it's not at all like that. My offenses arose from a feeling of inadequacy, not potency. I never had any power in my life" (quoted in Masters 1991, 185). Contrasting with Nilsen's serial killer is our potentate, our man on a quest, constructed in part with the help of the term *serial killer* itself. Nilsen suggests that the term is misleading because of the implied intention to repeat: "Each one seemed to be its own last time. . . . You might as well call Elizabeth Taylor a serial bride" (Masters 1991, 265). Why should we inscribe the figure of the serial killer with power, and what relation might that construction have with culturally acceptable meanings of power? What relation might there be between that inscription of power and the fact that the majority of serial killers' victims are those commonly perceived as weak, as lacking cultural presence: single, unemployed "drifters", prostitutes, or women in general?

According to a psychologist called to the witness stand, Dahmer's collecting of human heads, limbs, and genitals can be interpreted as a reenactment (in his own special way) of a benign and familiar role. While noting that "it was very, very bizarre behavior," the witness added that considering that hunters display animal heads without being considered psychotic or paraphiliac, it was also a "pretty realistic way to keep trophies" (quoted in Ullman 30). Similarly, Wilson and Seaman argue that serial killers who retain certain body parts do so "for much the same reason as the big-game hunter mounts the head and antlers taken from his prey" (68). When we find ourselves conflating images of serial killers with roles created by, among others, Ernest Hemingway in order to find the former legally sane, perhaps it is time to find ways of foregrounding what it is we consider normal. Instead of interrogating Dahmer's past (and especially his childhood) in our search for, say, the "key" to his motivation, perhaps we need to examine the relation of dreams of violence, of racial or sexual purity, of closure, of death, to our dominant culture and its dreams.

Much of Michel Foucault's writing is concerned with the demarcation of social normality. In *Madness and Civilization* he claims that he is writing a history of the Other, positing Madness as outside the spheres of (and separate from) Reason (which oppresses Madness and thus forces it to the margins). Part of this book will be spent looking at or looking out from the representations of Dahmer in order to see how neatly or uncomfortably they lie in our histories of the Other or of the Same. The serial killer is represented as "mythical Other" (Jenkins 1994, 112), as a dangerous outsider who fulfills a "critical social function in defining conventional morality and behavior by providing a *ne plus ultra*, against which normal society readily finds common ground" (112), but at the same time I will suggest that the myth is constructed in a manner which also problematizes the finding of that common ground. Arguing that the roles played for us by the serial killer, and those that we play, the roles we play for him, are unstable, get confused (and not necessarily by accident), I will suggest that in certain instances our representation of the serial killer makes redundant the opposition of self and other, that "civilization" not only depends on "perversion," but that the "perversion" which the serial killer represents can be said to be the fulfillment of what goes for "civilization," the fulfillment of normative expectations. Another way of saying this is that "normality" and "perversion" exist together on a dynamic continuum as much as they are oppositional structures giving each other meaning.

The stories of serial killers which perhaps most threaten the divide between normality and perversion are those which describe a slow progression from nonviolence to violence. As well as contradicting the presumption of "evil" from the beginning, the idea of a gradual descent (as opposed to one giant leap) helps to destabilize the idea of a secure divide between self and other, between the normality and the abnormality of the serial killer. Such an idea may appear not too discordant with an approach to crime which considers beastliness and criminality to be a latent quality of all of us. From such a perspective self-control is that which marks the civilized from the savage: "There will always be a dark side of human nature," says a Milwaukee psychiatrist in one of the books on Dahmer; the dark side is the motivation for us to master and grow with it, managing it the best you can. There will always be mass murderers" (Davis 1991, 265). But the need for "other control" can be expressed as fervently as the need for "self-control." For *Halloween* director John Carpenter, "liberal" horror movies, those which say that "the evil is within our tribe and inside of us," contrast with the "conservative" ones like the science fiction movies of the fifties, those which say that "the evil is outside of us and our tribe—demons we have to fight off" (*People Weekly*, 1 April 1991: 70). I hope to exclude myself from both approaches to crime (hope, in other words, to mess up that all-inclusive binary) by removing nature from the equation. Without nature, without the sense of inevitability it engenders, we are left with uncertainties, with a world which we have created, with a world which only we can change, and perhaps a world in which there will not "always be mass murderers." In other words, without nature it all comes back to us, to ourselves, to our perception of the self and of the other. And if we remove nature, perhaps we also reduce the criminal's perceived power (and therefore attraction), or at least the power which comes from being perceived as enduring, *true*. A possibility I explore is that this partnership of nature and crime has been, in effect, a partnership *in crime*, that there is a connection between the naturalization of the criminal and the expectancy and the reality of victimhood.

"With the new year," writes Don Davis, Dahmer "was about to send his awful scoreboard into double digits" (1991, 126). We like to talk about serial killing in terms of sports. It gives us a framework for assessing just how important we should consider a serial killer to be: "Can you give us some indication as to what would be a range, a ball park figure as to what crimes this individual has likely committed?" asks the Chair in the House of Representatives Hearing on serial killing (*House* 71). Helping to make those sport metaphors seem more appropriate, and concurrent with the recent glut in baseball player trading cards, is the availability of serial killer trading cards. As well as offering the illusion of possessing and controlling our favorite monsters, the fun of collecting serial killer cards, as with any other trading cards, is comparing statistics. Listed on the Jeffrey Dahmer card would no doubt be the following data: Born in 1960; white male; seventeen male victims; victims killed in Wisconsin and Ohio between 1978 and 1991; victims mostly gay, mostly black or Hispanic; had sex with, mutilated, and sometimes ate his victims. Information which would not appear is that he "came from what might be construed as a typical, all-American middle-class family" and that he "apparently did not come from an impoverished or deprived background" (Norris 1992, 265).

In order to offer some answers to the questions mentioned in this introduction, or at least in order to find some more questions to ask, I have focused on our representation of the man who will no doubt prove to be one of the most enduring of serial killing superstars. I discuss how books, movies, magazine and newspaper articles, jokes, and network talk-shows all contribute to the construction of the Dahmer myth. I also consider how we have perceived other serial killers of the last decade or so and how we have previously read or created the idea of monstrosity. I pay attention particularly to Thomas Harris's *The Silence of the Lambs* and its movie version. Harris's novel and Jonathan Demme's movie were of crucial significance to the way Dahmer was represented, owing to their content and contemporaneousness with the breaking of Dahmer's story. They also provide for us, perhaps more than any other contemporary texts, the opportunity to drool over and get turned on by repeat murderers.

As I have suggested in this introduction, the representation of Dahmer includes both elements of denial (denial that the serial killer has any connection with normality) and of celebration (of the serial killer's perceived transcendence of normality), a release from that denial, the expression of those repressed dreams, so to speak. The structure of the book—if we can stretch this mind metaphor just a moment longer—might be read as inducing a move from the assumed safety of conscious denial to those subconscious spaces which inform our collective fantasy life. Part 1 is a discussion of the "forces" of that denial, of the police and the police mentality which simultaneously constructs and polices abnormality (as a means of exonerating normality). In chapter 1, I suggest that the FBI has appropriated from psychiatry the power to define for us the meaning of contemporary monstrosity. The importance of the monster that emerges lies in its function as ultimate referent for policing discourses, in its naturalizing the power of those discourses, and in its justifying increased policing powers. In the remaining chapters of Part 1, I describe discourses which cloak investigative policing with the benignity of investigative journalism, discourses we all speak without questioning their values and assumptions. I aim to examine their centers, their constructions of unspeakableness, and to identify what they mystify. The unspeakable, I will suggest, does not stay silent.

In Part 2, I describe the different ways we construct the serial killer in our own image. I suggest that we are both thrilled and horrified by what we see, that we exist in a kind of horror movie which we write and perform for ourselves daily. The jury rejected the argument of Dahmer's attorney that Dahmer "became enamored, overwhelmed, caught up in the character in *Exorcist III*" (*Los Angeles Times*, 31 January 1992:A4). However, like readers of a postmodern mystery, a genre which David Richter notes "revolves around the use of labyrinths, mirrors, auto-referentiality, and other analogues to the self-conscious use of textuality" (Richter 106), we are unable or unwilling to distinguish between observation of and involvement in teleworld or movieland. In an age in which collective dreams seem more easily realizable, more likely to surface, the nature of those dreams, I argue, becomes all the more important. The blurring of *particular* fantasies (fantasies of power, especially male power) with reality (or in other words, the realization of those fantasies) is contextualized, I suggest, by what Margaret Morse calls this "cultural shift away from the forms of realism, literacy, and objectivity which have been dominant in Western culture since the Renaissance and the age of industrialization" (Morse 76). The suggestion of a connection between fantasy and behavior is of course contentious. Debate took another turn in 1996 when John Grisham, claiming Oliver Stone's *Natural Born Killers* inspired the murder of his friend, William Savage, called for films to be subject to product liability (reported in *Variety*, 17 June 1996: 11–12). My comments in Part 2 turn on the idea that bridging the gap between fantasy and a violent reality is perhaps made a little easier when we regard real-life killers and their victims as characters in a fantasy world, when our representations of real-life killers are indistinguishable from movie heroes (ideas which, Oliver Stone would argue, *Natural Born Killers* explores). In the concluding chapter of Part 2 I describe in more detail how the serial killer figure and its others are constructed in relation to ideas of power and weakness. The intention is to suggest how that opposition can be defamiliarized.

Some readers will no doubt feel offended by the assumption of their participation in the discourses under discussion, an assumption expressed by the constant use of the term *we*. It is a term whose meaning will shift considerably. Sometimes it will refer to "we men," those of us whose sense of self is constituted in part by the history of and by expectations of masculinity. Sometimes it can signify "we white men and women." At other times it can refer to those of us who consider ourselves or who are considered "heterosexual," or "educated," or "middle-class." And of course it will refer at times to a combination of these and other ways we define ourselves. I haven't needed to pass through a swinging door in the back of a used-book store or to subscribe to an obscure cable channel in order to find the quotations I use in this study. Mostly they have been taken from magazines with large circulations, from newspapers claiming national status, from television shows with the highest ratings. When I read the *New York Times* or watch *The Oprah Winfrey Show*, I read and watch with the assumption of belonging to a readership or viewing audience that has a semblance of common beliefs and understanding. I feel I am one of a crowd. *We* will signify that crowd or that illusory crowd, that mass readership or mass viewing audience to which I imagine the words I read and hear are addressed.

I write for the possibility that those who see themselves as wholly outside of my representation might feel momentarily that it resonates with their perception of normality, that they will at times pass over that *we* unquestioningly. And yet perhaps I construct for myself a privileged position. I may open the *New York Times* or switch on to *Oprah* and be a part of mass culture, but I allow myself the belief that I am able to locate my position within "the mass." I assume powers of self-reflexivity. The serial killer I see haunts his common representation. He is the monster within, or rather he is monstrous normality within the monster of serial killer mythology. Identifying myself with the normal and remarking on its monstrosity is to have a contradictory perspective, allowing me to confess, Frankenstein-like, that the serial killer I see is my monster, my creation—that I write the serial killer and I write my self.

PART I

Policing the Serial Killer

We even told [the investigators] where [a suspect] would live and the type of dogs he would have. In this case, Doberman pinschers or German shepherds. The only reason we said that—not that we have anything against Doberman pinschers or German shepherds—is it is just that we believed he was a paranoid individual. (An FBI officer explaining the benefits of personality profiling at a House of Representatives Hearing on Serial Killing, *House* 22)

Reflecting on *The Order of Things,* Foucault in *Power/Knowledge* remarks: "My problem was to ascertain the sets of transformations in the regime of discourses necessary and sufficient for people to use these words rather than those, a particular type of discourse rather than some other type, for people to be able to look at things from such and such an angle and not some other one" (211). In chapter 1, I suggest that we are using different words to describe criminal monstrosity. Our dominant policing discourses, used both within and without the police community, describe a world threatened more by inexplicable horror than by various forms of medically and legally defined insanity.[1] The horror evoked is beyond the reach of psychiatry, is indicative of a madness which cannot be treated, and consequently imprisonment or execution (as opposed to hospitalization) are perceived as the state's only suitable response. Central to such discourses is the idea of evil, the widespread acceptance of which, I suggest, allows those who protect society from its monsters to once again assume an aura of priestly authority.

Many of the discourses' terms are those favored by and indeed first used by the National Center for the Analysis of Violent Crime (NCAVC). This FBI service is located at the FBI Academy in Quantico

1. The majority of states, including Wisconsin (the state in which Dahmer committed the majority of his crimes), apply the test for insanity established by the American Law Institute in 1962. According to Section 4.01 of the Model Penal Code: "A person is not responsible for criminal conduct if at the time of such conduct as a result of mental disease or defect he lacks substantial capacity either to appreciate the wrongfulness of his conduct or to conform his conduct to the requirements of law."

and is run by agents of the Behavioral Science Unit. In 1984 its establishment was formally announced by President Reagan, who gave it the primary mission of "identifying and tracking repeat killers." It is responsible for the creation of systematic personality-profiling techniques known as the Criminal Investigative Analysis Program. In recent years its reputation as a locus of power and knowledge has grown considerably. NCAVC is the center to which Wilson and Seaman refer when they state that "clearly, there [is] only one oracle to consult" on the problem of serial killing, and they call its members the "FBI's renowned 'A Team' " (117). It is also home to the *The Silence of the Lambs'* Jack Crawford and Clarice Starling.

The policing discourses I describe are becoming dominant in "the media" (not always distinguishable from the judiciary when trials are televised). They are spoken by those presented by television as experts on serial killing, and by those cited in magazine articles. In an age in which the concerns of entertainment are the concerns of the police, in which representations of the police dominate our mass media, and in which many of our television and cinema heroes are real or fictional members of elite police chapters, the particular ways we construct criminal monstrosity indicate, I suggest, an intensification of what might be called a cultural "policing mentality."

In chapters 2 and 3, I discuss some specifics of this policing mentality: processes of individualization upon which dominant policing discourse relies; the construction of "family" and "childhood" as origins of the serial killer phenomenon and consequently as spaces which can and should be policed; and the simultaneous construction of and investigation of "the unspeakable." In chapter 4, however, I examine how attempts to police the idea of normality can founder when Dahmer unsettles traditional distinctions between the civilized and the savage.

16

1

Defining the Monster
Serial Killing and the FBI

For years the Marquis de Sade has been an object lesson in how a monster ought to behave. Bataille uses the term *volupté* in reference to the wicked Frenchman, a term Jane Gallop explains, "is characterized by the exceeding of a certain quantitative level. The prevalence of quantification and categorization and the vast number of victims in Sade's text account for Sade's unprecedented success in doing violence to humanistic notions of man's dignity and individuality. The Sadian hero appears as someone with an insatiable quota to fill, someone with an heroic task which does not afford him any simple pleasure" (Gallop 30). In Downtown Milwaukee, Jeffrey Dahmer, or "The Man Who Could Not Kill Enough" as Anne E. Schwartz describes him in the title of her book, does his best to emulate the aristocrat of murder and mayhem. Or so the story goes. Never mind Dennis Nilsen's assertion that the term *serial killer* is misleading on the grounds that each murder is intended to be the last. Our monsters are on an (anti)heroic quest for the biggest score possible. For the Sadian monster, this task is mingled with everyday life, a combination which constitutes his monstrosity: "The intensity which is the seriousness of *volupté* becomes intolerable by being deflected onto everything, onto the innocent little pleasures of everyday life. The result is not pure violence, but the violently impure" (Gallop 33). On one level Dahmer's life seems to have been the pursuit of those simple pleasures. But he always managed to mess up, get it wrong somehow. Sharing a beer with friends would have been fine until one of them opened the refrigerator. Lunch with his colleagues at the chocolate factory would seem like a nice way of breaking the monotony. Only Jeffrey has to spoil it all by filling his sandwiches with leftovers from the night before. Dahmer can be the Sadian "monster

17

within": the perverse within the mundane, the unnatural within the natural, the animal within the social, the antiheroic within the unheroic. He is the archetypal figure of impurity, the representative of a world which needs cleansing.

If Sade is too aristocratic or too foreign, then there are models to be had much closer to home, namely, those familiar monsters of the nineteenth-century novel. Dahmer is "the average-looking man" (Schwartz, picture caption), a "former tennis player, the son of middle-class parents" (Davis 1991, back cover), who has the appearance of being "a nice guy" (Norris 1992, 1). But Dahmer, the boy next door, is also he who emitted "wolflike howling" and "demonic screams" (Norris 1992, 8) when he was arrested, and when we read that "many witnesses quoted in the press have attested to his extraordinary Jekyll-and-Hyde transformations when drinking" (Masters 1991, 266), we have little trouble in constructing Dahmer as the latest descendant of Stevenson's character(s). When we tell stories about our monsters, we like to imply that their monstrosity is everywhere, only hidden from view, concealed within. The figure of the serial killer is "violent impurity" personified, and it is a construction that necessitates figures of violent purity to confront it. The expulsion of the perverse from the mundane, the unnatural from the natural, the animal from the social are heroic tasks, and the heroes who perform them need to be mirror images of the men who threaten man's dignity and individuality.

Mary Douglas has written extensively on the involvement of the opposition of pure and impure in the way we classify the world around us. She suggests that "reflection on dirt involves reflection on the relation of order to disorder, being to non-being, form to formlessness, life to death" (Douglas 5). Describing oneself as an agent of cleanliness is a tried and tested way of justifying one's actions. Having a crack at appealing to our sense of order, the self-proclaimed "Streetcleaner," Peter Sutcliffe, explains, "The women I killed were filth, bastard prostitutes who were just standing round littering the streets. I was just cleaning the place up a bit" (quoted in Beattie 81). Historically, to be designated society's Mr. Clean has been a good way of gaining state-sanctioned power. With reference to nineteenth-century Britain, Peter Stallybrass and Allon White note that "the discursive elision of disease and crime suggested an elision of the means with which to cope with them: like crime, disease could be policed" (Stallybrass and White 133). "Policemen and soap" thus become "analogous: they penetrate the dark, public realm" (134). In our own society Jack Henry Abbot identifies such an elision of disease and crime and sees it as instrumental in the production of "the policeman mentality" that makes us believe "there is such a thing as a relentless enemy in human society that requires eradication and cannot ever be reconciled with human society" (Abbot 61). Represented as a new form of beastliness, the serial killer seems to invite existing policing/purifying powers to redefine themselves or concede to discourses for whom the new beast functions as ultimate referent: "Not really a traditional form of murder . . . this crime is actually a form of disease. Its carriers are serial killers who suffer from a variety of crippling and eventually fatal symptoms, and its immediate victims are the people struck down seemingly at random by the disease carriers. It is the disease of serial murder that is rapidly becoming an epidemic in American society today and one of the patterns of violence that the office of the U.S. Surgeon General has called one of the top-priority issues of public health" (Norris 1988, 12).

Before the serial killer, society had plenty of other diseased and filthy beasts with which to deal. Foucault identifies the homicidal maniac as the monster who sustains and justifies the power of nineteenth-century psychiatric discourse. Homicidal mania is "a necessity . . . linked to the very existence of a psychiatry which had made itself autonomous but needed thereafter to secure a basis for its intervention by gaining recognition as a component of public hygiene. And it could establish this basis only through the fact that there was a disease (mental alienation) for it to mop up" (Foucault 1980, 202). Foucault dramatizes the psychiatry profession's reasoning thus: "How can it be proved that madness constitutes a danger except by showing that there exist extreme cases where madness, even though not apparent to the public gaze, without manifesting itself beforehand through any symptom except a few minute fissures, miniscule murmurings perceptible only to the highly trained observer, can suddenly explode into a monstrous crime?" (Foucault 1980, 202). At the end of the twentieth century, the FBI are more willing to agree with, among others, Joel Norris, who says that the serial killer "is an entirely different criminal" (Norris 1988, 17) from any that came before. This change makes the beast less detectable to the old diagnosticians, lessens the ability of psychiatry to figure itself as society's agent of cleanliness, and increases the dominance of the police mentality, increases the powers of law enforcement—specifically, the FBI. The disease of serial killing as constructed by the FBI does not adversely affect the mental state of those it strikes. It is a disease which can be recognized by particular biographical facts. It is one which, in the void left by the absence of insanity as a credible judicial concept, can assume the appearance of that age-old and most flexible of estrangement tools, evil.

A Milwaukee journalist remembers, "When a local Baptist minister and his wife went to Dahmer's apartment and performed an exorcism, complete with speaking tongues and guttural growls as the evil spirits

19

filled them, we watched on television" (Schwartz 140). We watch the exorcism of Dahmer's apartment and don't flinch when we hear his attorney telling the jury that Dahmer's favorite movie was *The Exorcist* and that he showed it to some of his victims before drugging them. When he is charged in court, he wears an orange prison jumpsuit with a black T-shirt underneath: "Halloween colors. They suited the mood," reports the *Washington Post* (7 August 1991: B1). When his trial begins, one of its headlines promises "Ghoulish Details" (31 January 1992). The language of good and evil transcends the barrier between "serious" and "tabloid" journalism, and it is prevalent in Dahmer's own version of the events which led to his arrest. He tells police before the trial, "I have to question whether or not there is an evil force in the world and whether or not I have been influenced by it. . . . Although I am not sure if there is a God, or if there is a devil, I know that as of lately I've been doing a lot of thinking about both, and I have to wonder what has influenced me in my life" (quoted in Schwartz 200–1). Dahmer's pres-entence apology begins with "It is over" and ends with a quotation from Timothy: "Christ Jesus came into the world to save sinners—of whom I am the worst. But for that very reason I was shown mercy so that in me, the worst of sinners, Christ Jesus might display his unlim-ited patience as an example for those who would believe in him and receive eternal life. Now to the King Eternal, immortal, invisible, the only God, be honor and glory forever and ever" (quoted in Schwartz 219). Dahmer talks of "the doctors [who] have told me about my sick-ness" (quoted in Schwartz 217), but it is a sickness which we inscribe with satanic overtones.

One of the doctors Dahmer might have spoken to is Joel Norris, "renowned psychologist" as the cover of his book on Dahmer de-scribes him, a cover dripping with embossed blood. Cameron and Frazer note that despite there being few serious writers who "would care to admit to an explicit belief in original sin," we are able to put "a Freudian gloss" on the supposition of everyone's potential for evil. Unconcerned with even a Freudian gloss, Norris's *Serial Killers: The Growing Menace* describes a particular individual sliding "into his troll-ing phase" (Norris 1988, 21), and is a book described by the author "as the mirror of the fine line that separates each one of us from yielding to the primal, instinctual, animal behavior that lurks beneath the veneer of psychological self-control and social convention" (Norris 1988, 6). In Dahmer's story of Good and Evil, the Devil is defeated, and Dahmer offers himself to and asks forgiveness from God. But it is an apology we don't want to hear. We are happier if our monsters remain gar-goyles. So rigid is our division of the world into good and evil, normal-ity and monstrosity, that the man who putatively beat Dahmer to death with a broom handle can be placed on our side. "I hope there will be no economic returns or celebration as a folk hero for the man that killed Jeffrey Dahmer," says Milwaukee County District Attorney E. Michael McCann (The *New York Times.* 29 November 1994: A1), fearing, presumably, "A Just Dessert" to be society's tabloid reaction to the man-eating monster's violent end.

With our construction of the serial killer, extreme realizations of the dark side of human potential are inscribed with permanence, whether it is "evil" or, to use Norris's phrase, "primal, instinctual, animal behavior." In a *Washington Post* article, Charles Krauthammer notes that "post-Hinckley," the "irresistible impulse" is in decline and "unless Dahmer succeeds in reviving this defense, we may soon return to the wisdom of the eighteenth-century English test that exculpates the defendant if 'he doth not know what he is doing no more than . . . . a wild beast' " (7 February 1992: A25). Dahmer "admits having acted like a wild beast up to and including eating his prey," says Krauthammer, but "what he must prove is that he was as unknowing of the nature of his act as a Bengal tiger." The "wisdom" of that eighteenth-century test seems to have been on the mind of the prosecution in Dahmer's trial. In his final argument, Michael McCann helps to win the day with his rhetorical question to the jury: "Do you think that was . . . . a wild-eyed madman?" (quoted in the *Washington Post.* 16 February 1992: A21). Dahmer, says an expert witness in the trial, demonstrates his sanity by "remembering to reach for a condom" before copulating with his dead victims. Dahmer, says McCann, demonstrates his sanity by selecting his victims on the basis that they have no cars and therefore are less easily traceable. To be found mad is to be found animalistic. To be mad one must be visibly so. One cannot look normal and be insane. One must be raving.

The construction of the sane and evil monster is the latest sign of our current desire to seek a language of condemnation which brings closure, of the desire for the distinction of our "selves" from our "others" to be complete and lasting. Sane beings motivated by evil can be imprisoned or capitally punished *and* estranged from the rest of us. Our latest monster allows us to morally condemn at the same time as we give his acts the appearance of intelligibility and therefore responsibility. The cause of the crimes, evil, is inexplicable, beyond scientific investigation, but the acts themselves are the acts of a sane man. We are thus freed from a tangle of legal and psychiatric discourse which is perceived as protecting those whose actions are deemed gratuitous, beyond causal intelligibility, discourse referred to in a *National Review* editorial on the Dahmer trial entitled "So Guilty They're Innocent" (2 March 1992: 17–18).

The struggle with evil elevates the FBI to a community service, above politics. As fighters of evil, the FBI can assume the powers of a priesthood: that is, the power of being both attached to the law and above it, the power of the confessor, the power of possessing the right to regard an individual as a battleground between Satanic and Godly forces. In contrast to psychiatric discourse—that to which the serial killer and his attorneys can turn in order to negate questions of culpability—is the lofty discourse of the FBI, which has the power to distinguish right from wrong. In contrast to psychiatric discourse— that which has itself become unsanitary, that which contributes to the creation of an environment in which the serial killer thrives and is protected—is the purity of FBI discourse. Underground in a former nuclear bunker at Quantico, entry to which is controlled by key locks and cypher, members of the NCAVC work in an environment atmospherically controlled to protect their state-of-the-art computers. This is sanitized policing: "Once signed in and tagged with a badge, visitors are escorted along a corridor and down by elevator to the Behavioral Science Investigative Support wing, a futuristic high-tech beehive of a crime-fighting center, the only one of its kind in the world. Its business is the analysis of violent crime, not the physical arrest of violent criminals. There are no cells here, no interrogation rooms, no 'Most Wanted' posters; only desks and computers" (Wilson and Seaman 118). The new disease of serial killing is fought with sterilized efficiency. And in order to justify the higher status of FBI discourse compared with that of psychiatry, the disease of serial killing is one whose carriers must be perceived as more of a threat than their monstrous forbears. The empowerment of the serial killer serves to validate the exalted discourse of the FBI, while the exalted discourse of the FBI empowers the serial killer.

The conflict between the FBI and the profession of psychiatry is above all a conflict over language, over the meanings of words, over which words are relevant. It is a conflict described as follows by the FBI's John E. Douglas for the House of Representatives Hearing:

Police are going to these people, these psychiatrists and psychologists for the profiles, for the assessments, and they are not too good. These other profilers are using terms such as paranoid schizophrenia, manic depressive psychosis, and paranoia. . . . What do these terms mean to law enforcement? It doesn't mean anything to us. . . . So we developed our own terms, and back in 1980 Roy Hazelwood and myself in an article we wrote on the 'lust murderer' . . . came up with terms called organized and disorganized. . . . What we mean by organized and disorganized is that the crime or the crime scene reflects organization or it

22

may reflect disorganization. What do [we] mean disorganization? Well, disorganization could be caused by the youthfulness of the offender, or that the subject at the time of the offense was under the influence of alcohol or drugs so that's why it appears disorganized, or appears disorganized because of some mental defect on the part of the subject. (House 3)

Compared, then, to the debased and parochial language of psychology, compared to what the FBI call "psychological jargon" (House 22), is the clarity, purity and universality of the language spoken by the FBI. But for the FBI's construction of monstrosity to gain credence, it must also be inscribed with the mark of *truth*, and in a world of knowledge still mostly divided between scientific fact and artistic interpretation, the mark of truth is conferred by science. The creators of the personality profile are celebrated in the serial killing hearing thus: "What they have achieved in being able to develop the actual science that they have and the expertise, the level of it, is something that is quite a milestone in the law enforcement profession" (House 8). Elsewhere in the hearing, as the credibility of psychiatry's role in crime is questioned, psychiatry's scientific methodologies are appropriated: "The task of the investigator in developing a criminal personality profile is quite similar to the process used by clinicians to make a diagnosis and treatment plan: data is collected and assessed, the situation reconstructed, hypotheses are formulated, a profile developed and tested, and the results reported back" (House 28).

As the FBI seeks to give its discourses an aura of scientific truthfulness, psychiatry loses the public's confidence in its scientific credentials. Reporting on Dahmer's insanity trial, Charles Krauthammer, in a *Washington Post* article entitled "The Insanity Defense on Trial" (7 February 1992: A25), suggests that "people react with disgust" at the "trivialization" of the law by "pseudo-psychiatry." Such a person is CNN's Sonya Friedman in an edition of her show entitled "The Criminal Mind" (*Sonya Live*, 1 March 1993). After making her guest, psychiatrist Richard Kraus, feel at home by saying, "Three psychiatrists often have four opinions," she throws in an aside guaranteed to needle the most hardened of talk-show shrinks: "hardly a science." In *The New Republic*, Lincoln Caplan notes that much of the media covering the Dahmer trial treated the insanity defense as "a cause and a symbol of various social ills" (30 March 1992: 19). Instead of regarding the insanity defense as giving criminal law its "moral authority," as a "narrow exception" which strengthens a system "rooted in the idea of individual responsibility," society, says Caplan, commonly regards it as a symbol of lawlessness. When instances of disorder seem to have increased to the extent that the normality of order is threatened, and when instances of, in this case, insanity apparently rise to an extent that calls into question the normality of sanity, it can make sense to clear the way for a new system of categorization, to re-demarcate self from other.

Implying temporary disorder and possible recovery, suggesting a continuum on which we can all belong, mental illness is replaced in court by a form of madness marked with permanence, one which is visible to the layman. In the process the life of the science to which it relates inevitably declines. And outside of the court, too, we are growing tired of hearing that our criminal monsters may be suffering psychologically. A guest on *Geraldo* who has written on serial killing notes that in each of the fifty-two cases she has studied there was an "element of multiple personality present" (29 March 1993). Our impatient host cuts her short, not wanting "to get off on that." Compared to the omnipresence of inconspicuous and inexplicable serial killers, the exploration of paranoid schizophrenia, manic-depressive psychosis, or psychopathology doesn't seem to entertain us much these days. Now it is not minds we want to hunt, but persons, or rather personalities. And seeking, presumably, to justify such a shift is our (sometimes confusing) differentiation of personality disorders from psychological ones: "Most experts now agree that serial killers suffer from severe personality defects but are not apt to have such mental disorders as schizophrenia," says a *Newsweek* article on Dahmer (5 August 1991: 41). With such diagnoses, serial killers are bound for imprisonment or execution because personality disorders disallow the possibility of an insanity defense.

With regard to the validity of its involvement in the law, the psychiatric profession itself is beginning apparently to doubt itself. On a CNN *Crossfire* (whose subject, in the wake of Dahmer's decision to plead guilty but insane, was the insanity defense), Richard Vatz (psychology professor and associate psychology editor of *U.S. Today*) said that the American Psychiatric Association in its 1983 statement on the issue of legal insanity "disavowed the ability of psychiatrists to ascertain whether people could control their behavior." The statement, he continues, argued "that the ability to discern between an irresistible urge and resisting the urge is the . . . difference between twilight and dusk." Richard Ratner, forensic psychiatrist, speaking in defense of psychiatry's involvement in the law, noted that "insanity is not a psychiatric term, it's a legal term," a fact which provoked Vatz to ask, "So, why do psychiatrists willingly participate endlessly attesting to whether a person is insane?" (*Crossfire*, 31 January 1992). If psychiatry is to leave the courtroom, FBI-speak is showing signs of taking its place. In Dahmer's insanity trial the FBI system of categorization described above came close to being employed in what would traditionally have been extrajudicial territory reserved for psychiatry. Defense Attorney Boyle attempted to persuade the jury of Dahmer's insanity by calling as a witness Robert Ressler of the FBI's Behavioral Science Unit, who was prepared to say Dahmer's actions fitted the pattern of a "disorganized killer." Judge Gram agreed with Prosecuting Attorney McCann that "Ressler's expertise in helping police to identify unknown serial killers did not apply in the case of a known serial killer such as Dahmer" (*Washington Post*, 1 February 1992: A8).

Although use of the FBI's categorization of society's dangerous individuals was denied in the case of Dahmer's insanity trial, FBI discourse does seem to have gained "definitional leverage" (to use a phrase of Eve Sedgwick's) beyond the boundaries of the law-enforcement community—gained, that is, the power to define society's monsters. It is the FBI definition which matters, and it is one which, at least according to a Dr. Radecki (a psychiatrist who heads the National Television Coalition on Television Violence), should inform our view of monsters from pre-Quantico days: "Serial killing is a relatively new phenomenon. Jack the Ripper, at the turn of the century, wouldn't meet the FBI definition for a serial killer, because you have to kill at least six people. This is a new phenomenon" (*Oprah Winfrey*, 4 September 1991). In an age in which the drama of law enforcement plays an increasing role in our lives, in our entertainment, the use made of the FBI's definitions of crime and crime scenes has had the effect of further discrediting psychiatric discourse. In contrast to the common representation of FBI detectives involved in tracking down serial killers as hard-nosed and streetwise, the psychiatrist, as Anthony Clare notes, is frequently portrayed as "eccentric or weird, certainly as disturbed as his patients, reflecting the widespread public assumption that one has to be a little mad to become a psychiatrist in the first place" (The *Sunday Times*. 8 August 1993: sec. 9:8). And in the spirit of the movie *Dressed to Kill* and of a *True Police Cases* cover headline which enquired "Did the Shrink Psych Himself Up for Murder?" (August 1992) is Thomas Harris's Hannibal Lecter, a character who embodies for us the idea that psychiatrists are not only mad but criminally so.

When purifying and policing are the same in our minds, then psychiatry, figured as an impediment to law enforcement, taints the justice system with its complications, explanations, and extenuations. If psychiatry coddles the suspect, the FBI takes *paternal* control. The conflict over ways of dealing with criminal monstrosity and how to define it can also be figured in gender terms, or more specifically, as a conflict between male and female parent roles. Joel Norris remarks on the difficulty of writing about serial killers in a way which is considered neither patriarchal or "motherly" (that is, overly forgiving, sympathetic): "In the glare of media publicity that made multiple killers larger-than-life characters, the issues of prevention and motivation got lost and were replaced by demands for vengeance and retribution. It was easy to see why no academic or political figure would stake his professional livelihood on a program that might be perceived as 'coddling killers' " (Norris 1988, 22–23). That Dahmer's attorney describes the doctors he called to support his client's 'guilty but insane' plea as "courageous" (*Larry King Live,* 17 February 1992) indicates the current status of the concept of insanity. On CNN's *Crossfire,* Robert Novak asks Richard Ratner to "be one of the regular guys for once" and agree that John Hinckley, for example, "was just a bad dude." A sister of one of Dahmer's victims, Eddie Smith, describes her opposition to Dahmer's plea of guilty but insane: "All of us want him to go to prison and take his justice like a man" (*Jet,* 3 February 1992: 18). Remarkable in our culture is the power of those discourses which seek the death or imprisonment of the convict by appealing not necessarily to justice but to (masculine) vengeance. Equally remarkable is the labeling of those who seek to explore the possibility of medical treatment for society's "others" as emasculated or unheroically feminine. The association of the desire for knowledge with weakness and of retribution ("no questions asked") with power is expressed by a caller to an episode of *Geraldo* that focused on "cannibal killers": "Could it be that the saying that the world is getting weaker and wiser is beginning to come true?" (*Geraldo,* 12 April 1992).

Foucault argues that the judiciary needs a father figure in the form of an extrajudicial element in order to conceal its own authority: "What is odd about modern criminal justice is that, although it has taken on so many extrajudicial elements, it has done so not in order to be able to define them judicially and gradually to integrate them into the actual power to punish: on the contrary, it has done so in order to make them function within the penal system as non-judicial elements; in order to stop this operation being simply a legal punishment; in order to exculpate the judge from being purely and simply he who punishes" (Foucault 1979, 22). As I have suggested, in recent years the psychiatric profession as one of those extrajudicial elements has been seen as failing to do its job as "advisor on punishment" by sending people to hospital and not to prison. However, a 1991 report in the *Bulletin of the American Academy of Psychiatry and the Law* says that less than 1 percent of all felony cases involve an insanity plea, and 75 percent of those are rejected. Levin and Fox quote studies suggesting that most people overestimate the number of persons indicted for felonies who obtain verdicts of not guilty by reason of insanity, and note that "at the heart of the public's distrust for the insanity plea is its perception that criminals . . . will 'get off' on an insanity verdict and spend little time incarcerated. To the contrary, statistics actually reveal that offenders judged legally insane generally do not stay for shorter periods of time deprived of their freedom than if they had been found guilty" (Levin and Fox 204). Despite the view prevalent among legal experts and psychiatrists that if Dahmer had been found insane, there would have been virtually no chance of his ever being released, much attention was given to the possibility that if found insane, Dahmer could seek parole within a year and "walk," playing on fears which help prepare the mind to "understand" the vigilante violence of, say, Charles Bronson movies. Similarly playing on such fears, the FBI has stepped in as a new, more "realistic" punishment advisor to maintain the idea of the criminal justice system as a "community service" and as being "above politics and dispensing 'justice for all' irrespective of class, race, sex, or religion," thus legitimizing "the state and those whose interests it wittingly, or otherwise, furthers" (Deleuze and Guattari 13–14).

Our different definitions of monstrosity affect both our notions of punishment and of what should be policed. The figuration of serial killing as a disease can be a way of reassuring ourselves that its origins lie outside the social body, or at least in regions of society which are considered to be feeding off mainstream, healthy America. The same reassurance is given when serial killing is perceived as being related to a particular abnormality of an individual, physical body. "Doctor is Allowed to Scan Dahmer's Brain," says a *New York Times* headline (11 November 1991: A11), while on CNN's *Sonya Live*, attention is given to Arthur Shawcross's XYY chromosomes and possible zinc-deficiency (*Sonya Live*, 1 March 1993). "To a very large extent," says Roger Depue, administrator for the FBI's National Center for the Analysis of Violent Crime at Quantico, "crime adjusts to the environment. We've become a highly transient, stranger-to-stranger society. Criminals are going to take advantage of that" (Michaud 41). Depue brings good news to those whose business is the policing of crime: crime and the criminal are always present; a "criminal element" in society is inevitable: only its nature will change. Depue's reasoning can lead to an opposition between society on the one hand and those indelibly marked with the disease of crime on the other. The serial killer, Depue can imply, is not related to the fundamental values of contemporary society. Instead, he is society's parasite. From Depue's perspective, the serial killer is the latest manifestation of The Criminal, an ever-present figure adjusting to a changing historical situation, one who has exchanged financial profit and other rewards of criminal behavior for the pleasure of killing strangers.

Few of us balk at "understanding" the criminal motivated by financial gain. The pleasure of killing "for its own sake" is another matter, and we deem the cause of our modern monster's crimes to be inexplicable, beyond the reach of scientific knowledge. FBI science is concerned with identifying the beast, not with what motivates him: "We don't get hung up on why the [serial] killer does the things he does. What we're interested in is that he does it," says FBI agent Roy Hazelwood (Porter 50). Faced with "motiveless" crimes we (and the police) ask ourselves, "If the crimes are motiveless, why should we be concerned with motive?" The serial killer has brought (or is the product of) a shift in our policing mentality: the disregard for motive. The desire for more reactive policing is expressed by a dominant conservatism which associates explication with sympathy. As Jack Levin's and James Alan Fox's touchiness demonstrates in their introduction to *Mass Murder: America's Growing Menace*, to do anything else but condemn our monsters in the most facile of ways is to run the risk of being interpreted as being in league with them: "We hope this study will help us to explain—not condone—what has seemed incomprehensible" (7). To question the serial killer construction is to speak the language of the serial killer. Instead we must play one big game of *Clue*, where the only thing that matters is finding where, how, and who, not why.

The "motivelessness" of our latest monster's actions allows us to turn away from uncomfortable questions. Gregg McCrary of the "elite 'A (for analyst) Team' " at Quantico tells us, "As it happens, most serial killers are white. No one knows why, but the statistics show it to be so" (quoted in Wilson and Seaman 123). The statistics only seem to matter in terms of aiding the detection of a criminal who has already committed his crime(s), not what they might tell us about how our society is put together. The "nature" of the serial killer we identify, what makes him "tick," is figured as a mystery, and for the most part we are content to leave it as such. Without "motive" but *with* Douglas's and Hazelwood's terms, "organized" or "disorganized," becoming part of everyday discourse (used in articles without quotation marks, used with no reference to their origins, used as part of a discourse which is self-evidently "scientific and true"), our construction of the serial killer becomes an inhuman figure, an automaton who is either out of control or follows a program whose writer remains unidentified. "It" is either in control, or it is not, either adult, sober, non-drug using, and sane, or some or none of the above. According to Hazelwood and Douglas (1980), the terms have the merit of demystifying the serial killer. But they also have the effect of mystifying, the same effect which comes from any other either-or categorization with no acknowledgment of shades of difference in between, from any attack on the plurality of difference, or indeed from staying silent. As one of our most respected authorities on serial killing, Hannibal Lecter, notes in an exchange with

Starling (having read Douglas and Hazelwood's comments? having attended the hearing, disguised? or having been invited?), the categories tell us very little:

> *Lecter:* They're dividing the people who practice serial murder into two groups—organized and disorganized. What do you think of that?
>
> *Starling:* It's . . . fundamental, they evidently—
>
> *Lecter:* *Simplistic* is the word you want. In fact most psychology is puerile, Officer Starling, and that practiced in Behavioral Science is on a level with phrenology. . . . *Organized* and *disorganized*—a real bottom-feeder thought that. (Harris 1991, 18–19)

They are antithetical terms whose oppositional nature can easily be threatened. Dahmer, says Robert Ressler, displays both "organized" and "disorganized" behavior: "All the buzz words apply to him, but from both sides of the house. . . . He would lure victims to his apartment, get people into his clutches, then he will go into bizarre rituals such as cannibalism and necrophilia that are not normally found in your organized type of offender" (Davis 1991, 169). As the only two categories which the FBI allows itself merge and cancel each other out, the image of the serial killer blurs and then disappears.

G. K. Chesterton's Father Brown asks, "What do these men mean . . . when they say detection is a science? . . . They mean getting *outside* a man and studying him as if he were a gigantic insect; in what they would call a dry impartial light, in what I would call a dead and dehumanized light. . . . It's pretending that something familiar is really remote and mysterious" (quoted in Porter 50). The discourse we use to describe our monsters, inscribed with the truth associated with the discourse of science, mystifies the criminal, constructs him above all as something different, alien. For Don Davis, Dahmer should be regarded "not only as a prisoner, but as a specimen to be studied by experts" (Davis 1991, 280). An edition of ABC News's *Day One*, devoted to Dahmer's story, concludes with an image of Dahmer in court framed in black. As the frame begins to fill the screen, Dahmer's image shrinks. It is an image which can serve to represent both our objectification of the serial killer and his objectification of his victim. Both are ways of denying connections between observer and object.

Our mystification of the serial killer is accompanied by mystification of his "rivals," elite members of the FBI whose job it is to track him down. As I mentioned earlier, the discourse which proceeds from Douglas's and Hazelwood's terms is figured as a purity with which to combat both the impurity of the serial killer and of the psychiatric discourse (that is, a discourse which has become stagnant through lack of relevance to the real world, a discourse which infects manly clear thinking with convolution and tortuosity). The FBI sees the serial killer as existing on a different plane, a plane on which traditional thinking on crime has no meaning. We respond to this figure by discounting language, by elevating the NCAVC onto that different plane, above and beyond mere mortals. The FBI we read about can resemble Thomas Harris's characters, Jack Crawford (*The Silence of the Lambs*) or Will Graham (*Red Dragon*). As Graham's colleagues expend their energies on new theories and new plans to catch their man, he spends his time in moody silences, in trying to leave the world of his family, or society, of discourse. That different plane he seeks is the site of supercops, superkillers, and no big words. It is a site requiring a special vision, not a special language: the horror of the serial killer is above all, the serial killer *appearing* from nowhere. Starling and Graham are successful in their detection the moment they dispense with the logic of language and are able to see what the serial killer sees. According to the serial killer myth, purity describes our monsters and the men (and occasional women) designated to capture them. The place they meet is characterized by being free of the trivialities of everyday living. It is the place where the serial killer metamorphoses from an archetypal figure of impurity to a figure pure in his transcendence of normal thinking, normal language, normal people—a figure who is a worthy adversary of the FBI.

That special place high above the confusing, amorphous, messy place we call society is one psychiatry could never reach, for psychiatry is a world of words. Psychiatry belongs where there are always at least two sides to every story. Our construction of the serial killer could never be defined or "captured" by psychiatric discourse because he exists beyond words, evades all but the most general categories. It is a construction that has a destructive effect on the perception of the world as ultimately controllable (by words, by reason). Dr. Ken Magid, clinical psychologist, sees "the serial killer and the severe psychopathic personality disorder as being the AIDS of the mental health community, that is, we don't have a cure for those people" (quoted on CNN's *Murder by Number*). For the mental health community, the serial killer represents a problem which needs to be solved not only because of his destructive effect on society, but because of his destructive effect on the status of psychiatry's discourse. And it is a representation which the FBI helps to engender. Meaninglessness and motivelessness are key concepts in the struggle between psychiatry and the police, and are figured in terms of disease in different ways. For the psychiatric profession, the meaninglessness of serial killing is a problem to be overcome; the unspeakableness of the serial killer represents a void of understanding which has to be filled with discourse. For the police it is a *natural* condition, a problem which is showing signs of reaching epidemic proportions, which requires ever more vigilance, ever more policing, and the power to exterminate.

The crimes of the serial killer are made more mysterious by our figuring them as originating in nature, and in the process exterminatory powers seem all the more justified. Nature represents an uncontrollable force, and so too does the serial killer. For Park Dietz, a forensic psychologist who works for the Behavioral Science Unit, serial killers "capture the public imagination because the risk seems so uncontrollable to most people" (CNN's *Murder by Number*). In the House of Representatives hearing on serial killing, the FBI refers to "behavioralists and futurists and other criminal scientists who believe that in the 1990s we are going to see an ever-increasing violent crime wave" (*House* 22). Metaphors which describe criminals in *natural* terms give authority to policing discourses, and metaphors which describe more obvious manifestations of "nature" in *criminal* terms make the "thinning out" of the "wildlife" among us all the more normal: "These days [Nanse] Browne heads a new support group for mountain lion victims, calling the wild cats 'serial killers' that should be systematically thinned out by state wildlife officials" (*Los Angeles Times*, 3 April 1995: 1).

Making our monsters analogous to mountain lions can make us feel more dependant upon the state for protection. Contrary to evidence that "the majority of [serial] killers tend to operate within one city or even one neighborhood" (Jenkins 1994, 45) is the myth of the increasingly mobile and transient killer who can strike anywhere at any time, a myth which justifies a more mobile police force moving unchecked from state to state, city to city, with increased powers of surveillance and entry. In Conrad's *The Secret Agent*, Vladimir explains to Verloc how stronger measures of law and order can be consciously incited, how society can be manipulated in this way by "effective" terrorism, that which cannot be explained away easily, that which will make society feel threatened for that reason: "A bomb outrage to have any influence on public opinion now must go beyond the intention of vengeance or terrorism. It must be purely destructive. . . . The attack must have all the shocking senselessness of gratuitous blasphemy" (Conrad 66–67). The construction of the serial killer is terroristic in the manner described by Vladimir, and has the same effect. Dahmer is "A Human Time Bomb" (chapter title, Norris 1992, 102) whose primer remains a mystery.

In their discussion about the construction of homicidal mania and its relationship to the discourse of psychiatry, Millot, in *Power/Knowledge*, remarks to Foucault, "You define here something like a strategy without a subject" and then asks, "How is this conceivable?" (Foucault 1980, 202). In response, Foucault plays down the idea of conspiracy: "I would be tempted to say that there was, in fact, a necessity here (which one doesn't have to call an interest) linked to the very existence of a psychiatry which had made itself autonomous but needed thereafter to secure a basis for its intervention by gaining recognition as a component of public hygiene" (Foucault 1980, 202). However, in the tradition of criminal ethnomethodology (praised by Stephen Pfohl for questioning "the uncritical use of official statistics on crime and deviance as reflective of crime itself" and suggesting that "the production of official statistics suggests more about the organizational work of control agencies than it does about the activities of deviants" [Pfohl 30]), CNN's *Murder by Number* offers the possibility that the FBI is knowingly involved in the exaggeration of the serial killer phenomenon. On the program, Richard Roth reports that in a letter to a 1983 Senate subcommittee, former FBI director William Webster pointed to the growing number of unsolved crimes and suggested that they were evidence of the work of serial killers. Using Webster's statistics, crime writer Ann Rule, who also testified to the Senate subcommittee, arrived at a figure of five thousand deaths per year which could be attributed to serial killers, a figure that Philip Jenkins describes on the show as "ludicrous" and that Eric Hickey suggests is not supported by empirical research. The show argues that the estimate "became the basis for funding" the unit at Quantico to study and analyze serial murder. Roth reports that, following a study commissioned by CNN discounting the FBI statistics,[1] the FBI admitted it might be wrong, and pointed to the fact that the information was collated in part from the media.

The CNN study can evoke the serial killer as a figure that functions for the FBI as a kind of ultimate referent for their procedures, their level of funding, and their discourse. As such, he must be, to some extent, a figure of mystery. The threat posed by the serial killer to society is as mysterious as the figure itself. In chapter 3 I describe in more detail our investigative procedures that construct the unspeakable. But while the

1. CNN claims that while the official summary made by FBI Behavioral Sciences and Investigative Support Units says that "since 1977 there have been 331 serial murderers and nearly 2,000 confirmed victims," "after removing duplicating cases, the total number of serial killers listed in the FBI's own supporting data is only 175 cases. After adding in serial murderers missing from the FBI data, the total number of known serial killers since 1977 is only 191. The actual number of confirmed victims—just 1,007—is slightly more than half the number of victims the FBI has claimed until now."

nature of serial killing is figured as mysterious, we are nonetheless keen to identify its symptoms. While its nature may be the secret of unworldly, satanic deities, we do our best to identify signs of its earthly manifestations. We look for and find those signs in spaces whose relation to society as a whole can go unnoticed. Our policing of the serial killer safeguards the idea of social order by identifying the serial killer's "asocial" origins. Since Freud we have figured childhood as the great origin of adult behavior, an origin easily framed as a space somehow belonging to nature and outside the realm of society. In the next chapter I suggest that explanations of serial killing rarely go beyond "individuality" (that is, "individuality" figured *in opposition to* society) and/ or "childhood," states whose relationships to dominant cultural concerns and values can be obscured.

2

Investigating the Serial Killer

The Seeking of Origins

THE SERIAL KILLER AND THE IDEA OF THE INDIVIDUAL

The human and social sciences have accustomed us to see the figure of Man behind every social event, just as Christianity taught us to see the Eye of the Lord looking down upon us. Such forms of knowledge project an image of reality, at the expense of reality itself. They talk figures and icons and signs, but fail to perceive forces and flows. (Mark Seem, "Introduction," in Deleuze and Guattari, xx)

They go for your mind in prison today—where before, it was all physical suffering. (Abbot 20)

"17 Killed, and a Life Is Searched for Clues" says the headline of a *New York Times* article on Dahmer (4 August 1991: A1). Even following the serial killer's capture, arrest, and conviction, policing proceeds unabated. It is not conviction which brings the illusion of closure, only that which we really seek: origins of the story of *his* violence, origins which we figure as belonging solely to the individual, to *a* life. Our discourse of detection continues by reconstructing the history of the individual serial killer as a case, as something to be solved, as something whose center begins (and usually ends) in the unspeakable. Like Victor Frankenstein, we build a monster, only to peel back the skin and see what's inside. And sometimes we do it in a manner which makes distinguishing ourselves from those under study not always an easy task: "We shall attempt a dissection with surgical precision" (Leyton 31) is Elliott Leyton's pep talk to the readers of *Compulsive Killers*, before mentioning in the main body of the text, in his discussion of the descendants of the most infamous surgeon of them all, Jack the Ripper, the number of medical titles attached to the names of the nineteenth century's serial murderers ("Dr. William Palmer, Dr. Thomas Cream, Dr. Marcel Petiot, and many others").

34

Investigating the Serial Killer: Origins

In the *New Republic* Lincoln Caplan notes that "it's fashionable to argue that Americans now take less responsibility for their actions than they once did. Insanity defendants are sometimes portrayed as emblematic of the trend, because they are seen as seeking an undeserved dodge" (30 March 1992: 20). Perhaps in response to the common perception of the criminal too ready to blame society for the crime, the 1980s and early 1990s have seen a questioning of the existence of society itself, a renaissance of the individual at the expense of society to the extent that the self is perceived as the only or at least the main form of reality. It is a renaissance important to the FBI's construction of monstrosity. In a climate of respect for "the individual," that "individual" is also the means by which estrangement proceeds. Violence in the name of sex is perceived as originating in the body of an individual instead of indicating misogyny. An unquestioning distinction is made between the individual and the social context, and the latter fades from view.

For Simone de Beauvoir, Sade is "quite right in cutting through sophisms and exposing the inconsistencies of a society that protects the very things it condemns, and which, though permitting debauchery, often punishes the debauchee" (Beauvoir 67). Like *In Cold Blood's* Officer Dewey, who finds it difficult to understand "how two individuals could reach the same degree of rage, the kind of psychopathic rage it took to commit such a crime" (82), and who fails to consider the possibility that such a "meaningless" crime could be shared, communal, social, we see only individual rage; we see monsters but are blind to monstrosity. We might *think* social groups, but we *see* individuals. For Don Davis, "Many people killing many other people is one thing . . . one person killing many people can be terrifying" (Davis 1991, 167). An edition of ABC's *Day One* opens with the screen filled with a close-up of Jeffrey Dahmer's eye and a voice-over telling us, "His name has come to mean simply murder" (18 April 1993). From what can begin as a shock to the social consciousness, giving voice to meanings of our shared world which have gone without saying, the representation of the serial killer can evolve into the loading of all that unspeakableness onto *a* name, *a* body. Figured as acultural, isolated from a cultural context, the serial killer is the spectacle whose brilliance dazzles us. Focused on him, we fail to see beyond.

Wondering "whether an individualism in which the self has become the main form of reality can really be sustained," the authors of *Habits of the Heart* argue that "philosophical defenders of modern individualism have frequently presumed a social and cultural context for the individual that their theories cannot justify" (Bellah et al. 143). Their main concern is that individualism "may have grown cancerous—that it may be destroying those social integuments that

Tocqueville saw as moderating its more destructive potentialities, that it may be threatening the survival of freedom itself" (vii). Philosophical defense of individualism—a defense which more often than not perceives the conflict as being between illusory abstraction and tangible manliness—is redundant in an age whose currency is personalities. On an episode of *Geraldo* entitled "Jeffrey Dahmer: Diary of a Monster," the host highlights our separation of personalities from social and political issues: "The conduct of the Milwaukee Police Department in this case, as you all know, is under intense scrutiny right now. Was it the fact that they thought this was a gay thing that made them so disinterested? Was it because most of the victims were minority people? What was it that caused them to essentially downplay or ignore these cries for help? . . . Our story, though, is not that story. Our story is the human aspect of this, and coming up, you'll meet more people whose lives were touched by Jeffrey Dahmer" (*Geraldo,* 12 September 1991). The "human story" we mostly hear is one which is celebrated as transcending less tangible "social questions." It is a story in which lives "touch" and which is given the quality of being "more real." While Dahmer's goal is, according to Masters, to make "depersonalized person[s]" (Masters 1993, 97) of his victims—and perhaps a depersonalized person of himself—his "success" brings to him the reality of "personality," one which, as a former classmate of Dahmer's suggests, can matter above all else: "I'm not surprised he made it to the cover of *People* magazine—in some way he was living up to [his home town's] high expectations" (Martha Schmidt, *Day One,* ABC, 18 April 1993).

Making "personality" more real, more relevant (as compared to the unreality, the abstraction, or the trivialization of those spaces without "personal reference") is the FBI's "personality profile." FBI officers list "age, race, employment, grooming habits, level of education, arrest and military history (if any), pastimes, marital status, socioeconomic status, type of residence and home environment, with whom he is residing" (*House* 35) as some of the characteristics upon which they particularly focus in assembling profiles of uncaught serial killers. The personality profile may indicate a change in the direction of law enforcement, away from the policing of a particular act and towards a particular type of person. Already the authority of the personality profile is such that it gives the police unprecedented powers of entry: "Profiling concepts have been used in search warrants in several instances where we have done a profile, and that has been used as part of the search warrant, part of the probable cause to search a particular individual or search an individual's property" (*House* 10–11). And it is also the means by which the police extend their influence beyond law enforcement and into the justice system: "We sometimes assist in the development of prosecutive strategies of the district attorneys. Pre-sentence, parole, and commutation opinions based on data base research—we have assisted in counseling Governors and in counsel-ing other individuals who are dealing with the issue of parole and commutation of a particular individual who is incarcerated for a serial violent crime. We have testified in pre-sentence hearings" (House 11).

"What, after all, is crime or the criminal but the exercise of the power of the state to control certain behaviors or people believed to have a certain criminal identity within particular historical circum-stances?" asks Stephen Pfohl (Pfohl 33). Cynics like Pfohl might argue that the FBI's personality profile, misused, or used to its full advantage, can be instrumental in the production and reinforcement of criminal stereotypes, that is, the connecting of personal characteristics to crimi-nal behavior. Of course the potential dangers of policing based on the assembling of statistics are that common knowledge of the "likely" char-acteristics of, in this case, a serial killer can lead to a common belief that the relationship between those characteristics and behavior is causal. The personality profile can be the basis for what amounts to a legal inscription of personal abnormality (as well as, of course, normality). Having figured serial killing as a parasitical disease afflicting our social body, or as an evil which manifests itself only in individuals, that is, having safeguarded the idea of our normality, we may feel exonerated and safe in aiming to eradicate all things that our serial killer "repre-sents." And when this mood is accompanied by a way of seeing our world as made up of only individual bodies, we may feel comfortable about selecting individual "characteristics" or "lifestyles" as targets of eradication. Dreams of the cleansing of humanity feed on the belief in a causal relation between individual characteristics and behavior. The extent to which the FBI's increased powers of surveillance over "devi-ant" individuals are perceived as justified depends on how entrenched the idea of policing as purifying has become in our common psyche. As well as being an aid to detective work, and supposedly a way of improv-ing the efficiency of the police,[1] the personality profile can also be a useful tool in the policing of values and in the policing of and construc-tion of criminal "types."

While we fail to see beyond personality, beyond individual types, Dahmer, we tell ourselves, takes his self a little too far away from the rest of us. His putative *selfishness*, his inability to relate to others socially (enabling him to regard them as objects, things) corresponds with psy-

---

1. The FBI sees the personality profile as a "cost-effective way and a more efficient way to reduce . . . investigative man-hours" (*House* 10)—important qualities to adver-tise, no doubt, when one is attempting to secure increased federal jurisdiction.

chology's definitions of psychopathy. According to a *New York Times* article headlined "Brain Defect Tied to Utter Amorality of the Psychopath" (7 July 1987: C1–2), "the term refers to someone with . . . the apparent incapacity to feel compassion or the pangs of conscience". Despite the headline's focus on the possible biological cause of or relation to psychopathy (a possibility pursued with much vigor in the case of Dahmer, with teams of psychiatrists and psychologists searching for genetic disorders, neurological impairments, and biochemical imbalances), many of those quoted in the article figure psychopathy as something which does not so much originate in the psychopath but rather circulates socially. It is noted, for example, that the "detachment may be partly due to problems in moral and intellectual development that can be dealt with through behavioral treatment" (C1). It is also suggested that in recent years psychopathy seems to be on the rise—an observation which if accurate is less likely to be explained by neurological changes than by social change. Later in the article, criminologist José Sanchez is quoted as follows: "The young criminal you see today is more detached from his victim, more ready to hurt or kill. . . . The lack of empathy for their victims among young criminals is just one symptom of a problem that afflicts the whole society. The general stance of the psychopath is more common these days; the sense that I am responsible for the well-being of others is on the wane" (C2). And Robert Hare, psychologist, notes that if the official psychiatric diagnosis of psychopathy is used, 50 percent of prisoners fit the definition; but he and other psychiatrists argue that "the diagnostic criteria focus too much on criminal misbehavior—because they were developed through the study of psychopaths who got caught—and too little on the underlying personality problems." (C2).

Also challenging the idea that serial killing results from individual pathology are the many cases in which murders are committed by two or more offenders. Philip Jenkins suggests that "group serial homicide" may "account for 10 or 20 percent of all serial murder cases" (Jenkins 1990). As Freud—who, in *Civilization and Its Discontents*, contemplates the problem of diagnosing whole civilizations as neurotic without the aid of a comparative context (Freud 1953b, 141–142)—might remark, we should be wary of diagnosing psychopaths within what can appear to be a context made up in part by psychopathy. If he could observe us now, existing in a world described by Christopher Lasch in *Culture of Narcissism* as one of radical individualism engendering a narcissistic preoccupation with the self, he might also consider us presumptuous for allowing the burden of proof in an insanity trial (as is the case in Wisconsin law) to fall on the defense.

If the ability to estrange with the use of psychopathy is made difficult by a context of social psychopathy, the idea of evil helps us out (once again) by giving momentum to our individualizing procedures. The confession we want to hear is one in which the crime originates wholly with the confessee. Judith Halberstam notes that our common perception of evil is that it "resides in specific bodies, particular psyches. Monstrosity as the bodily manifestation of evil makes evil into a local effect, not generalizable across a society or culture" (Halberstam 37). With our condemnation of Dahmer as evil, we say, simply, *he happened:* there is no need to explain the crime, to speculate about context, only to deal with him, the criminal. Unlike insanity, a concept which requires continual rewriting and substantiation, evil has a relatively unchanging history, a history of going without saying, and is something which, as we search a serial killer's life for clues, can lead us to the safety of silence instead of the risk of further explication.

While we, with religious zeal, can condemn Dahmer as evil, we have no time for the idea that evil forces took possession of him, that evil has an external source. It is an irony of which Dahmer is apparently aware: "Is it possible to be influenced by spirit beings? I know that sounds like an easy way to cop out and say that I couldn't help myself, but from all that the Bible says, there are forces that have a direct or indirect influence on people's behavior" (quoted in Masters 1993, 112). Evil is a concept of which only the prosecution can make use. When Dennis Nilsen was tried in 1983, the jury, split on the question of Nilsen's legal insanity, sought help from the judge, who consequently declared that "a mind can be evil without being abnormal" (quoted in Masters 1991, 269). While a judge can be taken seriously (at least by the jury) in condemning Dennis Nilsen, for example, as evil, and while the notion of evil functions for society as a whole as a means of condemnation, a defendant's references to such notions generally are rejected.

Halberstam argues that "modernity has eliminated the comfort of monsters because we have seen, in Nazi Germany and elsewhere, that evil works often as a system, it works through institutions as a *banal* (meaning 'common to all') mechanism" (Halberstam 37). But our current preoccupation with individualizing by use of the term *evil*, with creating monsters and ignoring monstrosity, indicates our nostalgia for the premodern, for the comfort that those old monsters offered us. Individualization and our serial killer construction are interdependent, naturalize each other, give each other meaning. Threatened by an unknown of unidentified, violent individuals, and respectful of policing powers of surveillance, we argue the need for "the assignment to each individual of his 'true' name, his 'true' place, his 'true' body, his 'true' disease" (Foucault 1979, 198). In the process, we fail to provide a cultural context which may enable us to identify normative expectations which both our heroes and our monsters fulfill.

"ARE YOU RAISING A JEFFREY DAHMER?"

She continued to suffer from long bouts of nausea; but now, a more serious form of rigidity developed, one which none of the doctors who saw her was ever able to diagnose exactly. At times, her legs would lock tightly in place, and her whole body would grow rigid and begin to tremble. Her jaw would jerk to the right and take on a similarly frightening rigidity. During these strange seizures, her eyes would bulge like a frightened animal, and she would begin to salivate, literally frothing at the mouth. (Lionel Dahmer describing his then wife, Joyce, carrying Jeffrey: Dahmer 33–34)

Phone-in caller:	We certainly haven't heard much about Jeffrey Dahmer's parents. Can you tell me if you see any connection between his upbringing and the crimes he's committed?
Mr. Boyle (Dahmer's attorney):	My job would have been a lot easier if I had found that there were some problems with his upbringing. The opposite was true.
	(Larry King Live, 17 February 1992)

The idea of the family does not contradict individualism but complements it. Bellah et al. describe a culture in which "the family is the core of the private sphere, whose aim is not to link individuals to the public world but to avoid it as far as possible" (112). They suggest that "the tendency of our individualism to dispose each citizen to isolate himself from the mass of his fellows and withdraw into the circle of family and friends, that so worried Tocqueville, indeed seems to be coming true (112). In the late twentieth century, families are individuated, not *extended,* and the idea of "family," like that of "individual," is constructed, and indeed celebrated, as an "asocial" entity. *Family values*—a controversial phrase in the politics of the nineties—are presented as the panacea to social ills by their making redundant the need for society and its institutions altogether.

If the crimes of a serial killer cannot be neatly and completely figured as originating in the criminal's individual identity, his family can function by mopping up the remaining meaning, leaving the rest of us untainted. "Clues to a Dark Nurturing Ground for One Serial Killer" (that strange, redundant "one" indicative of an out-of-control desire to individualize?) reads the headline of a *New York Times* article (7 August 1991, A8) which figures Dahmer as growing up in a self-contained plant-pot of an existence called "family." The struggle between the acknowledgment of and the denial of a relation between society and Dahmer's actions is played out in an edition of *Oprah* entitled "Are You Raising a Jeffrey Dahmer?" (4 September 1991). In response to the suggestion by one of Dahmer's classmates that Dahmer's actions may have been related to cultural homophobia and racism, an audience member says, "I think that's up to his family to take care of that, and the people that are around him when he's growing up. That's not the whole society in general." The classmate's assertion that "families don't exist in a vacuum" has little meaning in the world in which the mythical serial killer exists, one composed only of family units, dysfunctional family units, and individuals lacking an assigned familial role. For Larry King an obvious question to ask Dahmer's attorney is whether "the victims' families show any anger towards [Dahmer's] parents" (*Larry King Live*, 17 February 1992). An answer came two years later when the parents of Steven Hicks, Dahmer's first victim, sued Dahmer's parents, alleging that their negligence contributed to the death of their son (*People Weekly*, 28 March 1994). And if there is no family to blame, the neighbors will do. Dahmer's neighbors complain of hate-mail, threatening phone-calls, shootings from passers-by, and bomb threats (Dvorchak and Holewa 238).

Foucault notes that homicidal mania was abandoned shortly before 1870, and one reason was "the idea of degeneration" (1978, 11), which made it no longer necessary "to make a distinction between the great monstrous and mysterious crimes which could be ascribed to the incomprehensible violence of *insanity* and minor delinquency" (11). In consequence there existed "a psychiatric and criminological continuum" which provided "a causal analysis for all kinds of conduct, whether delinquent or not, and whatever their degree of criminality" and which also "permitted one to pose questions in medical terms at any level of the penal scale" (12). A comparable continuum is described by the Behavioral Science Unit, allowing the potential for being a serial killer to be identified in childhood. The connection between a "dysfunctional" family background and the phenomenon of serial killing is described in the House of Representatives' hearing on serial killing. After noting that "certainly our society is more mobile. We are hearing, and perhaps we are just now discovering these instances of child abuse, the type of chaotic childhood that you are talking about. We have more working parents today and latch key kids and all that goes with it," Chair English asks his FBI guests, "Does that, on a per capita basis, lead you to believe—the FBI to believe—that we will see more of this phenomenon as these young people grow up and mature?" To this question of whether there is a continuum between "working parents" (presumably he means working mothers), "latch key kids" (and "all that goes with it"), and serial killing, the FBI responded positively: "I think very well we will" (*House* 53). And the continuum of which the serial killer is a part also apparently includes "peeping

Tom." "Is there a pattern to at least give some hope of identifying these individuals in the future? In other words, do they go from, say, being a peeping Tom to assault, to rape, to murder? Is there a pattern that fits in there in which we can predict that this person is a likely candidate to be a serial murderer?" asks English. Again responding positively, FBI Officer Douglas talks of the need to identify "these young children at school age years" (*House* 54).

In the hearing, a constant theme is the physical, social, and economic mobility of the serial killer, a mobility which makes him difficult to identify. It is a stable familial role which especially gives an individual meaning, renders him visible, *immobile*. In answer to English's question, "Is there some key that would indicate—that would trigger this type of phenomenon?" (*House* 53), Officer Douglas replies, "That's a very good question. . . . In our research with serial murderers, we found that, for example, the backgrounds, without exception, everyone had a chaotic early childhood, a lot of mobility, a lot of transientness in their family, abusive parents, absent parents . . ." (53). Stallybrass and White refer to Henry Mayhew's definition of nomads as possessing habits which are not "domestic" and who "transgress all settled boundaries of 'home' . . . simultaneously map[ping] out the areas which lie beyond cleanliness" (Stallybrass and White 129). They see his definition as "a demonized version of what Bakhtin later defined as the grotesque" (128). Notwithstanding evidence which suggests that "among perpetrators of homicide, almost 60 percent are relatively close to their victims in the sense of being spouses, family, or acquaintances" (Jenkins 1994, 46), our policing discourses describe a world divided between families and nonfamilies, fixity and transientness, noncriminality and criminality, meaning and nonmeaning, cleanliness and dirt—oppositions which are frequently conflated.

Conflating several is Anne E. Schwartz: "The state of Wisconsin, specifically Milwaukee, has become a welfare magnet, since neighboring states have drastically cut their welfare benefits. In 1991, Milwaukee's record year for homicides, police say the victims and perpetrators are not local but from Illinois, Michigan, and Indiana. They flock to Wisconsin because of our lucrative welfare benefits" (176). The image Schwartz presents is a twentieth-century version of Mayhew's. After quoting Mayhew who refers to "pregnant and pestilential diseases, and whither all the outcasts of the metropolitan population seem to be drawn," Stallybrass and White remark, "That last phrase is troubling, implying that the 'filthy' are *drawn* to the filth" (132). Schwartz conflates the poor with transiency and criminality and figures them, like Mayhew, as beings who unconsciously are drawn to, attracted to, flock to things and places which satisfy their animalistic urges. And as

Stallybrass and White note, once such metaphoric relations have been established, they can be reversed: if transients or, in the case of particular representations of Dahmer, failed transsexuals (or indeed most other embodiments of transgression) *are* criminals, then criminals *are* those who lack fixity in the way which is perceived by, among others, English and Douglas.

We identify a link between "abnormal family" backgrounds and serial killers, and we conclude that the link is causal. To come to that conclusion, we ignore other possibilities. When we spot "abnormalities" in serial killers' family backgrounds we, like Douglas, seem to forget the majority who come from what we would consider normal family backgrounds, and we find it easy to ignore Westley Allan Dodd's remark that "I was never abused. I was never sexually abused. I was never physically abused. I wasn't neglected. The family had plenty of money, owned our own house, two cars, a trailer. I had a happy childhood" (quoted on CNN's *Murder by Number*). We ignore the majority of those who suffer child abuse and never go on to commit crimes such as Dahmer's, and we ignore the possibility that "victims of abuse are just as likely, if not more likely, to grow up and become ruthless businessmen and victimize unsuspecting consumers for pleasure—not just for profit—as they are to grow up to become serial killers" (James Alan Fox, quoted in Schwartz 145). We prefer not to consider the possibility that the causal link we identify can prove troublesome to certain individuals of whom society expects the worst. In Sonya Friedman's previously mentioned show, "The Criminal Mind" (*Sonya Live*, 1 March 1993)—possessors of criminal minds being, according to Friedman, "career criminals" who start "very young"—one of the show's guests describes the pressure exerted by a society that expects those from violent homes to become violent adults, those who were abused as children to become adult abusers. Lorenzo Carcaterra, whose book describes growing up in a violent and abusive home dominated by a father who had murdered his first wife, calls the idea of "the cycle of violence" an "unfair burden" and says, "One of the reasons I wrote the book is people who grow up like I did are labeled that [potentially criminal], that we're going to do that, we're going to repeat that." We ignore the possibility that with the reduced demand for reproduction in the context of consumer capitalism, a decreasing need for kinship in a more mobile society, and the declining importance of gender roles in the division of labor—all factors which helped naturalize the idea of the traditional family—the "collapse of traditional values . . . [is] in a sense the result of the very success of the capitalist societies these value systems had helped engender" (Altman 1982, 90–91). Fetishizing detection and surveillance,

43

we largely disregard such possibilities and prefer to channel our energies into "identifying these young children," a decision based on the conclusion that "we will see more of this phenomenon [of serial killing] as these young people grow up and mature" (House 53).

Births and origins go together naturally enough, and when we trace the origins of a particular serial killer, we can find ourselves dwelling on the image of the newborn with its mother. If we find no familial trauma, our stories can begin and end with this image. "So many of us wanted to believe that something had traumatized little Jeffrey Dahmer, otherwise we must believe that some people simply give birth to monsters," writes Ann E. Schwartz (39). She would have rested a little easier if she had watched an episode of *Inside Edition* in which Jeffrey's father and stepmother, Shari, told the interviewer that his natural mother, Joyce, took medication for her bouts of anxiety depression while she was pregnant with Jeffrey. In their books on Dahmer, Norris and Brian Masters both dwell on Joyce's mothering of little Jeff. Norris's account suggests that Jeffrey suffered from a condition caused by his mother's medication (prescribed to alleviate the most "feminine" of ailments, anxiety depression). He also notes that Joyce was "a very 'hyper' person" (Norris 1992, 62)—another "feminine trait" according to patriarchal myth? Masters remarks on Joyce's decision not to breastfeed and, while mentioning that "thousands of mothers in the Western world decline to feed their offspring at the breast," admonishes the mother who "may not reflect that by denying her breast to the infant she is placing self before benevolence." Masters concludes that the lack of breast-milk can explain Dahmer's sense of loss throughout his life.

While Jeffrey's biological mother takes most of the hits, Shari fails to escape being connected with the actions of her stepson. When Geraldo asks someone introduced as a "friend of the Dahmer family" whether Shari is "a wicked stepmother," the friend replies that she "is the epitome" of one (*Geraldo*, September 12, 1991). Although on the same show claims are made that Dahmer was molested by his father when he was eight years old,[2] it is our monster's mothers or stepmothers who usually receive the most attention. Typical of the attention given to Dahmer's origins (and typical, perhaps, of small-town America's desire to connect itself with national concerns, however tenuous or befouled the link may be) is a front-page headline of the *Chippewa Herald Telegram* (25 July 1991): "Mother of Accused Mass Murderer Lived Here."

---

2. A notation in Dahmer's probation files refers to a statement by his father, suggesting that Jeffrey was abused by a neighbor's boy. Dahmer has denied being abused by anyone (see Dvorchak and Holewa 35).

As we read *In Cold Blood*, struggling to identify the meaning of the killer's acts, we can find ourselves interrogating the killers in the manner of Detective Church, insisting that they "tell us something about [their] family background" (Capote 217). Once there, in that mysterious origin of life's meaning, we tend to give a disproportionate amount of attention to the mother and not much to the father (at least, not his presence). The mother of Church's interviewee is quoted as saying, "People are looking at me and thinking, Well, she must be to blame somehow. The way I raised Dick. Maybe I did do something wrong" (Capote 287). The dysfunctional family unit is largely figured as a place lacking the father. With patriarchy absent, matriarchy rules, and the results are perceived as monstrous: "Serial killers are almost invariably found to have experienced environmental problems in their early years. In many cases they stem from a broken home in which the parents are divorced or separated, a home with a weak or absent father-figure and dominant female, sometimes a home-life marked by a lack of consistent discipline" (Wilson and Seaman 40). With the family figured as the originator of the meaning of our lives, the amount of structure in our lives depends on the type of family from which we come. And we have come to expect that to defy the law of the father is to disperse meaning, that matriarchally produced narrative is inevitably chaotic. Like Dahmer, whose life, in the words of Oprah Winfrey, "spun out of control" (*Oprah*, 4 September 1991), the individual growing up in a female-dominated family (Dahmer lived with his grandmother after his parents were divorced) is commonly perceived as an unpredictable figure whose actions appear motiveless.

A woman who knew much about both narrative and monsters is Mary Shelley. In her introduction to the 1831 edition of *Frankenstein*, she tells us of her agreeing to her publisher's request for an account of "the origin of the story." Making an analogy between text and monster, she ends her introduction by bidding her "hideous progeny go forth and prosper." But Shelley, weary of people asking her how "she came to think of and to dilate upon so very hideous an idea," might tell us not to locate the *truth* of a monster in his mother, not to figure mothers as the origins of their sons' stories, and thus not to add to the anxiety of the mothers of our monsters, or potential mothers-to-be like Anne E. Schwartz, whose nightmare is to give birth to something akin to what she writes about: "I wondered if I would give birth to a two-headed child someday, to serve as a constant memory of the biggest story of my life" (Schwartz 15).

Do we fathers or potential fathers-to-be feel anxious about the possibility of fathering a monster? According to common wisdom, if we do, it should be because of our absence, not our active participation. While

Lionel Dahmer feels guilty for not spending enough time with his son, masculinity's involvement in the "creation" of Jeffrey is represented negatively, as a "good" force not implemented. From the perspective which sees men as the originators of structure, of a sense of place, of visibility, the serial killer, the archetypal purveyor of meaninglessness, can only be the product of femaleness. The struggle between our law enforcers and the serial killer is represented as the struggle between the law of the father and the disorder of the mother, between post-Oedipal language spoken by the police and heard nightly on crime shows, and pre-Oedipal language spoken by the killers, by "mamma's boys" who never grew up to be real men. Our policing discourses, implied to be and valorized as masculine, conflict with feminine discourse, discourse lacking motive and logic.

We perceive this conflict as pertinent to the case of Dahmer. With homosexuality associated with the feminine, those little men, those mamma's boys—like "the homosexual mass murderer" Dean Corll, who "had become a mother's boy" (Wilson and Seaman 271) because of his father's being out of town—are people we like to figure as naturally tending towards homosexuality and criminality, or rather a criminality inscribed with homosexuality, or homosexuality inscribed with criminality. Possible links between the serial killer and patriarchy and masculinity are effaced by our tendency to originate his story in terms either of his individual asocial being or his dysfunctional family, a family deemed dysfunctional by the absence of the father and the presence of the mother. Within this apparatus, detection of the serial killer becomes the detection of all that is perceived as weakening the structure built in obedience to the laws of the father; investigation and policing of ideas about the individual and the family are naturalized; and the dependency of the meaning of those ideas upon ideas of mainstream society and culture is negated.

With the psychiatric profession being commonly perceived as failing in its (fatherly) duties of punishing the suspect, the FBI has stepped in to carry out those duties as an extrajudicial element in the penal system and to naturalize the metaphor "child as potential criminal" by its figuration of serial killing as originating in preadulthood. In the process, the prevention of serial killing is restricted to the policing of childhood, an activity which is instrumental in the *construction* of our idea of childhood, that is, it is a space to be policed. Discussing *The Silence of the Lambs*, Elizabeth Young argues that the success of Clarice's "coming-of-age as an FBI agent means that she is now fully trained to enforce the power of the state through modes of invasion, surveillance, entrapment, discipline and punishment that not only parallel but literalize, as Foucault's work helps to remind us, the operative modes of psychoanalysis itself. This plot development, in other words, twins psycho-analysis, the metaphoric FBI of the psyche, with the FBI, that literal enactment of psychoanalysis" (Young 25). In locating the origins of se-rial killing in childhood, our policing discourses (those that we speak as fluently as the FBI) reenact the simultaneous construction of and inves-tigation of the space with which psychoanalysis has been especially preoccupied. However, we are happy also to reverse the metaphor's terms (criminal as child), to regard the relationship between police and criminal as one of father to child, a move which can help to normalize the inscription of all us who are not part of the "law enforcement com-munity" as children/potential criminals, and to normalize the idea of members of that "community" as apolitical patriarchs. The stories we tell about serial killing have the effect of sustaining the mystique of patriarchal/police power, and indicate a "childish" trust, a "childish" respect for that power.

3

Investigating the Serial Killer
Silencing the Unspeakable

He's an extraordinary looking man, yet I really can name nothing out of the way. No sir; I can make no hand of it; I can't describe him. And it's not for want of memory; for I declare I can see him at this moment. (Richard Enfield describing Mr. Hyde)

Patterns of murders committed by one person in large numbers with no apparent rhyme, reason or motivation. (The subject debated by a 1983 Senate Judiciary committee formed to discuss the impact of serial killing on American society)

The hunt for a serial killer is frequently described in Gothic terms, and especially as a Gothic quest for knowledge of the "beast." Guy Le Gaufey refers to the vogue in the nineteenth century for vampire novels in which "the aristocracy is always presented as the beast to be destroyed" and in which "the savior was a bourgeois" (Foucault 1980, 1). The saviors/detectives in the serial killer myth can represent a similar antielitism: the FBI rejecting those big words of the psychiatric profession; Clarice Starling as cheap, white trash made good. But the stories about Dahmer generally lack heroic saviors. Instead they recount the inability of the police "to do their job," or the failure of overtolerant or naive psychiatrists and counselors to identify Dahmer's potential for violence. Dahmer is figured as "slipping through the cracks": presumably those cracks appearing in the once-solid and stable society—the less liberal, less wordy, and safer society of old, a society defended by recognizable protectors.

An exception is the story told by Anne E. Schwartz. Her book on Dahmer acknowledges "the men and women of the Milwaukee Police Department, whose cooperation with a reporter has always been at considerable risk to their jobs: You are my heroes and I am grateful to your trust" (ix). Her book begins with some of these heroes assuming the aura of chivalric manliness: "For cops on the beat, the sweat would trickle down their chests and form salty pools under their steel-plated

48

bulletproof vests" (2). Presumably of the Teutonic Order is Officer Rolf Mueller, "of German origin," who "sported a mass of perpetually tousled blond curls on top of his six-foot frame" (1). Playing opposite such heroes is the story's heroine. The author tells us that while other reporters are sleeping with their answering machines switched on, she (wearing "black underwear under white shorts" [6] we are informed, helpfully) was "the last person who was not a police official to leave [Dahmer's] apartment alive" and that "the experience of seeing the apartment and witnessing the horror of the residents that night was [hers] alone" (11).

The lonely heroine confronting (male) horror is a familiar subject of the Gothic. But in Schwartz's case, the villain has already been arrested, and presumably wouldn't have been interested in her anyway. And while we have grown accustomed to the idea of such villainy disguised as respectability, Schwartz, unlike Clarice—who seems as much at risk within the confines of Quantico or at a funeral surrounded by police as on the streets chasing serial killers—finds nothing creepy in the ranks of the law enforcement community: villains are villains and cops are cops; heroes and heroine, police and journalist, are as one. The discourse reproduced by the book is one of benign policing: part journalese, part police jargon, a discourse of detection which only reaffirms existing notions of what constitutes social order.

The Gothic, that place where we play with the fear of the text's extratextuality, of its unspeakability, is where we find it natural to place the serial killer, he about whom we can't stop talking and he who leaves us speechless. It is in the Gothic novel where ideas central to the way we perceive ourselves and our society seem particularly threatened, and where language itself seems vulnerable to an impending silence. In *Poe, Death, and the Life of Writing*, Gerald Kennedy explores Poe's responsiveness to the relation of writing to this potential void of meaning:

> Poe sounded the abyss not simply through existential motifs, through scenes of annihilation and expressions of dread. In less obvious ways he interiorized the void of meaninglessness as a problem of writing and explored through his own practice the emergent relationship between the new death and the act of inscription. He sensed a momentous cultural transition and projected this awareness in texts which reflect the desperate situation of a subject striving through an always inadequate system of "mere" words to give coherence to unspeakable fears. (Kennedy 185)

If in Poe we can read an acknowledgment of language's lack of certainty, of the voids which destablize its meanings, our particular use of the Gothic is invariably to maintain that aura of unspeakability, to hint at what may lie within the closet but to keep the door closed. Our Gothic tales are generally without the moral questioning, without the "shattering of the protagonists' image of his/her social/sexual roles" which another commentator says is characteristic of that tradition (Gross 62). If the tales appear to spring from "fears and uncertainties arising from instabilities in personal, social and political realities" (Graham 261), they are blind to the potential disorderliness of order.

One of the novels with which Dahmer is frequently associated is Stevenson's *Dr. Jekyll and Mr. Hyde*. Andrew Jefford has written on the opposition of speech and the unspeakable in Stevenson's novel. He identifies, on the one hand, the cozy world of well-lit interiors, of hearths, of speech, and on the other the cold, dark world of the unspeakable. For Jefford, "Hyde's realm is essentially that of signifier, and his effectiveness in the narrative is reliant upon the free movement of that signifier: *evil*" (62). "Hyde's real crimes," says Jefford, "must always be other, and elsewhere" (63). Jekyll describes the matter of Hyde as "one of those affairs that cannot be mended by talking" and asks Utterson to "do one thing . . . respect [his] silence." Utterson (his name, as Jefford notes, "speaks of speech"), the lawyer, and his associates, Lanyon (a doctor) and Enfield ("man about town"), form a band of respectability to which Jekyll belongs. When they discover a monster at the heart of their world, their language becomes less prosaic: "they become," in the words of Nabokov, "artists," finding themselves confronted by a shock to their well-ordered lives. Dahmer is our latest version of the monster of violence secreted behind outward respectability: "Like many people before them, [Dahmer's victims] were bamboozled by the courteous Dr. Jekyll side of Jeffrey Dahmer's personality" (Davis, 1991, 76). But our version is one whose duality is rarely questioned, one whose violence is never respectable. It is one which does not inspire us to question the opposition of sanctioned heterosexuality and unspeakable homosexuality, one which does not alert us to the possible connections between that which is condemned as unspeakable and the discourse which condemns it.

"I always covered up for that 'inner me' that I loved. He just acted and I had to solve all his problems in the cool light of day. I could not turn him in without also destroying myself. In the end he lost. He still lies dormant within me," says Dennis Nilsen (quoted in Masters 1991, 265). According to John Wayne Gacy, his crimes were committed by an evil part of himself called "Jack" (Wilson and Seaman 274), while Ted Bundy's Mr. Hyde was "the Hunchback" (Wilson and Seaman 262). The "Jekyll and Hyde" scenario we construct is reproduced by serial killers themselves. At other times their acts "just happen." Dahmer speaks of "compulsion" (quoted in Masters 1991, 266), describes waking up to find the dead body of Stephen Tuomi, with no memory of actually killing him: "Where that rage came from or why that happened, I don't know. I was not conscious of it" (quoted in Masters 1993, 109). Nilsen says: "My sole reason for existence was to carry out that act at that moment. I could feel the power and the struggle of death . . . of absolute compulsion to *do*, at that moment, suddenly" (quoted in Masters 1991, 266). According to Brian Masters, Nilsen "claimed he had no power of responsibility at the time, and that afterward he was inhabited first by fear, then by 'a massive and suppressed remorse' " (Masters 1991, 266).

The idea of sudden, inexplicable violence can be a way of exonerating the serial killer, or at least the Dr. Jekyll half of him. "It just happens" says "it" happens *to* me or *to* us, and there's nothing one can profitably say about "it." Figuring the self as the site of a struggle between competing personalities or forces is a move we dismiss as an attempt to have the serial killer's actions excused. Dahmer's "confession" (spoken by an actor for ABC's *Day One.* 18 April 1993) that he "made [his] fantasy life more powerful than [his] real one" was widely interpreted in this way. But whereas we condemn the serial killer for this apparent attempt to avoid culpability, for this neat divide between his self and other, *we* strenuously attempt to maintain such an opposition, continue to differentiate between his unspeakability and the normality which is his outward appearance, continue to place him in turn within and separate from, normal society. One of the ways we do this is to resort to the idea of nature. Brian Masters' article for *Vanity Fair* is entitled "Dahmer's Inferno," and in it he describes Dahmer "as disconcertingly ordinary, even unremarkable, until the secret dissolution of his personality finally erupted upon the world" (Masters 1991, 184). Masters reproduces that image in *The Shrine of Jeffrey Dahmer:* "Every human being has dark, shameful, nasty impulses—the combined inheritance of the species. . . . In Dahmer's case, the constraints failed, the inhibitions collapsed, and Dionysus broke loose" (Masters 1993, 19). The metaphors that often come to mind when we attempt to describe the serial killer figure him as a natural disaster, beyond the knowledge, the words, and the control of man. Nature is where things just happen.

However, as I described in chapter 1, another tool we use to estrange is the idea of evil. The concept of evil can help us avoid the idea that, in the words of criminologist Steven Egger, "[serial killers] enjoy it—it's as simple as that" (quoted on CNN's *Murder by Number*) or that they "do what they want to do" (Jack Levin on *Geraldo*, 4 December 1991); that is, it helps us to avoid the possibility that their actions are the result of "human desire." And when unspeakableness has a direct correspondence with *dominant* culture, our language becomes a little more strained in order to cover the gaps, the silences. The actions of the "heterosexual" killer cannot be figured in sexual terms—his sexuality is left unspoken—and what is left unsaid by our maintenance of the opposition between speech and unspeakability continues to haunt our language. Like Nilsen, when "it" just happens, we have difficulty in turning "it" in without destroying our notion of our selves, without unraveling the discourses which structure them.

Brian Masters begins *The Shrine of Jeffrey Dahmer* with the words which Dahmer's defense attorney uses at the start of his opening statement at the trial: "Ladies and gentlemen of the jury, you are about to embark upon an odyssey" (Masters 1993, 1). In his article for *Vanity Fair*, Masters, constructing his trip as a descent into the unknown, journeys into Dahmer's neighborhood, an area which "contrives to feel dislocated, apart," one whose houses "stand like ghosts of a happier time," one in which you do not walk "without listening for footsteps behind you" (Masters 1991, 184). Fellow questers Robert Dvorchak and Lisa Holewa describe Dahmer's 25th street as "getting more down-at-heels" and then, presumably by way of explanation, note that "in the past ten years, the neighborhood had changed from 37 percent black to 69 percent black" (Dvorchak and Holewa 15). Meanwhile, Ann E. Schwartz, the first journalist to enter Dahmer's cryptic crypt, apartment 213, Oxford Apartments, for whom "foul smells are as much a part of the inner city as crime" (Schwartz 4), finds what she is looking for in the smell of death. The smell of death is above all the smell of mystery: "Ask a veteran cop what death smells like and he or she will say, 'Once you've smelled it, you'll never forget it. There's nothing else like it. . . . I have smelled death on a number of ride-alongs with the police department, and they are right" (7). But the "stench inside Dahmer's apartment" is apparently even more mysterious, even more threatening. It signifies "something more, just as those killed there were not merely murdered but had their lives unspeakably ended" (7). The construction of that "something more" is familiar in our representations of serial killers. It is a space into which we can place all that we are not or do not want to be. Not that such mystification can be sustained for long. The smell of death, which for Schwartz is like nothing else, is later compared, less mysteriously, "to meat left to rot in an unplugged refrigerator" (7).

Schwartz's quest for knowledge of what that "something more" might be leads her down to downtown Milwaukee and the city's gay bars. Her story is of the descent from her "neighborhood of manicured lawns" (6) to where the underclass live, to a world peopled by

Dahmer's "facilitating victims" (see chapter 4, p. 70). Here, presumably, is where the "criminal mind" is formed and allowed to express itself freely. If the construction of society's monsters reflects upon the fears and anxieties of a particular historical period, the period in which I write is especially nervous about threats to the ideologies that constitute what we like to call "middle" America, that condition or space that has been central to the idea of America itself, so much so that discussion of social class is often perceived as inapposite. It is a space defined by financial status, social stability, family structure, sexuality, and still, perhaps, race.[1] It is a space located antithetically to that of the criminally unspeakable. Noting that British criminal law "defines only some types of avoidable killing as murder: it excludes, for example, deaths resulting from acts of negligence," Stephen Box argues that "we are encouraged to see murder as a particular act involving a very limited range of stereotypical actors, instruments, situation, and motives" (Box 9). Likewise, in America, the perpetrators of murder, rape, robbery, and assault are "focused on by state officials, politicians, the media, and the criminal justice system," and are distinguished from the abstract, faceless, colorless, genderless, sexless "middle."

Perhaps above all, middle America sees itself as *domestic.* Harold Schechter suggests that the serial killer represents "the savage force roaming in the dark, as the nuclear family huddles terrified inside the home" (quoted in *Los Angeles Times,* 3 May 1992: "Calendar," 49). Noting that she writes for a "family newspaper" (8), Schwartz reminds us that police officers like Rolf Mueller were prepared to leave the relative safety of that family, prepared to fight that savage force and enter neighborhoods full of "drug dealers, prostitutes and the unemployed mentally ill"; and that, nevertheless, he "could not wait to go home" and was "anxious to see his wife and daughter" (2). The nuclear family is the space which, in the American myth, represents financial as well as social stability, and contributing to the fear and bewilderment of that family, and to the present ascription of meaninglessness to the serial killer's crimes, is the inability to explain them with reference to financial gain. Andreano and Siegfried in *The Economics of Crime* blank out at the prospect of actions being motivated by anything other than money: "For crimes against persons (murder, rape, assault) we have no theory as to the value of such offenses, and hence no theory as to what would affect the returns from such crimes" (14).

As any psychoanalyst will tell us, however, that blanking out can

---

1. In the next chapter, with particular reference to the representation of Jeffrey Dahmer, in which questions of sex and race overlap, I will describe dominant or middle-American culture's construction of the serial killer in the context of sexuality and race.

also say something about ourselves. What is the horror in the horror stories we tell? For Elliott Leyton it is that middle-class success depends on others' suffering and that the failed will come back to haunt the successful. Describing the serial killer as a "product of his age," Leyton notes that "the pre-industrial multiple killer was an aristocrat who preyed on peasants; that the industrial era produced a new kind of killer, most commonly a new bourgeois who preyed upon prostitutes, homeless boys, and housemaids; and that in the mature industrial era, he is most often a failed bourgeois who stalks university women and other middle-class figures" (Leyton 269). A study of the backgrounds of thirty-six serial killers suggests, however, that we could describe the serial killer as an archetype of bourgeois success instead of failure: "Almost all were white males, usually the oldest child, in a home with a stable source of income that provided a self-sufficient economic level" (Dvorchak and Holewa 136). In his apparent ability to sustain two lives, in his familiar form of outward success and inner failure, the serial killer, like Jekyll, is representative of a society which seems prone to conceal secrets behind respectability: the brothel-visiting banker, the transvestite clergyman, the broker whose interest in stocks is as much sadomasochistic as financial.

If the serial killer construction is anything to go by in a middle-class society which, naturally enough, equates meaning with middle-classness, what proves horrifying is the possibility that the way we make sense of the world actually depends on what we construct as nonsense, that our certainties depend on uncertainty. In discussing the shock caused by the murders described in *In Cold Blood,* Sol Yurick notes that our particular meaning of meaning is central to our definition of *middle-class:* "It is the middle class which is responsive to and outraged by that violent dislocation, by that apparent unmotivation of certain acts which it is stylish to call irrationality or absurdity in literature. The very words argue the exception that tests a pervasive condition, an everyday state of being. And after all, it is the middle class which has created a social medium whose very nature is shored up by an ideology that stresses volition, cause-effect, reason, logic, historicism" (Yurick 80). And Yurick notes the fear that that which is presented as antonymous to middle-class meaning actually lurks within: "Anything that appears to violate this order is shattering, outrageous, deserving of the death penalty; the very presentation, the very special pleading, of *In Cold Blood* implies the *unusualness* of the murderer's act and so becomes diversion, entertainment in case history, and tries to persuade us that what are in fact common patterns of behavior are aberrations" (author's italics, 80). Horrified by an abyss of meaninglessness, we are intent on persuading ourselves that serial killers' patterns of behavior have no relation to the dominant ideologies of the day, that the apparent randomness and motivelessness of their violence is not nurtured by a violent culture characterized by urban anonymity, that their transientness—which the FBI seems to fear most—has no correspondence with a society that requires a highly mobile labor force.

In the case of Dahmer, the task of such persuasion can seem a little easier. With Dahmer, the killer of mostly single, poor, nonwhite gays, the nuclear family is more likely to express moral outrage than fear. He whose victims are without "cultural significance" is robbed of some of the mythology which informs our perception of other serial killers. As Don Davis notes, "No one in Milwaukee even knew that a serial killer was on the loose" (108). Essential to the idea of the middle class is the naturalization of heterosexuality, and the moral of Dahmer's story reaffirms much of what constitutes middle-class ideology. Our stories of moral questers "descending" from positions elevated by those ideologies corresponds with Gross's reading of John Rechy's novel, *City of Night*. Rechy, says Gross, "shapes the imaginative vision of urban gay life to Gothic form. An example of this style is the narrator's description of a prototypically decadent gay/Gothic party. . . . Count Dracula is the evening's host and the dead, soulless guests the leftovers from the bar and bath set" (62–3).

Those who wouldn't be seen dead at such parties—who may nevertheless be somewhere in attendance—are the regular guys at the head of that nuclear family, who are still struggling to keep it together. Cameron and Frazer note how the representation of a crime as "meaningless" helps to obscure the link between fantasies of power and masculinity, benign or otherwise: "The FBI clearly recognizes, despite the language of 'persons,' that serial killers are *men*, but the discourse of serial murder downplays the gender factor, perhaps because commentators prefer to stress the meaninglessness of the crime, relating this to what is seen as the increasing alienation of the individual from society, especially modern North American society" (158). The world created by the tabloids is, Cameron and Frazer say, "stalked by motiveless 'fiends' whose 'brutal lusts' remain forever unspecified, their connection with masculinity somehow obvious, yet unexplained" (44).

Although Cameron and Frazer note that 'we just have not been able to find any women who fit our concept of a sex-killer" (23), since their study was published (1987), there have been several instances of women who fit the concept, at least a concept acceptable to others.[2] But their pointing out of the existence "of a disproportionate volume of

2. Philip Jenkins states that "perhaps 10 to 15 percent of known American serial killers are women" (Jenkins 1994, 151).

material about murders committed . . . by women" (23) is still relevant today. Despite there being only one female serial killer, Christine Falling, discussed in the first part of CNN's Special Report, *Murder by Number*, it is her image with which the program begins, and the impression given in the show is that serial killers can with equal likelihood be men or women (or indeed be white or black). Presenter Richard Roth's way of evening up the odds for all of us is by telling us that "serial murderers come in all varieties—short and tall, black and white, men and women" without mentioning that black serial killers and female serial killers are the exception rather than the rule. Roth plays our particular version of *Clue*, a version that I suggested in chapter 1 was designed with the help of the FBI—the identity of the killer being potentially that of any character, any one of us, anywhere and everywhere. (But, as I argue later, it can be a game in which we like to think supercops—or superkillers like Lecter—hold all the clues, have possession of that little black envelope).

The failure to make the connection between the meaning of masculinity and serial killing is demonstrated in a *Psychology Today* article which describes the growing number of what it calls "inexplicable" violent crimes: "Overwhelmingly, the victims of bizarre murders are women or children; the killers are almost invariably men" (Porter 46). The word *bizarre* crops up rather frequently when the fact that most serial killers are men is mentioned. Jack Levin, author of *Mass Murder*, notes on an edition of *Geraldo* (the focus of which, in the wake of the Dahmer story, is cannibalism) that "eighty-five percent of all homicides are committed by men and when you look at the really heinous, bizarre crimes, the number gets to be up to ninety-nine percent." He concludes that "Men, for one reason or another, are simply more violent than women" (*Geraldo*, 4 December 1991). Meanwhile in *Serial Killers* Colin Wilson and Donald Seaman note that "many 'motiveless murders' involve rape or other forms of sexual violence. At first this sounds like a contradiction in terms until we recall that most 'motiveless murders' involve boredom and resentment. The murder of Bobbie Franks is a case in point. Leopold and Loeb had originally meant to kidnap a girl and rape her. Yet even if they had done so, the murder would still be classified as a motiveless crime, since the motive was not sex, but a desire to prove themselves 'supermen' " (Wilson and Seaman 16). Ignoring the history of male dominance being expressed through sex (that is, making an unprovisional distinction between sex and power), Wilson and Seaman contribute to the mystification of this desire for omnipotence, this desire which elsewhere we generally associate with masculinity, this desire to prove oneself a super *man*. Later in their study they talk of the "apparently motiveless murders being committed nationwide: 'motiveless' in the sense that there was no apparent connection between killer and victim" (86). Here, the lack of a *personal* connection between killer and victim is enough to warrant use of the term *motiveless*. To use the term here is to deny the possibility of nonpersonal connections between individuals that are formed by cultural expectations, connections which guide our behavior toward people we do not know. Just as there are connections between a lecturer and an anonymous audience or a prison guard and a new prisoner— connections which inform if not dictate the form of relationship when personal contact is made—there are connections between killer and anonymous victim which can, I suggest, be described; they need not be entered into the realm of the great unspoken.

Judith Butler sees gender as an identity gained over time, an identity which coheres from a process of repeated performance: "Gender ought not to be construed as a stable identity or locus of agency from which various acts follow; rather, gender is an identity tenuously constituted in time, instituted in an exterior space through a *stylized repetition of acts*" (author's italics; Butler 140). The idea that *The Silence of the Lambs'* Buffalo Bill might be seen as enacting a "violent version" of Butler's conception of gender is suggested by Elizabeth Young (Young 16). The murderous acts of serial killers are often represented as consequences of severe anxieties about gender. About Peter Sutcliffe, the killer of female prostitutes, Joan Smith says, "The most compelling explanation is that he had a compulsion to destroy the thing he feared in himself; fearing the pronounced feminine side of his character, he projected it onto women and ritually destroyed it, time after time" (Smith 2). In a similar vein, Joel Norris argues that "John Wayne Gacy killed male prostitutes because he was extremely homophobic, and he was killing the hated homosexual part of himself" (quoted in *People Weekly*, 12 August 1991: 36). The motivation of serial killers is frequently explained in terms of the need to expel: to expel the feminine, to expel the homosexual. The idea that serial killers kill repeatedly in order to demonstrate their manhood (and its associate, heterosexuality) is expressed in the negative; that is, they are represented as attempting to destroy manhood's "opposites(s)." Such maneuvering allows masculinity to be literally silent. In a *Time* article ("The Mind of the Mass Murderer," 27 August 1973: 56–57), psychiatrist Shervert Frazier suggests that among the common traits found among the sixty-five murderers and serial murderers he analyzed was that they did not "know how to be men" because many had grown up in fatherless homes or suffered "repeated brutalization by a father who was inconsistent or unpredictably violent." In a world of binaries, if they didn't know how to be men, then what they did know would presumably have more to do with our perception of the feminine than the masculine. The question (and the problem) becomes not masculinity but femininity, or rather femininity's invasion of masculinity. The serial killer becomes someone who attempts to overcome his insecurities about his gender by killing what he perceives as a threat to his manhood. It is an act we find easy to condemn, but what escapes condemnation, or at least critique, are the meanings we give to the term *masculinity*. It remains the untouchable, the unkillable, the eternal, the natural. It is never the "hated" part, the part to be killed. We know that Buffalo Bill is a failed transsexual; that he desires the removal of his penis, his masculinity; and that his killings are the consequence of his failure to legally transform his masculine image into a feminine one. We know that his female victims are the means to an end: the destruction of his masculinity, which the state has denied him. And yet what we see is not serial murder as the result of a failure to expel masculinity, but the "evil" of femininity having invaded a masculine realm, an evil which is perhaps best represented by the image of Buffalo Bill, having concealed his penis between his legs, opening his Dracula cloak to flash his "vagina" to the camera.

"The serial murderer doesn't simply go back to pumping gas," says Alfred Regnery, administrator of the federal Office of Juvenile Justice and Delinquency Prevention; "a senseless murder is not just committed once" (*Time*, 14 November 1983: 47). We are content to attribute meaning, a recognizable motive, to single murders. Multiple murders, however, which might suggest a pattern, are more likely to be entered into the world of nonsense. Elizabeth Young identifies the serial killer as a figure who makes explicit the connection between the isolated and individual misogynistic act and the misogyny which permeates society as a whole:

> For the particular creepiness of *The Silence of the Lambs* is that it locates the way in which, when a male killer strikes against women again and again, in secret and at random, his actions seem to carry the threat of a single act of violence to its logical conclusion: serial murder. At the same time, this conclusion is itself without conclusion, since its very repeatability suggests that there is no end to misogynist murder, but rather an endless stream of such crimes spilling not only from film to film but beyond the borders of all film, to the non-film "real world" itself. (5–6)

There being "no end" to the story of misogynistic murder makes the telling of that story problematical. As I noted in chapter 2, we are keen to give beginnings to that story, but they are beginnings which lead nowhere, at least nowhere we are willing to go. The absence of a definite ending disrupts the idea of a definite beginning; like most things we deem inexplicable, the serial killer becomes a figure of nature, and in the process misogyny, for example, becomes "natural."

The idea that violence just happens, just happens naturally is often accompanied by reference to the aggressor's fantasy world. Describing a particular serial killer, an FBI officer, for example, says, "Often killing at random and in a senseless manner . . . this individual is a human predator seeking out his prey to fulfill his fantasy and kill" (House 5). "Senselessness" is frequently associated with fantasy and desire, and in the process they can assume the stature of irreducibility. Barbara Ehrenreich, for example, remarks that

> As a theory of fascism, [Klaus Theweleit's] *Male Fantasies* sets forth the jarring—and ultimately horrifying—proposition that the fascist is not doing "something else," but doing what he wants to do. . . . The reader's impulse is to engage in a kind of mental flight—that is, to "read" the murders as a story about something else, for example, sex . . . or the Oedipal triangle . . . or anything else to help the mind drift off. But Theweleit insists that we see and not "read" the violence. . . . What is far worse, Theweleit forces us to acknowledge these acts of fascist terror spring from *irreducible human desire.* Then the question we have to ask about fascism becomes: How does human desire—or the ceaseless motion of "desiring production," as the radical theorists call it—lend itself to the production of death? (My italics; from the foreword to Theweleit 1987, xi–xii)

Reading Capote's *In Cold Blood,* we can experience this pull between the notion that violent criminals are "doing what they want to do" and the notion that they are "doing something else." While Dick is apparently "convinced that Perry was that rarity, a 'natural killer'— absolutely sane, but consciousless, and capable of dealing, with or without motive, the coldest-blooded deathblows" (Capote 55), we might share Tony Tanner's view of Capote's text as a gathering together of "groups and clusters of related facts so that the sudden bout of blood-spilling is retrieved from its status as an isolated fact and provided with a complex context in which it becomes the focal point of converging narratives" (Tanner 98). The book's narrative can help us deny the act's isolation, its motivelessness. It can interrogate the book's title. And reading the book can replay the choices we face in representing the serial killer. In accord with Theweleit's perception of the German Freikorps, I suggest that serial killing should not be explained away as "something else," but that the serial killer is "doing what he wants to do," making his fantasies come tragically true. But to figure the violence of the serial killer or the fascist as the result of "natural"

59

dreams or of Ehrenreich's notion of "irreducible desire" is another act of denial, another failure to take responsibility. It is a failure to take responsibility for those dreams, fantasies, and desires, and perhaps it is a way of authorizing them.

During the House of Representatives hearing, Representative Jim Lightfoot says, "I think it is hard to believe that those individuals could both develop a desire to commit such violent crimes and also get away with as many as they did before they were apprehended" (3). Lightfoot's remarks imply that such a desire means lack of control, that desire means incomprehensibility, that desire of this sort "takes over" as Hyde takes over Jekyll. This association of desire with a loss of control has its uses in the legal defense of sex-murderers and rapists—with victims figured as inciting that desire, as originating the narrative of the crime—but it can also be a factor in our failure to take responsibility for collective fantasies, for the fantasies of a violent society. Park Dietz, a forensic psychologist, believes serial killers learn to enjoy murder, that "what motivates Jeffrey Dahmer or Ted Bundy are not delusional beliefs. They are personal preferences—preferences for what kind of things are sexually stimulating. And that's learned—learned in the same way that men become breast-men or leg-men by exposure during critical moments of development" (*Murder by Number*). Supporting Dietz's suggestion is Westley Alan Dodd who says "I wasn't sure I could kill so in my mind I had to make that exciting. I had to fantasize about it. To be able to kill, I had to make that thought exciting, and in a matter of just a couple of weeks, I was able to do that and I was ready to kill" (*Murder by Number*).

The idea that murder can be exciting is not a strange one. In order to make the idea strange, perhaps we can learn from Dennis Nilsen, who on the one hand says that he had no control over the "compulsions" which overcame him and on the other seems to imply that they were of *his* making: "The need to return to my beautiful warm unreal world was such that I was addicted to it even to the extent of knowing of the risks to human life. . . . The pure primitive man of the dream world killed these men. . . . These people strayed into my innermost secret world and they died there" (quoted in Masters 1991, 265). Here is something of a shift from denial to an acknowledgment of responsibility: they are *his* dreams which caused the deaths. Perhaps we should similarly examine our fantasies of power, of transcendence, to see what it is we dream of transcending. Perhaps we can tease out meaning from the most "bizarre" occurrences and acknowledge the reality and the presence of real men and real women who get caught up in those fantasies. But mostly we reassure ourselves that such desires are a natural mystery, beyond our knowledge and control. We may suggest that serial killers enjoy what they do, that "it's as simple as that," and then we tend to leave it at that. On CNN's *Murder by Number,* Richard Restak responds to the argument that serial killers must be crazy because of the nature of their actions by saying that the argument is "a way of eliminating or, should I say, refusing to look at the outer limits of human freedom and even human evil if you will." Restak here acknowledges, as does Ehrenreich in her reading of Theweleit, the denial of the possibility that these men are doing what they want to do, but his comments indicate the way we figure these actions as the epitome of freedom, as proof of transcendence, of power, of the way we naturalize the lust for murder.

"Lust for murder," "murderous lust": the confusion of desire and violence is made to seem normal in a variety of ways. The proponents of stricter censorship of television frequently argue not for a reduction in violence and violence-oriented sex, or for a reduction in violence on the one hand and nudity and sex on the other, but simply for a reduction in "sex and violence" per se. The history of the representation of sex as an act of violence is naturalized by this easy pairing-off, by this failure to disentangle "nonviolent" sexual images from violence. Sex, apparently, just *is* essentially violent. That the destruction of the desired object is an unsurprising consequence of desire is presumably an assumption behind this remark from an FBI official: "What is the motivation of these serial killers and killers in general? And often times you can't just look at the attractiveness or unattractiveness of a victim" (House 18).

We deny that violence against women or the idea of women can be an expression of a culturally inscribed masculine power by framing that violence as a natural phenomenon, in particular as an expression of a male sexuality grounded in nature. Our bodies and our minds are not always our own, we insist: sometimes nature takes over, and nature is a violent place. It is a maneuvre in harmony with Bataille, who says, regretfully, "that life, the register of the possible, necessitates comprised sexuality," whereas the fiction of Sade "makes possible the revelation of the 'true nature of sexual attraction, that is, violence, which in life remains hidden behind the fog of affection' " (quoted in Gallop 32). The effect of figuring rape and rape ending in murder as "sexual," as the expression of the "true nature of sexual attraction," is to negate the possibility that the violence is an act of cultural domination, an expression of a masculine power. It also obscures the possibility that the actions are related to the particular way we perceive power, that is, as the presence of masculinity achieved by the absence of femininity (an opposition which, as I suggest in chapter 4, is as relevant to the construction of homosexual serial killers as heterosexual ones).

Winifred Woodhull is among those who contend that rape should be desexualized and figured "simply" as a crime of power: "Rape should be seen as a logical outcome of political, economic, and social processes that generate and foster men's domination over women in every cultural domain" (Woodhull 170). Perhaps unknowingly supporting Woodhull's contention that rape is not an expression of apolitical sex, of sex distinct from power, representatives of the FBI note that "there is often a progressive pattern that takes place, that while at the early stages, there may be more rapes, the longer this individual commits these kind of crimes, the more likely it is that murder will be also involved" (House 72). Such "progressive patterns" might indicate that rape belongs to a narrative ending not necessarily in ejaculation for the aggressor, but in destruction of the victim. The idea of progression figures an escalation in violence not only as a pattern of action performed by someone whose sense of responsibility has apparently diminished with every unpunished previous rape, but as a "purification" of the violent act, a purification which ends in final closure, death.

But even when we desexualize violence and regard it only in terms of power, nature is prone to linger in the equation, for the histories of power and nature intertwine. Wilson and Seaman quote Ernest Becker—"We are all hopelessly absorbed with ourselves. . . . In childhood we see the struggle for self-esteem at its least disguised. . . . [The child's] whole organism shouts the claims of his natural narcissism"— before linking this "natural" self-love to the "urge to heroism" and "self-assertion" which, they say, when frustrated can turn to resentment and finally to murder (20). For Wilson and Seaman, the acts of the serial killer have nature as their origin. For them, serial killers belong to the "dominant five per cent," an elite which nature apparently assembles in other species: "Observations of zoologists like Lorenz and Tinbergen indicated that this applies to all animal species: five percent are 'dominant.' A psychologist named John Calhoun made an equally interesting observation: that when rats are overcrowded, the dominant five percent becomes a criminal five percent. Overcrowded rats express their dominance . . . in [ways] completely uncharacteristic of rats in natural conditions: for example, in rape and cannibalism" (Wilson and Seaman 226). If rats can be criminals (as opposed, presumably, to being law-abiding), then presumably it is only natural to figure our most violent criminals as those who are sufficiently strong and independent to escape *our* rat race. For Wilson and Seaman, Ted Bundy was a member of that dominant elite "who need success as much as they need food and drink." As such, Bundy is someone deserving of commiseration: "It is difficult to imagine anything more frustrating than a dominant male (or female) stuck in a position that allows absolutely no expression of that dominance" (282). The idea that the serial killer's acts originate in nature is often supported in studies on the serial killer by reference to Abraham Maslow's theory of human motivation, the "hierarchy of needs," presented in *Motivation and Personality*. Wilson and Seaman, suggesting that it can be applied to the "history of criminality over the past two centuries," summarize it thus: "If a man is starving to death, his basic need is for food. . . . If he achieves his aim, then a new level of need emerges—for security, a roof over his head. . . . If he achieves this too, then the next level emerges: for love, for sex, for emotional satisfaction. If this level is achieved, then yet another level emerges: for self-esteem, the satisfaction of the need to be liked and respected" (14). The acts of the serial killer are thus figured as continuous with the craving of food, as one of the more recent and extreme examples of man fulfilling his ever-changing needs.

In CNN's *Murder by Number*, the presenter warns the audience that "what you are about to see is a difficult subject to talk about," and by his suggestion that "the number of serial murderers is low, but the impact is like that of other unlikely tragedies: a plane-crash, a bolt of lightning. It appalls us, it plays on some primeval fear. We are obsessed, fascinated and it seems more so all the time." How much easier it is to comprehend the serial killer as akin to a bolt of lightning than as something whose origin lies within histories we can write for ourselves. Having constructed a barrier between nature and our culture, a barrier whose position depends on the absence and the presence of language, depends on those things we feel that we can talk about and those that we cannot, we expel the unspeakable serial killer to the natural world. How much easier it is to live with ourselves by finding him difficult to talk about. Condemning all our ideas of otherness to the unspeakable, we attempt to negate plurality, that which problematizes the idea of ourselves by complicating the process of defining what we are not. In our stories of serial killers, we feel the need to create "others" in order to colonize them, to investigate various "dysfunctional" families or various gay communities. As we enter each unfamiliar family structure and describe it in the same old paradigms, as we homogenize each homosexual world, difference is obscured, except for the difference which separates the colonized from the colonizers. Our quests for knowledge invariably take the form of transferring our own unspeakability, our own secrets, onto others or other worlds, worlds where words do not reach. The mysteries we encounter on our Gothic quests remain mysteries. The life represented in the movie *Jeffrey Dahmer—The Secret Life* remains a secret. Content to spread an epidemic of unknowing, we ask open-ended questions without anticipating answers. Unwilling to pursue questions of motivation very far, we fall back on the tangibilities of capturing the serial killer. Capture becomes the visualization of he who is mythically invisible, becomes all that matters. Replacing the world in which the serial killer is at large, a world of meaning permeated with meaninglessness, use polluted by uselessness, is the indisputable fact of the individual's presence. Against the certainty of vision, abstract questions about cause have little importance.

But when we are being reasonable, we know also that the "unreasonableness" we construct is our own. As Freud tells us, denial and unreason go together. The idea of nature conserves and conceals meaning, can account for the cryptic quality of our language. Encryption is, however, redundant. We know that language is not only surrounded by silence and nature, but is punctuated by them. We know that they are of language and can conceal and mark our secrets. Our serial killer can provoke the speaking of the unspeakable, the voicing of silence. We signify that unspeakableness with words. We go on talking about how unspeakable he is. We figure him beyond the pale of language only to discover that he is merely beyond the language that comes naturally. We are left with a figure of monstrosity whom we are unable to comfortably condemn to unspeakableness, who stubbornly remains *of* language. We are left uncomfortably with only language, language with no "other."

4

Jeffrey Dahmer

Gay, White Cannibal

Why should bodily refuse be a symbol of danger and of power? Why should sorcerers be thought to qualify for initiation by shedding blood or committing incest or anthropophagy? (Douglas 120)

Been surviving on McDonalds. Need to start eating at home more. (Jeffrey Dahmer, in a 1990 home video shown on *Dateline NBC*: quoted in *Entertainment Weekly*, March 1994: 47)

While not mentioned in the criminal complaints (assuming within the law the aura of the great unspoken), Dahmer's cannibalism, described by Geraldo Rivera as his "macabre snacking" (*Geraldo*, 12 September 1991), was the most sensational aspect of his case, that which separated him from other serial killers. In the movie version of The *Silence of the Lambs*, Starling tries to map out the norm regarding serial killers by suggesting that "most serial killers keep some sort of trophies from their victims." Lecter, distancing himself from that territory (and picking holes in the FBI's attempts at categorization), counters by noting that he is an exception to Starling's rule. Starling's response, "No, you ate yours," concludes an exchange which corresponds with a *New York Times* article on Dahmer, similarly demonstrating an apparently irreducible desire to distinguish normality from abnormality, no matter what the subject matter. There are, apparently, your average repeat murderers, and then there is Jeffrey Dahmer: " 'The trophies [souvenirs of victims] are usually identification cards or pieces of clothing. But few, Dr. Dietz said, are driven by their loneliness to keep pieces of their victims' bodies. An *ordinary serial killer* would have the sense to try to mask the smell,' Dr. Dietz said. 'It's awfully careless not to' " (my italics, 7 August 1991: A8).

The regarding of the body as something that can be hoarded, reassembled, or consumed is a form of abnormality with which currently we seem particularly fascinated. The early nineties witnessed the discovery of cannibalism's marketability. In the same year (1992) that *The Silence of the Lambs* won five Oscars, Francis Ford Coppola's *Bram Stoker's Dracula* was released. In the following year Disney's Touchstone Pictures released *Alive*, the story of how survivors of a plane crash in the Andes managed to eat in the middle of a snowy wilderness. The offering for 1994 in the category of human consumption was the film version of Anne Rice's *Interview with the Vampire*. In court Dahmer holds up a copy of the *Weekly World News* bearing a headline stating that he had eaten one of his cellmates. The masthead, however, is replaced by Dahmer with that of *The Milwaukee Journal* (reported in The *New York Times*, 15 February 1992: 10). If the switch is an ironic comment on the distinction between "serious" and tabloid journalism, Dahmer has a point. Exaggerating Dahmer's claims of cannibalism (he confessed to eating part of one of his victim's arm muscles), Courtland Milloy tells us via the *Washington Post* that "by his own admission, Dahmer befriends you, then cuts your heart out, then snacks on it after eating your brains" (1 August 1991: C3). Although Milwaukee Police Chief, Philip Arreola told reporters early in the investigation that "the evidence is not consistent" with Dahmer's contention of cannibalism, cannibalism was perhaps the major focus of most of the Dahmer stories. Dennis Nilsen speculates that Dahmer's claims of cannibalism were probably "wishful thinking" (quoted in Masters 1991, 268), and perhaps it is as much wishful thinking on our part as his. The intensity of speculation may indicate a cultural demand for cannibalism that exceeds the supply. Is there an argument to be made about a contemporary cultural fascination with this particular form of uncivilized behavior, a fascination strong enough to turn the disputed contention of an individual whom we regard as either sick or evil into one of the unquestionable truths of his being? If Clarice is *The Silence of the Lambs'* heroine for tracking down Buffalo Bill, Hannibal can be its hero for his quest to consume all the indignity in the world. Eating people, it would seem, is not necessarily wrong. It depends on who's doing the eating and who's being eaten. It depends on table manners. Would it be improper for me to suggest that we are finding cannibalism rather sexy at the moment? What function might the putative presence of cannibalism in our culture serve?

While Joel Norris seems to regard Dahmer's cannibalism as an act of nutritional replenishment, as an alternative to a trip to the health-food store—Dahmer, he says, eats "the vital organs of his victims to refortify himself with iron and vitamins that had been depleted through his alcoholism" (Norris 1992, 39)—it is generally perceived as being motivated by the desire for "spiritual empowerment." Dahmer's attorney, Gerald Boyle, explains his client's cannibalistic behavior thus: "He ate body parts so that these poor people he killed would become alive again in him" (Schwartz 195). The connection between cannibalism and empowerment is also present in Dennis Nilsen's assessment of Dahmer. In a letter to Brian Masters, Nilsen suggests that "[Dahmer's] unfolding aberration escalates in accordance with to what degree he is detached from reality (for example, what is termed NECROGRAPHY is an extreme example of extreme detachment). This is manifested in 'going all the way' in eating the heart of one's victim/spouse. (If you have the power to eat a man's heart this demonstrates your extreme power to possess and his extreme passivity). The painting and display of the victim's skull is a constant reminder of one's potency" (quoted in Masters 1991, 186). Is this idea of empowerment a delusion restricted to the imagination of a "sick" individual, or might it have currency in a cultural context?

There are differences in the way we perceive Lecter's cannibalism and Dahmer's, and the differences seem to be related to the differences we perceive in their sexuality. In this chapter I discuss the correspondence between Dahmer's putative sexuality, his color, and his supposed cannibalism, a correspondence that also hints about the relationship between cannibalism and mainstream culture, a culture which in many ways continues to present itself as being essentially heterosexual as well as white. In particular I will discuss with reference to Dahmer's representation our attempts to conflate oppositions such as civilization/cannibalism, self/other and heterosexuality/homosexuality, and the difficulties we get into when we do so. That Dahmer is perceived as deviant in more than one way complicates and sometimes impedes our essentializing notions of civilization, of heterosexuality, of our sense of self, and of what are perceived to be their opposites. The plurality of his deviancy, I suggest, might be the cause of an apparent unease about how to represent Dahmer, about this moment when the words do not come naturally, when openings seem to appear in what Roland Barthes would call the logosphere. Before the openings are smoothed over again, I hope an exploration of our construction of "civilization" as used in the stories we tell about Dahmer will yield more questions about our obsessions, fears, and desires.

The language used to represent Dahmer may best be described as "anthropological." Our representation of his putative homosexuality and the "homosexual world" he inhabits has the air of an investigation, the gaining of knowledge about what the *New York Times* describes as "the fringes of society" (4 August 1991: 30), those blurred areas on our horizons where transsexuality fades into homosexuality and where both are synonymous with transiency. In *The Man-Eating Myth* Arens says, "In ordering the material on other cultures, anthropology . . . serves as a medical category between us and them, represented by those who have lived in the two worlds and therefore claim to understand both the savage and the civilized mind" (169). As I have noted previously, medical metaphors are common in the representation of serial killers and their detection. With the moral integrity of a physician, we begin our quest for knowledge, make our entry into the mind of the killer, or, as in the case of Milwaukee journalist, Anne E. Schwartz, his neighborhood: "I hopped into my brown 1979 Chevy Caprice and, pushing the accelerator to its limit, drove from my neighborhood of manicured lawns into the bowels of the city to my reporting beat of darkened tenements, burned-out streetlights, and wary looks from the locals" (6). Clearly the natives aren't friendly, and those bowels need a good colonic irrigation.

Helping us see how our predecessors saw the colon in colony, Stallybrass and White, referring to Victorian England, remark that "at one level, the mapping of the city in terms of dirt and cleanliness tended to repeat the discourse of colonial anthropology" (Stallybrass and White 130). For Kenneth Lynn, it is a discourse which, in its American form, takes on a distinctly Christian quality. Expressing an ambivalence towards the city—the city constructed as, on the one hand, a place of "glittering amusement and technological marvels and on the other hand of social exploitation and spiritual degradation" (Lynn 137)—the discourse, prevalent in American literature and folklore from "all centuries of our history, all sections of the country" signifies "a familiar American concern, at heart a religious concern, with the question of whether honor, charity, and other traditional values of Western civilization [are] capable of surviving in the modern city" (137). The city, so the story goes, is where we find our most extreme examples of unnaturalness and criminality, qualities which the zoologist Desmond Morris, cited in Wilson and Seaman's *The Serial Killers*, obviously associates with homosexuality: "Morris remarked that cities are 'human zoos,' and added: 'Under normal conditions, in their natural habitats, wild animals do not mutilate themselves, masturbate, attack their offspring, develop stomach ulcers, become fetishists, suffer from obesity, form homosexual pair-bonds, or commit murder' " (Wilson and Seaman 227). When, following news of Dahmer, maps of gay cruising areas are produced by a local ABC affiliate as part of its four-part series on gay life in Milwaukee, *Flirting with Danger*, contemporary versions of the speakers of colonial anthropology find their way to downtown Milwaukee, home to the city's gay bars, which form an area that Dvorchak and

Holewa tell us was recently known as the "gay ghetto" (70). And when claims of cannibalism are heard, we find justification for our fancy-dress combo of pith helmets, white coats, and dog collars.

Arens reflects on the tendency to seize upon and exaggerate claims of reputed savagery: "The obvious preference runs in the direction of transforming those suspected of being cannibals into confirmed ritual endocannibals and, in the twentieth century, into gustatory exocannibals on a grand scale. The Aztec case is a classic example of this trend, which took on momentum without the accumulation of additional evidence on the act itself. The idea and image of cannibalism expands with time and the intellectual appetite" (165). The anthropological discourse present in Dahmer's representation can serve "as a reviver and reinventor of the notion of savagery" (Arens 66) and, especially when medical and medicinal in tone, can naturalize the need to eradicate (like a disease) the types of people or lifestyles we figure the serial killer as representing. With the reinvention of "savagery" being an essential part of the trouble-free evolution of the concept "civilization," the desire to change the concept of savagery may indicate a fear that "civilization as we know it" is threatened.

However, with Dahmer, as Courtland Milloy indicates, our traditional method of constructing savagery goes out of the window: "When I was growing up television shows frequently portrayed Africans as doing that kind of thing—turning some Great White Bwana into a happy meal. At least ten of Dahmer's victims were black. Police suspect that Dahmer hated blacks. But here is this all-America-looking white guy sucking on black people's bones like they were pork knuckles" (*Washington Post*, 1 August 1991: C3). Dahmer, in case we forget, is white. He is, according to racist ideology, the embodiment of a contradiction in terms: the white savage. And while, as Anastasia Toufexis notes in an article on the insanity defense, "Juries are more likely to send blacks to prison, whites to hospitals" (*Newsweek*, 3 February 1992: 17)—while, we are more willing to attempt to civilize white savages than black, more willing to perceive white criminals as erring only temporarily (their crimes the result of their white bodies and white minds being only temporarily out of control), more willing to perceive black criminals as beyond redemption, requiring punishment not therapy—Dahmer is rather too much beyond the pale, beyond being someone whom we can reasonably allow on this side of the border separating paleness from otherness.

When we see Dahmer—this white boy with a privileged background, from an industrious, well-educated family—how do we redefine savagery and civilization? What or whom is being defined as savage/uncivilized? In the representation of Dahmer's story others carry the mark of 'uncivilized' besides the perpetrator of the crimes. An appendix to Anne E. Schwartz's book on the Dahmer case lists his victims' criminal records along with their age and race. In the main text she says, "All of Jeffrey Dahmer's victims facilitated him in some way, which is not to say that they deserved to die, but rather that their life-styles and unnecessary risk-taking contributed to their deaths. That many of Dahmer's victims had arrest records was also a characteristic of a victim who was instrumental in his own demise" (114). Her comments follow reference to a Master's thesis written by a Milwaukee police lieutenant, Kenneth Meuler, in which he identifies four types of victim: "innocent non-participating victims" ("Neither their life-style nor their actions immediately preceding their death attracted the killer"); "innocent facilitating victims" ("Law-abiding people who made it easier for the killer"); "criminal facilitating victim" ("People whose death was the direct result of being involved in some criminal activity"); "criminal precipitating victims" ("People who were the first aggressor"). Schwartz implicitly identifies Dahmer's victims as belonging to Meuler's third category, "criminal facilitating victims." And it is their lifestyle which warrants this identification: "Many of Dahmer's victims went to a stranger's apartment because they wanted to make a few bucks by taking off their clothes and posing nude. The youths who left gay bars with men they didn't know were leading lives full of risks and, in the end, were killed as a result of their own negligence and recklessness. They were looking for nameless, faceless sex" (115). The same theme is replayed by police-union lobbyist David Orley, quoted in the *Wisconsin Light* (a Milwaukee lesbian and gay newspaper): "These gays all choose the life-style which gets them killed" (cited in *The Advocate*, 10 September 1991: 57).

To his neighbors, Dahmer explained the stench emanating from his apartment as "a sewer problem." Schwartz and Orley, holding their noses, describe the whole scene they encounter in downtown Milwaukee in much the same terms. As Milwaukee State Representative Polly Williams notes, such a morality can be expensive: "Because of the conditions here, we have our black men now that will fall prey to this kind of stuff because they don't have jobs, they don't have money. So if somebody comes and offers them a hundred bucks to pose for a picture, they'll take it, because they need to live" (*Nightline*, 7 August 1991). And, countering the type of claims Schwartz makes, someone who managed to escape from Dahmer's apartment tells *Newsweek* that "[Dahmer] was coming on as a friend and a nice guy. You could hear this man crying for help—that was my weakness" (3 February 1992: 46). By stating that Dahmer's mostly nonwhite victims were partly to blame for their deaths, we can reemploy the traditional method of defining savagery that we initially rejected. This is especially so when we invoke the myth which associates "sexual deviancy" with "racial deviancy" (and whiteness with heterosexuality), the myth evident in a question posed by Don Davis in his book on Dahmer: "How did Jeffrey Dahmer, a white man, work so smoothly with gays and minorities?" (1991, 255).

On a different tack, we might play down the fact that Dahmer is white by playing down the factor of race altogether, by playing down the fact that Dahmer's victim's were mostly black or Asian. Thus Dahmer is a "gay killer" or a "homophobic stalker" (Norris 1992, 262) but never a "white monster" and rarely a "black killer." Dahmer's possible racism is much more of a taboo subject than his sexuality, and that taboo helps to shield the partnership of whiteness with civilization. But it is a partnership protected not only by silence, but by inscribing his victims with *incivility*, by figuring Dahmer not as the white killer of blacks but as the white man tempted by and lost in a black, savage world. It is a world whose inhabitants speak a language which apparently requires translation: "And I, you know, I ain't got no quarter on him [she did not know who he was], I just seened him" is how Schwartz reports part of a neighbor's telephone call to the police telling them of Konerak Sinthasomphone, a fourteen-year-old Laotian, fleeing from Dahmer's apartment. We can only wonder about how much energy would have been spent tracking down the criminal records of the victims if they had all been white and heterosexual. Such attention in the representation of Dahmer implicitly links the victim with the killer, places him in "the world of serial killers," a "netherworld," an uncivilized world where anything goes, and of course a world distinct from ours.

For Milwaukee psychiatrist Ashok Bedi, Dahmer's sexuality is a sign of abnormality: "His personality disorder, the alcohol addiction, the pedophilia, the necrophilia, his ego and homosexuality, all were layers of his dysfunction" (quoted in Davis 1991, 264). In an edition of *Sonya Live*, the host notes that "Jeffrey Dahmer and [John Wayne] Gacy . . . were sexual sadists when it came to males," and that "Ted Bundy and [Arthur] Shawcross [were] sexual sadists when it came to females." She then asks her expert guests, "Was that just spurious, something that just happened, or is there something in the background that leads one in one direction or the other?" In response, Richard Kraus, forensic psychiatrist, says that "the Gacy and Dahmer cases revealed a lot of sexual orientation disturbance," whereas Shawcross "had something to prove, mainly that he was potent in a heterosexual world" (*Sonya Live*, 1 March 1993). The distinction Kraus makes between the "homosexual" killer and the "heterosexual" killer is representative of the way we perceive the acts of the former as a consequence of something gone wrong (that is, the individual has a sexual orientation "disturbance" and begins to like men), and the acts of "straight killers" as a consequence of a desire which is considered normal, which others have and most others putatively fulfill. Gacy's and Dahmer's homosexuality is framed as unnatural, the result of something gone awry, whereas Shawcross's "problem" is not his sexual orientation but his sexual impotency.

This choosiness when it comes to serial killers and their sexualities is evident in our referencing of Dahmer to *The Silence of the Lambs'* monster-as-hero, Lecter, and monster-as-gargoyle, Buffalo Bill. While Dahmer's cannibalism links him to Lecter, he mostly finds himself cast as Buffalo Bill because of the way we regard his sexuality. *People Weekly's* John Tayman, for example, suggests that "Jeffrey L. Dahmer may have more in common with *Lambs'* other nightmare man, the skin-stitching Buffalo Bill—a furtive, gender-obsessed character who was less mad genius than helpless psychopath" (12 August 1991: 36). In the movie, Buffalo Bill provides context to a good old-fashioned heterosexual story between two star-crossed lovers, separated by class, by prison-bars, and finally by the restraints of courtesy. His Bad Guy identity is reinforced by our conflating transsexuality, transvestism, and homosexuality and by his character being made up in part by the gay stereotype. The 1992 Oscars host, Billy Crystal, can be confident of getting an opening laugh by being wheeled onto the stage as Doctor Lecter, complete with restraining suit and hockey mask, but would be nervous about setting the tone for an evening of glamour and fun by wearing Buffalo Bill drag, speaking with an impediment, and carrying a poodle. Mike Kinsley can get away with referring to his cohost on CNN's *Crossfire*, Robert Novak, as Harris's more popular and more powerful monster—"Hannibal Lecter and I will be back in just a moment" (*Crossfire:* 31 January 1992)—but presumably would not if he implied a resemblance between Novak and the monster we commonly perceive as gender-confused, helpless, and impotent. *Newsweek's* Alex Prud'homme can compare and contrast the *"brilliant* mass-murdering psychiatrist in *The Silence of the Lambs"* to the "creature" from Milwaukee (my italics; 5 August 1991: 26). It is the mad but heroic genius we love, not those with abnormal sexualities, not those who love fluffy dogs and speak with a lisp.

The move to identify monstrosity and savagery in homosexuality is a familiar one in the representation of other "gay killers." In *Mass Murder*, Levin and Fox describe Dean Corll's murders in Houston: "Twenty-seven bodies of young boys were excavated in Houston, Texas, after Elmer Wayne Henley confessed to his part as an accomplice in the *homosexual rituals* of Dean Corll" (my italics; 20). "The macabre British homosexual serial murderer" (28) is how Elliott Leyton manages to infuse and confuse homosexuality (not to mention the murderer's nationality) with other-worldliness. Like the actions of "gay killers," those of "straight killers" are considered to arise from an inability to control themselves sexually, but because heterosexuality is naturalized, it is the (individual) killer's inability to control himself which is condemned, not his sexuality and not the "lifestyles" which are considered as essential to that sexuality. The heterosexuality of a "heterosexual killer" mostly *goes without saying*. Two separate groups are discernible in Wilson's and Seaman's list of illustrations for *The Serial Killers* (viii). There are "types" whose particular "perversions" are named, who are identified as "a necrophiliac lust killer," "a psychopath described as 'an accident of internal wiring,' " and John Wayne Gacy, "a homosexual serial killer," and then there are those who glory in sobriquets, who have earned the right to be nicknamed, those who are supposedly heterosexual: the "Boston Strangler," "the Night Stalker," "Son of Sam." When, as in the case of Ted Bundy, the victims and killer are assumed to be heterosexual, our tendency is not to group victim and killer together and exclude them from us, but to figure the victim as representative of our world, our civilization, and to figure the killer as a senseless monster from without or below. In such a case our tendency is not to explain the act in terms of varying degrees of "victim facilitation," but to mystify the act, describing the killer as striking motivelessly and striking at innocence.

To mystify or not to mystify, to regard as senseless or to find explanation—we are faced with many choices. For a heterosexual culture, the Dahmer case represents an opportunity to explain acts of savagery by referring to his putative homosexuality, to confuse homicidal with homosexual tendencies, confuse "sexual homicide" (Norris 1992, 255) with homo sex. Speculating on Dahmer's motivation for cannibalism, Brian Masters suggests that it is "possible that Jeffrey Dahmer dimly feels some kind of 'shared' tragedy with the victims, as if they have all suffered from indifference and neglect and [are] united in this dramatic denouement," and that "the desire to identify with the victim, to be at one with him, to share his fate, cannot in the end be more graphically expressed than by eating him" (Masters 1991, 266). In those representations of Dahmer which similarly describe his life as "tragic," a major flaw of Dahmer's, to put the tragedy in Aristotlean terms, is his homosexuality. A *Time* article on the Houston murders (27 August 1973: 56) takes seriously the idea that what it calls "aberrant sex" is "causally related to mass murder" before generally rejecting it (quoting a Harvard Medical School "expert on multicide" as saying that there is "no connection between homosexuality and murder per se"). Two decades later, however, plots which construct murder or serial murder as an event arising from homosexuality are not only of the subplot variety. On an edition of *Geraldo* we hear of Dahmer being "homosexual or freaky or whatever" with a potential victim (12 September 1991). The *Los Angeles Times* describes Gerald Boyle, Dahmer's attorney, conjuring up for the jury an image of Dahmer who, as a fourteen-year-old, "realized he was a homosexual and first fantasized about having sex with a corpse" (31 January 1992). And Masters, apparently inspired by Dahmer's guilt about his sexuality, presents us with an image of homosexuality as a harmful influence taking hold of a young, innocent, and *heterosexual* Jeffrey:

> Before the trial he started to have fitful dreams. . . . They were pleasant homosexual dreams accompanied by feelings of warmth and calm, with no violence or stress. Even these he distrusted, however, and declared his intention to free himself from them. First, the Bible forbade homosexual behavior, and he hoped he would in time be able to banish homosexual thought. Second, it was the homosexuality in him which led to his becoming a murderer. Had he not encouraged it, none of this might have happened. . . . It was possible, at least, that in the depths of his being his orientation was not homosexual at all, but that it had been diverted onto that by his extreme social awkwardness as a child. Dahmer's rejection of his homosexual dreams may have reflected a subconscious wish to rediscover his earliest self. (Masters 1993, 219)

Conspicuous by their absence are speculations about heterosexuality descending like a cloud on the young selves of future "heterosexual" serial killers. Rather than a suffering of "indifference," to use Masters' term, perhaps a more accurate description of the gay experience of heterosexual culture is a suffering of difference. I have in mind Eve Kosofsky Sedgwick's comment that "the nomitive category of 'the homosexual' has robustly failed to disintegrate under the pressure of decade after decade, battery after battery of deconstructive exposure—evidently not in the first place because of its meaningfulness to those whom it defines but because of its indispensableness to those who define themselves as against it" (Sedgwick 1990, 83). The representation of Dahmer connects the idea of savagery with that of homosexuality as a means of defining heterosexual culture against "Jeffrey Dahmer, homosexual."

The history of how we define the uncivilized is full of different versions of the "homosexual." Jeffrey Weeks comments that "in the mythology of the twentieth century, the homosexual is the archetypal sexed being, a person whose sexuality pervaded him in his very existence" (Weeks 107). The mythology is revived in Dahmer's representation. After quoting a former paramedic who says that 95 percent of the homes of gays he visited had a "strange odor" of "exotic perfume," "animal odors," and the like, Don Davis, in *The Milwaukee Murders*, discusses the police's unwillingness to get involved in disputes between gay couples, and mentions the claim of police who "go into the homes of such people" that "pornographic books and pictures are the norm" (10). For the writers of a *Newsweek* article, "Secrets of a Serial Killer," Milwaukee's gay bars "line up like tarts in the nights" (3 February 1992: 45). And according to Rick Bowen, director of *Jeffrey Dahmer: The Secret Life*, homosexual desire will override just about anything: "Gays are going to love [the movie] because I treat the love scenes sensitively. Besides, we used cute guys" (quoted in *The Advocate*, 3 November 1992: 93).

The myth described by Weeks can arise in more subtle ways. Ideas that homosexuals are "less choosy," that homosexual relationships are much more easily available than heterosexual relationships, that heterosexuality is something one moves towards as one becomes more civilized are the bases from which we can make sense of a quotation from Ashok Bedi included in Davis's book: "[Dahmer's] is what I call a defensive homosexuality. It's a retreat to homosexuality because these men or women have not *evolved the art* to connect with heterosexual encounters and reach across the sexual lines. So they connect with a group that will respond to them promptly" (my italics; 1991, 262). Comforting to a *white* heterosexual audience is the idea that Dahmer is prey to his sexual desires, that he is his sexuality's victim. It is an idea implicit in the term "homosexual overkill" that officials and press borrowed from the earlier case of Joachim Dressler. Robert Dvorchak and Lisa Holewa paraphrase Milwaukee County Medical Examiner Jeffrey M. Jentzen's testimony about the term as something that "is done by a man with deeply repressed homosexual feelings or a homosexual who acted in a frenzy against a gay lover" (Dvorchak and Holewa 209). Joel Norris notes that an "expert from a local university" commented at the trial that cases of homosexual overkill "usually involved torture or mutilations of the sexual organs" (Norris 1992, 45). *Overkill* was also the title of a CBS television movie about Aileen Wuornos, depicted in the press as the lesbian, man-hating, "first female serial killer." The idea of the savage homosexual is an antigay myth satirized in the following excerpt from an imaginary exchange between two Milwaukeeans (written by journalist Joel McNally in a piece pulled by editors of the *Milwaukee Journal*): "Give me good old normal heterosexuals anytime. They kill people just the right amount" (quoted in Schwartz 129).

Weeks also notes that the mythological homosexual "threatens to corrupt all around him and particularly the young," and that "the most pervasive stereotype of the male homosexual was as a 'corrupter of youth.' " This aspect of the mythology seems pertinent to one of the most highly publicized aspects of the Dahmer case. After a naked and bleeding fourteen-year-old Laotian boy, Konerak Sinthasomphone, was seen pursued by Dahmer on the street outside of Dahmer's apartment, neighbors called the police and then checked back later:

Caller: I wondered if this situation was being handled. This was a male child being raped and molested by an adult.

Officer: Where did this happen?

          [*She was transferred to another officer.*]

Officer: Hello, this is the Milwaukee Police.

Caller: Yes, there was a Squad Car No. 68 that was flagged down earlier this evening, about fifteen minutes ago.

Officer: That was me.

Caller: Yeah, uh, what happened? I mean my daughter and my niece witnessed what was going on. Was anything done about this situation? Do you need their names or information or anything from them?

Officer: No, I don't need it. No, not at all.

Caller: You don't?

Officer: Nope, It's an intoxicated boyfriend of another boyfriend.

Caller: Well, how old was this child?

Officer: It wasn't a child. It was an adult.

Caller: Are you sure?

Officer: Yup.

Caller: Are you positive? Because this child doesn't even speak English. My daughter had, you know, dealt with him before and seen him on the street, you know, catching earthworms.

Officer: Yeah—no, he's—it's all taken care of, ma'am.

Caller: I mean, are you positive this is an adult.

Officer: Ma'am. Like I explained to you. It is all taken care of. It's as positive as I can be. I can't do anything about somebody's sexual preferences in life. (Excerpts of transcript released by the Milwaukee Police cited in *The New York Times*, 2 August 1991: A10; *Geraldo*, 4 December 1991; and Davis 1991, 47–51)

After having been persuaded by Dahmer to allow the boy to be returned to his apartment, where the boy was killed minutes later, one of the officers who had been called to the scene sent the by-now infamous message to the dispatcher: "The intoxicated Asian naked male [*laughter heard in background*] was returned to sober boyfriend and we're ten-eight" . . . [*officers sent to a battery complaint*] . . . "Ten-four. It'll be a minute. My partner's gonna get deloused at the station [*laughter*]" (cited in Schwartz 93).

We can of course only speculate as to whether the officers truly believed the boy to be an adult, and we can only speculate about how they would have responded to a naked, bleeding, fourteen-year-old white girl or boy being pursued down a suburban street, or what they would have done if Dahmer had been black, or if the women complaining had been white. But the mythology that surrounds the "netherworld," that space inhabited by nonwhites and nonheterosexuals, that space which, if entered, apparently requires one to be deloused, might explain in part what Milwaukee Police Chief Arreola described as "inexplicable." We all know that vision is not a passive quality, and from the point of view of a culture which attempts to lump together all its "others",[1] the sight of a "self-confessed" homosexual with a naked Asian fourteen-year-old might appear "normal," might appear as if it belonged to a world in which law and order and reason did not and need not apply. Certainly it seems not to have applied when the officers left Dahmer with Konerak without filing a report or making a computer check, which would have revealed that Dahmer was on probation because of a conviction for molesting Konerak's then thirteen-year-old brother. And if Konerak did appear as an adult, the failure "to intervene in an apparent instance of domestic violence between gay partners" (Jenkins 1994, 179) can be explained by reference to the mythological homosexual, who is *undomestic* and all that that implies, to the idea that *domestic* is a heterosexual condition, to the idea that violence suffered by Konerak at that point had done no violence to the culturally prescribed notion of domesticity.[2]

"Did you buy the judge's explanation today that this was kind of a repressed homosexuality which caused the acts when [Dahmer] took them in his house, because of the shame?" Dahmer's attorney is asked on *Larry King Live* (17 February 1992), following the trial's conclusion. The *Milwaukee Journal* refers to Dahmer as a "gay misfit" in one of its headlines. The connection between Dahmer's homosexuality and the killings and putative cannibalism is made with reference to the "in the closet"/"out of the closet" construction of gay experience. In contrast

1. Milwaukee police officer Sgt. Leonard Wells, president of the League of Martin, an organization of black officers named after the Rev. Dr. Martin Luther King, Jr., stated at the time, "If you're poor, black, Hispanic, gay or lesbian, then in the eyes of many on the Milwaukee Police Department, you are engaging in deviant behavior" (quoted in The *New York Times*, 2 August 1991: A10).

2. This apparent association of homosexuality with natural disorder is of course not peculiar to the United States. London's gay community in 1993 complained of the lack of police monitoring of the murders committed by Colin Ireland (see Joan Smith).

to the statement of a former lover of Dahmer's that Dahmer was "an active member in the gay community in Milwaukee" and not a "homophobic gay person" (*Donahue*, 23 September 1991), much media attention was given to Dahmer's guilt about his homosexuality. The comments of James Alan Fox are representative of such diagnoses: "If he at all feels uncomfortable about his own sexual orientation, it is very easy to see [him projecting] it onto these victims and punishing them indirectly to punish himself. . . . He hated anyone who was more gay than he. This was his method of punishment. He could be attracted to these people and then feel extremely horrible about it, and he lashes out at them as opposed to himself. So it's a combination of his hatred for these victims, mixed in with some racial hatred, combined with fantasies that do involve this idea of cutting people up" (quoted in Schwartz 148). David Van Leer, among others, has argued that to a heterosexual audience "coming out" is often a confession to the guilt of one's sexuality, that to be homosexual, is to *be* guilty. In much of Dahmer's representation, homosexual existence is seen as a secret world of guilt and self-hatred, and conspicuously lacking is the idea that that guilt is misplaced. The idea of the closet, that structure created by or created because of homophobia, is made tangible in Dahmer's representation. His sexual closet, a world of guilt-ridden fantasies, is conflated with the closet which is his apartment, his "lair" (Davis, 1991, 134), his "chamber of horrors" (*Geraldo*, 12 September 1991), his "den of death" (Davis, 1991, cover), which we discover to be full of the stench of rotting corpses. This cryptic closet is presumably the reason why Dahmer's voice, as he attacks Tracey Edwards with a knife, "sounded as if it came from the bottom of a tomb" (Davis 1991, 24). Every new killing is seen as the result of that which lurks within the closet making itself known.

In a culture in which the guilt for one's homosexuality is naturalized, murders by (self-hating) homosexuals are figured as the natural consequence of homosexuality. And perceiving Dahmer's acts as homophobic—as caused by a violent repression of homosexuality—is another way of individualizing/aculturalizing the crime, of concealing the possibility that Dahmer's actions could be related to homophobic culture. Jonathan Dollimore notes how gay homophobia is usually figured in subjective, psychic terms rather than as something which circulates culturally (Dollimore 245), the consequences of which encourage "a way of thinking whereby the aggressor in homophobic violence is somehow identified with his or her victim: both are homosexual, the one repressed, the other overt" (242). Helping to localize the crime to homosexuality is the term *gay killer*, used to refer to both Dahmer and

Colin Ireland. Does the term mean the killer is gay, or that his victims are gay, or both? The confusion contributes to the depiction of a "gay world" characterized by violent criminality. It is a world depicted as excluding heterosexuality, not as something constructed by heterosexual culture's homophobia. It is a world in which sex and hate mingle: Dahmer's crimes are presented as either sex crimes, which are the expression of homosexuality, or as hate crimes, with that hate perceived as an enduring presence *within* homosexuality.

"He kind of talked and told me what he was—you know, what he wanted me to do." "And then he started acting like that, you know?" Tracey Edwards, "The Only Surviving Victim of Serial Killer Jeffrey Dahmer," as the *Donahue* show titled him (23 September 1991), recondemns homosexuality to the world of "the unspeakable," a world which can include all kinds of indescribable phenomena. We cannot say what is there, but what it is, "we know." But we also like to make it clear that this knowledge is not *intimate*. Heterosexuality's appropriation of culture (as opposed to individuality)—that is, appropriation of the idea of the *social* body, that body from which homosexuals are excluded because they are not involved in recognized kinship systems—helps to protect the full cultural presence of heterosexuality (a presence, that is, untainted with homosexuality) from the idea of a homosexuality "within," from a homosexuality which is fundamental to, not parasitical of, heterosexual structures. Homosexuality is figured as something which affects individuals, something individuals either assert, or must come to terms with, or repress; heterosexuality, on the other hand, is the bond which unites culture.

Some of Norman Mailer's thoughts on homosexuality resonate with the representation of Dahmer as someone who kills to assert his manhood, as someone wanting to gain acceptance in a heterosexual world by killing the homosexual within himself. Dollimore notes Mailer's opinion "that anyone who has succeeded in repressing his homosexuality has earned the right not to be called homosexual" (Dollimore 46; the view cited in Altman's *Homosexual Oppression and Liberation*). For Mailer, repression is a heroic act, an act one struggles to achieve alone and which, if achieved, allows one to be initiated into society and obtain cultural recognition for one's efforts. It is the history of the struggle to move from slavery to freedom. Perhaps anxious about the possible instability of the oppositions of heterosexuality/ homosexuality and civilization/savagery, Mailer in *Advertisements for Myself* states that to understand "the ills of the homosexual . . . one had to dig—deep into the complex and often foul pots of thought where sex and society live in their murderous dialectic" (Mailer 199).

The construction of the repressor of homosexuality as the repressor of precivilization wildness is identified by Joan Mellen in the movie *Deliverance:*

> In the primal event of the film Ed ([played by Jon] Voigt) and Bobby ([Ned] Beaty), but not Louis ([Burt] Reynolds), are captured by two rural degenerates, men primitive enough to act out those forbidden sexual impulses "civilized" men like our heroes repress and deflect into more acceptable manifestations, such as hunting animals or contact sports. Ed is tied to a tree. Bobby, a fat, ineffectual man, is ordered to drop his pants and is raped. Both men are threatened with having their "balls cut off," whether or not they cooperate. The terror evoked is not just that of being violently mutilated by degenerates but of being forced to express latent homosexual feelings, and in a passive vulnerable, re-ceiving manner. . . . As if in shuddering reaction to what has been seen, the film now turns to an advocacy of male force, in contradiction of its earlier irony toward Louis's macho flaunting of his strength. Now homosexual need and male eroticism for other males are associated with dark, savage, and primitive needs *properly* repressed by civiliza-tion. If civilization limits us, going native means that the dark forces of the id, symbolized by the ghoulish hillbillies, as malevolent as gar-goyles, will overtake us. *Deliverance* is, in sum, a Freudian fable of the dangers of our instinctual life. If the price of civilization is the curing of male vitality and release, the consequences of going back are surrender to the savage animal world of rape and violation of the weak by the strong. (author's italics; Mellen 318–19)

In a commonly heard story, Dahmer similarly goes on a journey into his psychic self. Revolted by what he finds, he attempts to destroy it. He fails, however, in his quest for deliverance: the beast will not die. Ac-cording to Michael McCann, district attorney in the Dahmer trial, Dah-mer *gave in* to sexual impulses. During cross-examination, McCann asks Doctor Wahlstrom, a defense witness: "Wouldn't we all be in trou-ble if we followed all our sexual desires, regardless of what those de-sires were?" (*New York Times*, 9 February 1992: A23). For McCann, we all have the potential for evil within us, and it has a name: sex. Sex is naturally something that will get us into trouble. This idea is also put forward by Camille Paglia in *Sexual Personae:* "Sex is the point of contact between man and nature, where morality and good intentions fall to primitive urges" (quoted in Masters 1993, 97). Sex, according to McCann, if not Paglia, needs controlling. But it's homo-sex which needs especially to be kept in check. Time and time again, repaying savagery with savagery, Dahmer attempts final destruction, final clo-sure. But it is a cycle only broken by his arrest. Dahmer proves his weakness, his "emasculation" by his failure to conquer homosexuality. And if we fail to question the association of homosexuality with savagery, perhaps our fascination for this story comes from the nightmarish possibility that his struggles are potentially ours, that deep within our notion of civilization we hear echoes of that which we define as civilization's other, that Dahmer's closets turn out to be our own. The perception of heterosexuality as the means by which homosexuality is repressed engenders a worrying opposition for "heterosexual civilization": a constraining heterosexuality versus the natural "freedom" of homosexuality.

We see, then, in Dahmer's representation and its stress on cannibalism a continuation of the colonizing of homosexuality by heterosexual culture, the conflation of heterosexuality with civilization and homosexuality with savagery. The homosexual, like all those colonized in history, is figured as both alien to and dependent on the parent culture. Dahmer, says Don Davis, "claimed to have killed seventeen of the most vulnerable members of Milwaukee's citizenry—children and homosexuals" (Davis 1991, 164–65). Davis's inscription of gays with weakness represents a paternalism (from a presumed vantage point of heterosexuality) which has less benign manifestations. Homosexuality is seen as dependent on heterosexuality for its tolerance—it is, so the story goes, a disease worthy of eradication—and for its civilizing qualities. Unless they are made of the stuff Mailer admires, however, the colonized can rarely cross the barrier separating the colonized from the colonizer. Brian Masters notes in his article how it is "suggested that [Dahmer] is a homosexual by default—that his sexual orientation was not a preference but a compensation for the impossibility of having a relationship with a woman" (Masters 1991, 189). Such a suggestion might lead to the uncomfortable conclusion that Dahmer's sexuality should be given the prefix *hetero*, that his actions were the consequence of a frustrated heterosexuality. Masters rejects the suggestion and calls Dahmer a "genuine homosexual." On the edge of heterosexuality, colonizers understand how Dahmer would want to be a real man, but an unreal man dressed in real men's clothes fools nobody, especially genuine heterosexuals.

The dependence of the colonizer on the colonized is downplayed. The idea of the dependency of heterosexuality on homosexuality is central to one of Eve Sedgwick's deconstructive arguments in *Epistemology of the Closet*. The "analytic move" her argument makes, she says,

is to demonstrate that categories presented in a culture as symmetrical binary oppositions—heterosexual/homosexual, in this case—actually subsist in a more unsettled and dynamic tacit relation according to

81

which, first, term B is not symmetrical with but subordinated to term A; but, second the ontologically valorized term A actually depends for its meaning on the simultaneous subsumption and exclusion of term B; hence, third, the question of priority between the supposed central and the supposed marginal category of each dyad is irresolvably unstable, an instability caused by the fact that term B is constituted as at once internal and external to term A. (Sedgwick 1990, 9–10)

Having blamed Dahmer's actions on homosexuality, heterosexual culture needs to repress the possibility that, to use Sedgwick's structure, homosexuality is internal to heterosexuality (and heterosexuality internal to homosexuality), and this need produces a frantic effort to stress homosexuality's externality or the need for that externality. I have suggested that one result is the extreme figuration of "the homosexual as cannibalistic savage" and that the structure is still not fully stabilized by this figuration. For the same move can be made to demonstrate that the opposition civilization/savagery exists in the same unstable state as heterosexual/homosexual, and that savagery is both internal and external to civilization.

Of course oppositions can always be shown to lack *intrinsic* stability. Theoretical demonstrations of their instability as a means of refuting essentializing arguments or denaturalizing oppressive ideologies have been perhaps the major and most useful recent activities of university English departments. However, I suggest that the apparent contemporary cultural fascination with savagery and especially cannibalism indicates that questioning the relationship of civility and uncivility has been as much the concern of what those English departments might call "dominant culture" as of the departments themselves. Historically, the nature of the relationship has always relied on context. In the absence of oppositions which are *essentially* different, estrangement relies on context. Context has always protected the idea of civilization from acts which appear savage. In *Alive*, the particular circumstances in which the survivors found themselves meant that few people condemned their cannibalism. While we know that cannibalism, as Brian Masters notes, "has a long history among some civilizations and has often been considered honorable by those tribes which have entertained it as a noble ritual," we may also like to dwell on the idea that "a strong echo still exists in our society, for what is more symbolically cannibalistic than the sacrament by which Christians take the body and blood of Christ into themselves?" (Masters 1991, 267–68). We've always *known* cannabalism; until now, however, we've done our best to deny it by calling it something else. Perhaps our current preoccupation with it shows us to be intrigued by the possibility that it is not the likes of Lecter and Dahmer straddling the histories of civilization and savagery but cannibalism itself. Are our ponderings not part of a healthy self-examination? Are they first steps in acknowledging that some of our prejudices have no reasonable foundation?

As we root around civilization in order to see how it works, to examine its internal circuitry, we find things which delight us, things which we do not need to displace onto others, homosexual or otherwise. "Civilized," we discover, has a prefix which has always been there, only hidden from view. And we're not too concerned about context, that which can "excuse" certain acts. Our attraction to the story of *Alive* seems to have at least as much to do with identifying "savage" behavior within our fellow civilians, as with acknowledging that context "legitimized" the cannibalism, made it less the behavior of savages and more that of the desperately hungry. We don't seem to feel the need to make excuses anymore. After journeying into the recesses of our psychic selves, our confession exhilarates us. In the context of Christian sacrament, Masters says, "it is interesting that Nilsen (who never admitted to necrophagy) frequently uses words like 'purification' and 'sacred' and 'this almost holy feeling' when describing his behavior towards those who died at his hands. Of his last victim, he wrote, 'Here in this cell he is still with me. In fact I believe he is me, or part of me' " (Masters 1991, 267–68). What we take great delight in seeing within us is not that which dilutes our powers of estrangement but that which gives us sacredness, holiness, mystery—that which connects us with the unspeakable force of nature. Perhaps our current fascination with cannibalism indicates a desire to appropriate those powers previously ascribed to the savage. Nilsen, as I mention in my introduction, remarks on the degree to which the figure of the empowered serial killer is a function of culture, and that he himself never had any power in his life—until, it seems, he gained some kind of spiritual and social power, the power that comes from consuming others, a power which makes sense in the language with which he, Lecter, and Dahmer are represented and with which we are all familiar.

That language, as I have suggested earlier, is the language of the anthropologist, or rather the anthropologist who has gone too far, whose sense of identity is hopelessly, madly confused: the civilized savage, the savage civilian. It is the language which Dahmer uses to compare human flesh to "filet mignon" (*Newsweek*, 10 February 1992: 31), the language which can make sense of Lecter reading cookery books for connoisseurs before feasting on his prison guards. It is the language of he who has "lived in the two worlds and therefore claim[s] to understand both the savage and the civilized mind," as Arens puts it, he whose certainties have been lost through such knowledge. We're not sure how to estrange Mr. Hyde and not too sure whether we want to. And perhaps this instability increases our sense of power. Occupying a no-man's-land where sanity is indistinguishable from madness, culture indistinguishable from nonculture, we have a great vantage point, we are able to see (and have power over) the mysteries of both sides. Discussing the medieval custom of expelling madmen in ships which became known as "ships of fools," Foucault, in *Madness and Civilization*, says that "if [the madman] cannot and must not have another *prison* than the *threshold* itself, he is kept at the point of passage. He is put in the interior of the exterior, and inversely. A highly symbolic position, which will doubtless remain his until our own day, if we are willing to admit that which was formerly a visible fortress of order has now become the castle of our conscience" (author's italics, 11). Perhaps we have alleviated our conscience by assuming that highly symbolic position ourselves.

But then, as I described at the beginning of this chapter, there are indications that we don't feel unstable at all, that ours is an anthropology which does not *move*, which does not enter into *discourse*. Perhaps the powers we have appropriated mean simply more of the same or that, with our appropriation of the savage, we are "merely" inscribing with mystery, with nature, practices fundamental to our existing sense of self. Thus the Lecter we see at the end of the movie, strolling down a street in what appears to be an Afro-Caribbean country, receives our adulation not only because he is about to dine on the despicable Chiltern, but that, once again, he demonstrates that his consumption knows no bounds. In the context of the movie, eating Chiltern might be excused as taking a bite out of misogyny. But, as I have suggested, context can be neither here nor there.

Postulating that "cannibalism is the elementary form of institutionalized aggression" and that "all subsequent forms of social aggression are related to cannibalism in some way" (Sagan 109), Eli Sagan argues that "the desire to kill and eat has been sublimated into the desire to dominate and oppress. Any form of domination and oppression is an act of aggression on the part of the oppressors. Cannibalism, aggressive warfare, and conquest have been replaced, in the internal affairs of civilized society, by subtler forms of domination: slavery, racism, religious oppression, and capitalism" (106). Perhaps the *sexiness* Hollywood identifies in the cannibalistic serial killer is not or not only akin to the sexiness Roland Barthes, for example, sees along the whole length of the border where we perceive culture and nonculture meeting, that "non-site" where he seeks to control "the contradictory interplay of (cultural) pleasure and (non-cultural) bliss" (Barthes 1975, 62). Perhaps it is the sexiness which Barthes for one writes against, the sexiness of power. Might not our contemporary construction of the empowered cannibal correspond with the normality we assign to sublimated forms of domination and oppression?

When answering, we shouldn't forget to bring race into the equation, for one aspect of normative power which both Dahmer and Lecter can be said to embody is that of racial power. As cannibals they are figures of power constructed in part with reference to race, to our ascription of power to the white man. As we speculate on *The Silence of the Lambs'* afterlife (or on an imaginary sequel: plans for Touchstone to make a second killing at the box office—perhaps followed by a third killing, a fourth, a fifth?—having now been dropped), the final image we have of Lecter is as a white cannibal among black natives. The acceptable face of cannibalism and serial killing is white. Lecter is the white man who represents the powers of civilization *and* of the appropriated powers of the savage. And these powers are reinforced by "that most tired of Hollywood racist conventions," as Elizabeth Young puts it: the final scene being of "fully realized white characters set against an undifferentiated backdrop of 'local color' " (Young 26). This is no transgressive monster. This is your arrogant, middle-aged, white guy with all the power in the world.

Hannibal the cannibal, he whose powers of consumption are limitless, is one of our latest heroes of consumer culture. Both he and especially Dahmer manage to confuse the consumption of food and sex in a manner we find powerfully intoxicating. Simone de Beauvoir notes that "eating can be a substitute for erotic activity only if there is still some infantile equivalence between gastrointestinal and sexual function. . . . [Sade] sees a close bind between the food orgy and the erotic orgy. . . . To drink blood, to swallow sperm and excrement, and to eat children means appeasing desire through destruction of its object. Pleasure requires neither exchange, giving, reciprocity, nor gratuitous generosity. Its tyranny is that of avarice, which chooses to destroy what it cannot assimilate" (Beauvoir 37–38). Peter Greenaway's *The Cook, The Thief, His Wife and Her Lover*, a vivid cinematic exploration of, among other things, our fetishization of food, might be a good illustration of a society finding "infantile equivalence between gastrointestinal and sexual function." And with our sex terminology celebrating consumption and closure instead of posivity, plurality, exchange, or rejuvenation, Dahmer's Sadean confusion of the sex orgy and the food orgy proves remarkably unshocking. Sex (as we keep telling ourselves) sells, and it is hardly surprising that as a consumer society we should sexualize consumption—or rather, when the maintenance of that society depends on consumers always wanting more, that we should sexualize the act of *unfulfilling* consumption. Beauvoir says, "If Sade's heroes

85

commit endless massacres, it is because none of them gives full satisfaction" (42). Likewise, Dahmer—he who, as Don Davis notes, goes on "one-stop shopping" (122) trips to the mall to pick up victims—is figured as the archetypal consumer. He is, as Anne E. Schwartz reminds us, "The Man Who Could Not Kill Enough." It is a figuration which can turn his victims' bodies, like the bodies of Buffalo Bill's victims which lie on "littered riverbanks amid the outboard-oil bottles and sandwich bags that are our common squalor" (Harris 1991, 70), into no more than waste from an unfulfilled consumerism.

A *Newsweek* article on Dahmer (who, incidentally, learned his butchering skills in the Army Catering Corps) notes that "in one study of thirty serial killers, seven were involved in the food business, as cooks, bakers, or owners" and adds "experts have no explanation" (5 August 1991: 40). Our cannibalistic serial killers seem to be spelling out for us a connection between their acts and consumption in the same way that George Romero's *Dawn of the Dead*, the plot of which involves zombies terrorizing a shopping mall, depicts "the worst fears of the culture critics who have long envisioned the will-less, soul-less masses as zombie-like beings possessed by the alienating imperative to consume" (Modleski 159). The nature of that connection is a matter for debate. Mark Seltzer suggests that "the question of serial killing cannot be separated from the general forms of seriality, collection, and counting conspicuous in consumer society and the forms of fetishism—the collecting of things and representations, persons and person-things like bodies—that traverse it" (94). But should we be identifying analogies or causal relations between consumer society and serialized killing? Referring specifically to the "repetitive ways of mass cultural representations" (93) and our addictions to them, Seltzer notes that accounts which "posit a pathological addiction to representation as the cause of violence . . . implicitly understand such media representations as impinging on the subject 'from the outside' " and that the addiction to representations "would consist then in the *contagious* relation of the subject to imitation, simulation, or identification, such that identification brings the subject, and the subject's desires, into being and not the other way around" (author's italics, 94–95). "Society made me do it" is the (mostly) vain cry of the defendant figuring himself diseased by culture's depravity. But while we are quick to dismiss such claims and to ask the criminal to take his punishment *like a man* (a request with which, as I noted in chapter 2, many serial killers seem more than happy to comply), we should be wary of taking "culture" out of the equation. The celebrity status of Dahmer, who killed apparently to satisfy an insatiable appetite, depends in part on his victim tally, and a culture which boasts of its levels of consumption has difficulty not only in estranging his putative conflation of sex and food, but also, in moments of self-reflexivity, in finding strange its methods for determining who deserves celebrity status and who does not.

Feminism has argued that patriarchy normalizes male sexuality as having more to do with consumption than creativity, more to do with a negation of difference than exchange. Dahmer's "tragedy" is explained in precisely these terms. But the tragedy is represented not as the tragedy of consumerism or of patriarchy but, as I mentioned earlier, of homosexuality. Dollimore notes that

> the homosexual is significantly implicated in both sexual and cultural difference, and for two reasons. First because the homosexual has been regarded (especially in psychoanalytic theory) as one who fears the difference of the 'other' or opposite sex, and, in flight from it, narcistically embraces the same sex instead. Difference and heterogeneity are sanctified, homogeneity is distrusted. The eminent Kleinian psychoanalyst, Hanna Segal, has recently declared the adult homosexual structure to be inherently pathological, disturbed, and perverse, and this because of an inbuilt, narcissistic desire for the same. (Dollimore 249)

Diana Fuss describes the position Segal takes as follows:

> The signification of "homo" has been linked to the politics of the phallocratic "same," whereas the meaning of "hetero" has been associated just as insistently with the more respectable politics of "Difference." When pushed to its extreme, Derrida's conviction that "phallocentrism and homosexuality can go, so to speak, hand in hand" posits the determination of phallocentrism *within* homosexuality (here coded as male); from this perspective, heterosexuality operates as the apotheosis of "heterogeneity" and functions to displace what is perceived to be the more conservative, reactionary, effects of the practice of "homogeneity." (author's italics; Fuss 111)

From the perspective which associates homosexuality with homogeneity, the repetitiveness of the "homosexual" serial killer's acts (unlike the repetitiveness of a "heterosexual" serial killer, whose acts, as I suggested earlier, are denied correspondence with heterosexuality) can be a *sign* of his sexuality. From such a perspective, the desire for more of the same is constructed as a sexual desire, as homosexual desire. But estranging homosexuality by associating Dahmer's cannibalism with this "homosexual" desire for the consumption of the other (desire, in other words, for the same) can run into difficulties, especially when we are intrigued by, flirt with, the possibility of cannibalism's presence within the history of the "civilized" self. While patriarchy will openly walk hand in hand with a consumerism that eroticizes food and the act of unfulfilling consumption, its relationship with homosexuality is still a closeted affair, and the confusion about how to represent Dahmer's cannibalism can be "resolved" by this unhappy axiom: Cannibalism is either (hetero)sexy or it is savage.

Our fascination with Dahmer is perhaps related to this inability to settle on how we are to depict him, to our inability to unproblematically conflate the oppositions heterosexuality/homosexuality and civilization/savagery. That we seem to be preoccupied with exploring the possibility that the latter opposition may break down can be indicated by our reception of Hannibal Lecter: civilized and savage, putatively heterosexual (or at least presumed heterosexual by his flirting with Clarice) and cannibal. Like Lecter, Dahmer is placed on a threshold of cultural constructions, and is perceived powerful as a result of his access to both sides of the border. And like Lecter, Dahmer is the white man appropriating the powers of the savage. But the civilization which made a hero of Hannibal can only make an unsung hero of Dahmer, for popularity is reserved for heterosexual savages.

PART II

Dreaming the Serial Killer

For the FBI, Ted Bundy "personifies [the] ruthless breed of serial killer who leaves a perceptible signature at the crime scene" (House 5). The serial killer's "signature" connects random events. It tells us what to read. The connected events become text produced by an unnamed author hoping to be read, a mystery whose solution lies in identifying its author. And yet it soon becomes much more. It teases the reader, challenges the reader to identify why such events are connected. It locates the burden of constructing meaning with the reader. The reader is forced to "write" the text, to assume authorship in order to anticipate what comes next. The signature is both a sign of the author's existence and an invitation into the mind of the serial killer which we show few signs of wanting to refuse.

The serial killer who leaves his mark and invites us to see things from his perspective knows that what we see will not necessarily catch us completely unaware. In the first chapter of Graham and Gurr's *Violence in America*, Richard Maxwell Brown identifies the denial of a dependency on violence as a central component of America's cultural psyche: "We have resorted so often to violence that we have long since become a trigger-happy people. Violence is clearly rejected by us as a part of the American value system, but so great has been our involvement with violence over the long sweep of our history that violence has truly become part of our unacknowledged (or underground) value structure" (Brown [1] 41). A central theme of part 2 is that the writing of serial killer mythology is increasingly contextualized by the *surfacing* of that "underground" value structure, by its going public, becoming central to the public spectacle.

5

The Horror in the Mirror

Average Joe and the
Mechanical Monster

To Randy Jones, one of Dahmer's neighbors, Dahmer seemed "like the average Joe" (*Newsweek*; 5 August 1991: 41). Helping us to disseminate a picture of Dahmer in court, a caption in Anne E. Schwartz's book describes Dahmer as an "average-looking man." To Tracey Edwards, whose escape from Dahmer's apartment led to Dahmer's arrest, Dahmer "seemed like a normal, everyday guy," and presumably in order to justify that characterization, Edwards agrees with Geraldo Rivera's suggestion that he and Dahmer were out to "hustle some chicks" (*Geraldo;* 12 September 1991). Dahmer "is a very gentle man" according to his attorney, and "that's what makes it so absolutely intriguing and unbelievable to see how a fellow like that you saw in court today could have done all these horrific acts" (*Larry King Live;* 17 February 1992). To make it even more intriguing, as a *Washington Post* columnist notes, Dahmer is not from one of the "nation's urban areas with more of a reputation for coldbloodedness," but from Wisconsin, "America's heartland" (1 August 1991: C3). As I noted in chapter 3, the idea that "appearances are deceptive" is repeated in article after article: "Concealed amongst all this normality lies dormant evil." Like the surrealists, in the banal we see, and perhaps like to manufacture, something extraordinary.

Average Joe often has a story to tell about himself and his friends that calls into question his claim to his name. This celebrated embodiment of middle America is often hiding something. His normality, we say, is an illusion. But when we look at our monsters and wait for the true gargoyle within to burst through that familiar shell, sometimes we experience a more horrifying or thrilling possibility: the monster that appears actually is Average Joe; what is unspeakable turns out to be impossible to put into words not because it is so extraordinary but because it is so ordinary. Thus, we have a twist on the story behind Daniel Vigne's *The Return of Martin Guerre* or Jon Amiel's *Sommersby:* not an intruder in the guise of familiarity, but familiarity in all its glory. It is a possibility that Hannah Arendt describes in *Eichmann in Jerusalem:* "[The prosecutor] wanted to try the most abnormal monster the world had ever seen. . . . [The judges] knew, of course, that it would have been very comforting indeed to believe that Eichmann was a monster. . . . The trouble with Eichmann was precisely that so many were like him, and that the many were neither perverted nor sadistic, that they were, and still are, terribly and terrifyingly normal" (Arendt 276). The "trouble" with Eichmann is the trouble with our serial killers, both new and old. "I shall clip the lady's ears off . . . wouldn't you?" asks Jack the Ripper in a letter to his fellow man. As Martin Tropp suggests, the writer "speaks directly to his readers, implying by his words and literacy (despite the [possibly intentional] misspellings) that he is one of them" (113) and that this is why he is so difficult to catch.

Halloween director John Carpenter, commenting on the success of *The Silence of the Lambs,* remarks, "I think we're all frightened of the unknown and also of the repressed people in our society. There's a duality that touches off sparks in all of us" (*People Weekly,* 1 April 1991: 70). Those sparks are theorized by Jonathan Dollimore thus: "Since, in cultural terms, desiring the normal is inseparable from and conditional upon not desiring the abnormal, repression remains central to identity, individual and cultural" (246). We often figure the serial killer as failing to repress the desire for the abnormal. Joan Smith, for example, figuring identity in hydraulic terms, says, "The otherwise inexplicable actions of a serial killer . . . can . . . be understood as a survival mechanism, a means of coping with intolerable stress. The fact that they commit such terrible crimes enables them to function normally in the periods between their crimes" (3). Our desire for normality, our fetishization of Average Joe, inevitably means that abnormality is constructed as something that *needs* to be repressed, something that inevitably becomes desirable, mysterious, sexy. As it comes into focus, our depiction of the serial killer as "letting off steam" is also a picture of Average Joe who has given in to his deeper desires. Our monster turns out to be not something monstrous disguised as Joe but Joe who has let it all hang out.

Attempting to satisfy our hunger for horror, we revert sometimes to what John Carpenter says indicates fifties' conservatism: the cheap scare. Our monsters, more animal than human, spring at us from behind bushes, prey on us, return to their lairs far from everyday, familiar society. At such times we might, like Dahmer's neighbor, John Bachelor, compare Dahmer to Jason in *Friday the 13th* (*Los Angeles Times*, 24 July 1991: A14)—he who, like Lecter, we like to conceal behind a hockey-mask—or we might, like Robert Dvorchak and Lisa Holewa, describe Dahmer's reported "wailing" and "screeching" when he is arrested as "all those forces seething inside him erupt[ing] to life" (Dvorchak and Holewa 8). But we are generally movie-literate people, and to truly scare ourselves, we want sometimes to be a little more subtle, to show that we can write and speak a little more fully, a little more *knowingly* about those "forces." At these times, we must be able to mistake our monsters for ourselves—or ourselves for them. We must build a house of mirrors.

If we are white, scaring ourselves in this way is a little easier. Average Joe is white, and so is Average Joe, the serial killer. Average Joe has power, the power of being average, of being a representative of middle America. And so does Average Joe, the serial killer. The sister of one of Dahmer's many black victims is curious about why her fellow guest on *The Maury Povich Show* should be so fascinated with Dahmer that she regularly attends his trial: "Did you want to read about the man [Joachim Dressler] that sat up there and cut up 11 people in Racine. Did you want to read about him? No, see, you don't even remember him. But he was—came from an insane place. But see, that's not big news. This white man that killed almost all minorities, he is big news" (*Maury Povich*, 4 February 1992). Not that the whiteness of a serial killer becomes an issue—but his "normality" does. We not only place the white Dahmer or the white Bundy or the white Gacy on the covers of magazines, we give them the power to look back at us. And that's a thrill.

Looking at our monsters is a good way of finding out who we think we are, or who we think we might be, or even who we want to be. They can be figures who have realized our frightening or fantastic potentials. The trick is to identify how subtle we are being. Take, for example, the representation of Dahmer as automaton. Seizing on classmates' memories of Dahmer's ritual walk to the school bus—four steps forward, two back, four forward, one back (Masters 1991, 267)—we deal with his lack of feeling towards his victims by constructing an image of Dahmer as boy-machine who develops into something which, when arrested, "looked so emotionless, so harmless, as if he were a robot being led away" (Norris 1992, 41). In court his face is "passionless" (*Geraldo*, 12 September 1991), his eyes "almost vacant" (*Newsweek*, 3 February 1992: 45). For the *Washington Post*, Dahmer, "his face . . . pale and impassive," "walked with the near-drop pace of a zombie" (7 August 1991:

B1). *People Weekly* magazine, countering the claims of his lawyer that he was in a "state of anguish," says, "but Jeffrey Dahmer was impassive in court as he was charged with first-degree murder" (12 August 1991: 32). While defense and state attorneys differ in their assessments of Dahmer's responsibility for his actions, their portrayal of him as unfeeling, inhuman, and machinelike are indistinguishable. Dahmer's attorney, Gerald Boyle, describes him in court as a "steamrolling killing machine," "a runaway train on a track of madness, picking up steam all the time, on and on and on," while Michael McCann for the prosecution describes Dahmer as a "cool, calculating killer who cleverly covered his tracks" (*New York Times*, 16 February 1992: 24).

Such estrangement can be of the unsubtle variety, a case of "pathologizing and thus disavowing the everyday intimacies with technology in machine culture" (Seltzer 98), but it can also indicate not so much a disavowal as an expression of anxiety on our part about modern humanity or, more specifically, modern man in "machine culture." Klaus Theweleit describes the masculine self of members of the First World War German Freikorps as "mechanized through a variety of mental and physical procedures: military drill, countenance, training, operations which Foucault identified as 'techniques of the self' " (Rabinbach and Benjamin in Theweleit 1989, xvii), and Mark Fasteau, among others, describes the stereotype of the contemporary male self in similar terms, a stereotype which we are still struggling to outgrow. In *The Male Machine* Fasteau describes the ideal image to which the title refers as

> functional, designed mainly for work. He is programmed to tackle jobs, override obstacles, attack problems, overcome difficulties, and always seize the offensive. . . . He has armor plating which is virtually impregnable. His circuits are never scrambled or overrun by irrelevant personal signals. He dominates and outperforms his fellows, although without excessive flashing of lights or clashing of gears. His relationship with other male machines is one of respect but not intimacy; it is difficult for him to connect his internal circuits to those of others. In fact, his internal circuitry is something of a mystery to him. (Fasteau 1)

Fasteau's "male machine" is a frightening but familiar image. It corresponds with the way we often figure our monsters: "If there's anything monstrous about [Dahmer], it's the monstrous lack of connection to all things we think of as being human—guilt, remorse, worry, feelings that would stop him from hurting, killing, torturing" (Davis Silber, quoted in Dvorchak and Holewa 141). It corresponds with the way we represent our mostly male psychopaths who can be diagnosed as such by demonstrating, among other things, "a shallow understanding of the meaning of words, particularly emotional terms" and by not showing "the surge of anxiety that normal people exhibit" when they are about "to receive a mild electric shock" (*New York Times*, 7 July 1987: C2). And, apparently keen to confer buddy-status on as many of society's others as possible, Fasteau's male ideal also corresponds with necrophiles and schizophrenics. "According to Eric Fromm's findings," says Brian Masters, necrophiles "often have a pallid complexion, and they speak in a monotone. . . . They are fascinated with machinery, which is unfeeling and antihuman" (quoted in Masters 1991, 266). *In Cold Blood* examiners of Lowell Lee Andrews produce a diagnosis of "schizophrenia, simple type," and by "simple," Capote tells us, "the diagnosticians meant that Andrews suffered no delusions, no fake perceptions, no hallucinations, but the primary illness of separation of thinking and feeling" (Capote 315). How different are our killing machines from our male machines? While we are familiar with and still sometimes valorize the male machine, how sensitive are we to the idea that it is logical for such machines also to regard their others as mirror-reflections of themselves, as unfeeling, interesting only as mechanical objects? While Dahmer the schoolboy explains to a classmate his reason for cutting up the fish he catches—"I want to see what it looks like inside, I like to see how things work" (Dvorchak and Holewa 41)—the adult Dahmer confesses to the police "in the uninflected language of an affidavit" that he disassembles his human victims "to see how they work" (*Newsweek*, 5 August 1991: 40). Our construction of the serial killer resembles a figure of masculinity, or rather a reassembled figure of masculinity, who has turned on all that frustrates masculinity either within himself or without. When we represent serial killers, necrophiles, psychopaths, schizophrenics, and a male ideal in similar ways, we sometimes refuse to identify links between them, but sometimes we allow the representations to merge, to form an almost conflated image in which the other is seen through the familiar self, the familiar self seen through the other. An uncanny effect, as Freud might say.

What Freud *does* say is that the uncanny hints at "nothing new or foreign, but something familiar and old established in the mind that has been estranged only by the process of repression" (Freud 1953a, 47). In the same essay he mentions the uncanniness of mechanization: "Jentsch has taken as a very good instance [of the uncanny] 'doubts whether an apparently animate being is really alive; or conversely, whether a lifeless object might not be in fact animate'; and he refers in this connection to the impression made by wax-work figures, artificial dolls and automatons. He adds to this class the uncanny effect of epileptic seizures and the manifestations of insanity, because these excite in the spectator the feeling that automatic, mechanical processes are at work, concealed beneath the ordinary appearance of animation" (31). A *Newsweek* article on Dahmer describes serial killers as "taking their cues from some deranged script" (5 August 1991: 40) and concludes with a quotation from Park Dietz: "These people are the most controlled people you can imagine" (41). While Dahmer was found to be *in control*, not out of it, his actions perceived to be those of a man who knew what he was doing, he is also represented as someone/something being controlled. The figure of the killer as unfeeling, programmed machine—the writer of the program remaining a mystery—is one with which the Gothic and our representation of serial killers are particularly occupied. And contributing to our sense of the uncanny is the defining characteristic of the serial killer, the repetitiveness of the killing act. For Freud, "repetition-compulsion" is "based upon instinctual activity and probably inherent in the very nature of the instincts—a principle powerful enough to overrule the pleasure-principle, lending to certain aspects of the mind their daemonic character" (Freud 1953a, 44). In other words, "repetition-compulsion" can signify oxymorons such as "mechanized nature" or "natural machine."

With Freud's understanding of the uncanny in mind, the mechanically repetitive serial killer is a construction which can suggest for us the power of "natural instinct," an instinct whose naturalness we may or may not wish to question. But whether we see the power of "mechanized nature" or of a "natural machine," our particular representation of the body as machine may appear as both a powerful fantasy and a fantasy of power. Mark Seltzer, who argues that "the matter of periodizing persons, bodies, and desires is inseparable from the anxieties and *appeals* of the body-machine complex" (my italics; Seltzer 98), refers to the type of fantasy which "projects a transcendence of the natural body and the extension of human agency through the forms of technology that supplemented it" (99). And just as dreams about technology can reflect more than just our anxieties, our construction of mechanized monsters, as I mentioned earlier, can indicate more than just our worries about humanity's "naturalness" or its future in a technological age. Gilles Deleuze says, "Types of machines are easily matched with each type of society—not that machines are determining, but because they express those social forms capable of generating and using them" (Deleuze 6). Reinventing Deleuze's comment, one might say that our constructions of automated monsters, rather than indicating what we fear machines are doing to us, indicate what kind of a culture is "capable of generating and *using them*."

In the mythology of modern America the serial killer is a character able both to scare and thrill us in unsubtle and subtle ways. He can be monstrous, but he can also demonstrate a monstrosity which is familiar. The figure of the mechanized serial killer—the serial killer as automaton, unable to stop—offers us a version of familiar, "natural," and to some extent "appealing" behavior "that has been estranged only by the process of repression." In part 1 I described how various other forms of the serial killer's "familiarity" are repressed or policed. In the remainder of the book I suggest that we also show signs not only of acknowledging that familiarity, but of infusing our acknowledgment with a kind of honor, a kind of veneration.

6

Confessing the Unspeakable

Dear Mr. Fleming,
As you may know I am Lionel and Shari Dahmer's agent, and I am in receipt of your fax
of May 6th to the Dahmers.
Regretfully, what you propose would conflict with our current Hollywood plans, and
we must therefore respectfully decline your offer.
Yours, Joel Gotler.
(Letter to Patrick Fleming, whose documentary film *To Kill and Kill Again*, focuses on a
model developed by California State University to represent the relationship between
physiological, psychological, and cultural factors involved in the "making" of a serial
killer)

A psychologist working for the Wisconsin Department of Corrections
says, "There may be some psychological dynamics to [Dahmer's] confessions. There could be some relief in being caught. Whatever pain he
had is finally over. Or there could be some charge for him for all this
confessing" (quoted in Schwartz 150). Whether Dahmer experiences
relief or a charge from his confessions, it is clear that we, as his confessors, experience the latter as we replay his story time and time again.
And readers of the magazine *True Police Cases* can read it for less than
fourteen dollars. An advertisement selling "The Jeffrey Dahmer Confessions" (copied, it says, from official files of the Milwaukee Police Department) notes how the product will tell "how he lured, drugged, killed,
had sex, and dismembered their bodies" and that you can "Order your
copy for ONLY $13.95" (August 1992).

Confession can be good business for confessor and confessee alike.
And sometimes the act of confessing seems more exciting than what is
being confessed. Suddenly everybody seems to have something to confess, to have, in other words, one of the things it takes to acquire celebrity status. But Dahmer has one of the best and biggest stories of them
all. His attorney is confident that Dahmer's 169-page confession is "the
longest confession in the history of America" and suggests that "this is
a man who wanted to rid himself of this after he was arrested" (*Larry*

King Live, 17 February 92). If Dahmer rids himself of his story, where does it go? "Dahmer could be making everything up or saying things in an 'eagerness to please' " (*Los Angeles Times,* 4 August 1991, A22), says John Liccione, a psychologist at the Milwaukee County Mental Health Complex. What is it Dahmer could say that would please his listeners? When Dahmer's neighbors in a poor Milwaukee community are offered fifty dollars for interviews by television networks and three hundred by national tabloids (*The Washington Post,* 7 August 91: B2), there must be pressure to get the story right, to satisfy the particular demand. And of course, like Dahmer's neighbors, we have no trouble in describing the nature of that story, in describing what it is we like to hear.

Henry Lee Lucas knew what that was. The Texas "drifter" confessed to killing 360 people across the country and was believed, without forensic evidence or witnesses to support his story. "The greatest serial killer of all time" (*Confessions of a Serial Killer*), the subject of *Henry: Portrait of a Serial Killer,* now says he only killed one and made up the rest in consultation with the Texas Rangers: "Every time they brought a murder case in . . . I accepted it" (*Confessions of a Serial Killer*).[1] Demonstrating a reversal of the traditional relationship between police and criminal, Donald Leroy Evans of Galveston confesses to killing more than sixty people, and police "are still attempting to prove his claims" (Davis 1991, 169). Dahmer insists on telling his story, one which the police can only partially verify: "The accounts of Jeffrey Dahmer's deeds come from his own mouth. There are no known witnesses, and in some cases there is no physical evidence to verify the statements written down by the police" (Dvorchak and Holewa 77). The FBI tells us that serial killers are "very cooperative during the interview. You just can't shut these guys up. They just want to talk about their crimes" (House 22). And we are good listeners. There is power in confessing, in having a good story—so much that for some it is apparently worthwhile to own up to things they didn't do. The storytelling spree gains as much fame as the killing spree. Confined to his cell, with only words and his imagination to pass the time, Lecter demands that Starling tell a story to match his. Watching the movie, we can see that everything and everyone are connected, that none of us are com-

1. Twenty Twenty Television's *Confessions of a Serial Killer* tells the story of Lucas's confessions and of attorney Viz Feazell who detailed discrepancies in Lucas's version of the murders. After challenging the Texas Rangers and the FBI for their handling of the Lucas case—he alleges that they ignored evidence which proved Lucas could not have committed the crimes—Feazell found himself charged with committing various crimes, including murder. He was found by the court to have been framed by the Rangers, and was awarded $58 million after filing a libel suit against a Dallas television station.

pletely innocent. As we cheer both Lecter's cannibalizing of Chiltern and Billy Crystal's impersonation of our favorite serial killer, we may for a moment or two forget ourselves and acknowledge that he is one of us. But what follows the acknowledgment? Do we question the confessor/confessee relationship? Do we feel a desire to identify and estrange our discourses which celebrate the serial killer? Or do we take pleasure in the power he represents?

Alain Grosrichard notes that "in most of the manuals for confessors or dictionaries of cases of conscience," there is "an article on 'morose delectation' which treats of the nature and gravity of the sin that consists in taking a lingering pleasure (that's the *morositas*) in the *representation*, through thought or speech, of a past pleasure" (author's italics; in Foucault 1980, 215). He then asks, "How is one to lend one's ear to the recital of abominable scenes without sinning oneself, that is, taking pleasure oneself?" It is a sin Hannibal Lecter makes no attempt to hide. Probing into the mind of Clarice, seeking an insight into her emotional psyche, he seeks images to get turned on by, words to fashion into pornography. Similarly, we needn't bother asking ourselves how we conceal taking pleasure in hearing of Dahmer's atrocities. Our interrogative discourses seek the truth of the confessee and find it within themselves.

In *Madness and Civilization* Foucault refers to the Lisbon *Temptation*, in which Saint Anthony sits facing the gryllos "born of madness, of its solitude, of its penitence, of its privations" (20). Foucault remarks that "it is exactly this nightmare silhouette that is at once the subject and object of the temptation; it is this figure which fascinates the gaze of the ascetic—both are prisoners of a kind of mirror interrogation, which remains unanswered in a silence inhabited only by a monstrous swarm that surrounds them" (20). The gryllos is "madness become Temptation; all it embodies of the impossible, the fantastic, the inhuman, all that suggests the unnatural, the writhing of an insane presence on the earth's surface—all this is precisely what gives the gryllos its strange power. The freedom, however frightening, of his dreams, the hallucinations of his madness, have more power of attraction for fifteenth-century man than the desirable reality of the flesh" (20–21). Constructing the figure of the serial killer as a seer and possessor of superhuman powers, we, like Clarice, dare ourselves to sit opposite him, ask ourselves and are asked what it is we see, and are fascinated to know what he sees. As we watch the televised court proceedings, Dahmer's eyes, like those of Lecter (Lecter, Clarice remarks, "sees very clearly—he damn sure sees through me"), seem to look straight through us: "He ambled into the Milwaukee County Circuit Court . . . his eyes drilling fearful holes in some of the camera lenses, as if he could see through the film and into the heart of anyone who gazed at him" (Davis 1991, 208). The power we ascribe to the modern monster is the power of the gryllos, that ability to transcend earthly matters, to move freely "above" everyday society, everyday language.

Hearing the serial killer's confession, we marvel that his/our words can't match his actions, that his actions escape the reach of words. He exists extratextually. Words, like flesh, can complicate things. We like to hear him talk, but we like his silences just as much. They speak volumes. Like Saint Anthony surrounded by silence, the world in which we find ourselves reflected in and through the eyes of the serial killer is surrounded by silence, a silence in which we can dream of action without words, of action without meaning. The silence with which we shroud the serial killer shrouds us too. For words are the enemy. Our serial killer seeks that which does violence to language, that which wrecks language, cannot be expressed by language, that which renders language silent. The confession purports to tell the truth, and yet we know it says nothing. Dahmer can tell us, "I knew I was sick or evil or both. Now I believe I was sick. The doctors have told me about my sickness" (quoted in Schwartz 150), but his words are, as he says, the words of doctors, and we don't allow the words of doctors to ensnare our monsters anymore. There in his silence, in his unspeakableness, is his secret. Perhaps we can see it, but rarely do we dare recount it. There's a power to his storytelling, and yet his power is also demonstrated by his ability to "escape" his story. He remains unrepresented, hidden from view. In the darkness he seems to ask us as many question as we ask him.

The confessor, seeing but not seen, is also concealed in darkness behind his inquisitor's lamp. Identifying closets and demanding their encryption, he hides within his own closet. Freud hides behind the couch. The confessor is also the voyeur, and he is one of our most celebrated embodiments of power. His is the power the state exerts over its confessees. The FBI's powers of surveillance—literalizing the modus operandi of psychoanalysis, as Elizabeth Young reminds us (Young 25)—are conferred on the prison system. Before his trial, Dahmer "is confined to a cell with a glass front, much like the fictional madman Hannibal Lecter. . . . Guards there record his movements in a log every five minutes" (*People Weekly,* 3 February 1992: 78). The Columbia Correctional Institution in Portage, Wisconsin, where Dahmer resides before his death, has "a glass-enclosed central-command station with twenty-eight video views of the facility" and offers wardens "the greatest ability to observe" (*Newsweek,* 3 February 92: 50). But we all like seeing in the dark, like the power of being fully present and invisibly so. It helps explain our loyalty to omniscient narrative—explains perhaps the attraction of books like *In Cold Blood*, its title referring to the murder *and* its representation, both acts "committed" without the appearance of emotional involvement. About Capote's "non-fiction novel" Tony Tanner asks, "Isn't it . . . that behind the mask of the dispassionate reporter we can begin to make out the excited stare of the southern-gothic novelist with his febrile delight in weird settings and lurid details?" (Tanner 101). Tanner sees the "truthfulness" of Capote's material as giving the illusion of "art laying down its tools as helpless and irrelevant in front of the horrors and mysteries of life itself" (101). Inconspicuous, the "artist" and the reader lie low, listen, watch. In their search for the closet of the confessee, they feel the need to conceal themselves within their own closet, that space from which they peer out, all-seeing, all-knowing.

Seeing without being seen is a way we gain knowledge about ourselves and especially each other. Its also a way of having fun, something the movie business has known for years. And when we go to the movies to get scared, the monsters we find there can see in the dark too. It's as though they might be sitting next to us. Cinema's serial killers observe (with us) potential victims through night-vision glasses. It's a power symbolized in *The Silence of the Lambs* by the cat. (Catherine Martin greets her cat before being attacked and carried away by Buffalo Bill, a scene we watch alongside our silent, nocturnal, all-seeing friend. And it is a cat which Starling—described by Lecter as having eyes the color of a tiger (22)—encounters as she explores the house of Buffalo Bill's first victim, Fredrica Bimmel). When Clarice shoots Buffalo Bill—when we see him lying on his back, insectlike, his glasses still strapped to his face like extended eyes—we can believe that by slaying this monstrous embodiment of the male gaze, she has managed to escape from the victimhood that that power had created for her, managed to disconnect herself from the narrative which makes the visual objectification of women continuous with their murder. The shooting of Buffalo Bill can be a shot in the eye for all those who had previously eyed her lecherously, including her fellow FBI trainees, passengers at the airport, Tennessee police, and of course Doctor Chiltern. But the celebrations following her graduation from the FBI are interrupted by a reminder of the constancy of men's vigilance. Lecter calls, assuring her that he has no intention of harming her. He declines her invitation to name his location. He could be anywhere. But he'll still be watching. No wonder that the novel ends with Clarice holidaying on the Chesapeake shoreline with a man who has defective vision. *The Silence of the Lambs* may be self-reflexive in its use of photography to portray murderous voyeurism, but even if we, Clarice, and Lecter all know that what he sees is (only) a construct, the power relation between observer and object stubbornly remains. The Lecter who exists in our collective consciousness—fashioned out of Anthony Hopkins' portrayal, the Lecter used as referent in representations of real-life serial killers, and our common perception of what a serial killer ought to be—retains to the end of the movie and beyond the power of the voyeur, the power of the silent confessor.

The discourse of our confessees becomes indistinguishable from that of the confessor. Imprisoned in a kind of mirror interrogation, both serial killers and their representers seem not unhappy about their confinement. But there are moments when, seeking confessions from our talk-show parade of strangeness, we feel the need to deny our voyeuristic tendencies, deny the extent to which we consume television's stories of other people's lives or images of other people's bodies. Tired of hostility from a *Maury Povich* audience, Jan Mullany, creator of trading cards featuring serial killers, points to possible hypocrisy on the part of his condemners: "Why is this show having me on? Why is there fascination with this? Why is the [Dahmer] trial being televised?" (*Maury Povich*, 4 February 1992). Povich's response—"the show is having you on . . . to try to convince you not to do it"—should be heard in the context of his teasing another show's audience about the content of the movie *Jeffrey Dahmer—The Secret Life:* "But just how explicit does the Hollywood movie get? When we return, we're going to show you a scene that might make you shiver" (28 September 1992). Geraldo Rivera can spare us the details of what Dahmer did to his victims because he does not "want Mom [the show's guest, whose son was murdered by Dahmer] to even hear what he did," but then proceed immediately with a rerun of a previous show in which a man who had escaped from Dahmer describes pictures he had seen of Dahmer's victims: "mutilated bodies, people handcuffed, you know, like he had been eating on them or something like that" (*Geraldo*, 4 December 1991). On another edition of *Geraldo*—whose subject the host describes as "the mind of serial killers and the women who love them" (29 March 1993)—details of serial killer case files are intercut with shots of the younger, prettier female members of the audience squirming at what they hear. We call what occurred in Dahmer's apartment "unimaginable horror" (*People Weekly*, 12 August 1991: 32) and then do our utmost to imagine it, demand to know every detail.

The pattern of denial followed by fulfillment of voyeuristic pleasure—a pleasure depending in part or wholly on the denial—is, as Judith Halberstam notes, reproduced in *The Silence of the Lambs:* "Prior to the autopsy, the camera has protected the viewer from close-ups of photographs taken of victims' bodies. Similarly, when Starling is being taken to Lecter, she is shown a photographic image of what Lecter did to a nurse . . . In the autopsy scene, the camera reveals all that it had promised to spare us: it lingers on the green and red flesh, the decayed body with two regular diamonds of flesh cut from its back" (42). But after such lingering, there is another stage. When Starling looks at a photograph and sees something in the victim's throat, "the corpse finally becomes object, thing": "The camera has framed the victim in much the same way as Buffalo Bill does as he prepares his lambs for the slaughter . . . And the camera also enables Starling to turn the corpse into a case" (43). Like Dahmer's camera recording every stage of the dismantling of his victims, Clarice's camera becomes a means to consume, cannibalize the body. And for our confessorial/policing selves, the construction of "the case" similarly depends on the objectification of the victim by the detective/viewer. As David Richter reminds us, we've had a lot of practice. The reader of an Agatha Christie novel, seeking "to duplicate from his or her armchair the deductions of the detective," is usually adept at limiting the extent to which he or she responds to the victims "as representations of real persons who act and suffer" (107). It is a maneuver as useful in real life as it is in fiction. For our real-life crimes to become transformed "believably" into a series of "cases," each shaped into a recognizable format, we must believe in the fictionalization of the victim's body.

Seeking the truth of the serial killer, we find it in the discourse with which we seek it. Sisters of two of Dahmer's victims (Edward Smith and Richard Guerrero) complain that Dahmer makes the covers of magazines while their brothers are largely forgotten. For them their brothers' lack of presence in the media amounts to their being condemned to meaninglessness, to an unreality, whereas Dahmer's celebrity status gains him the power of presence: "They could put these boys on the front of *Newsweek, Time* and everything to show that these boys were real. If it wasn't for these boys, he wouldn't even be existing" (*Maury Povich,* 4 February 1992). Dahmer's presence is gained, as the women suggest, by their brother's absence (absence in reality and in the representation of the crime). The proposal of Dahmer's attorneys "that the victims be referred to in court by numbers instead of their names" (*Los Angeles Times,* 27 January 1992: A10) was rejected, but the makers of *Jeffrey Dahmer—The Secret Life,* claiming sensitivity, remark that they did not "use the names of the victims, there were [only] composite victims" (*Maury Povich,* 28 September 1992). These anonymous, made-up victims are opposed by the unmistakable and named presence of Jeffrey Dahmer. "Why should we go to the families for truth?" asks Carl Crew, the writer and "star" of the movie. While the Dahmer character appears "real" in this cinematic blurring of fact and fiction, the makers of the movie defend themselves against claims from Shirley Hughes, mother of victim Anthony Hughes, that they seem to have made no attempt to represent the reality of her son by asking, "Is your son starring in this movie?" and "Do you think that you're any more special than the other families of other victims that have been killed by other serial killers that have had movies made of them?" The possessors of power as perceived by the dominant culture win the right to be named, to have presence. They have claims to the new reality created from the debris of the old: the reality of celebrity, the reality, that is, of an age in which to have identity is "to have one's personality mediated by the media" (Black 153). For Shirley Hughes, Carl Crew (who Maury Povich reminds us bears "an uncanny likeness to the real thing" and who Povich tells us was once "an embalmer at a mortuary"), "is no better than Jeffrey Dahmer." In the representation of the serial killer, the presence of the "powerful" and the absence of the "weak" reproduces what Dennis Nilsen believes to be the aim of the serial killer: the creation of a fully present self defined as such by the violent erasure of the other.

"You try to understand what makes a person a murder victim" says FBI Special Agent John Douglas (*People Weekly*, 1 April 1991: 64). Families of victims complain that the inscription of the victim with victimhood—that quality which, in the words of Douglas, makes a person a murder victim—represents a second death. It can be the death of a body figured as inhuman. Wilson and Seaman, for example, describing the ease with which Jack the Ripper found potential victims, note that "whores were as thick on the ground in the East End at night as were fleas in their doss-house bedding" (39). It can be the death incurred by a body reduced to an object. Speculating about why the Victorian collective imagination associated its monsters with doctors, Martin Tropp argues that in the "popular mind" there was "a common denominator linking the activities of doctors, vivisectionists, pornographers," namely that of reducing "another body to an object and gain[ing] pleasure in subjecting it to the will" (118). Our embodiment of the serial killer contrasts with our disembodiment of his victims. In portraying the serial killer in superhuman terms while objectifying his victims, we construct our own dehumanizing, pornographic fantasy. And when we judge victims of violence as they tell their stories on television, when we identify the "faults" in their behavior or their lifestyles which we perceive as leading to their victimization, we are part of that process of victimization. And placing ourselves in the position of the rapist, of the serial killer, we empower ourselves at his victim's expense. Our discourse becomes that which Roland Barthes defines as the discourse of the powerful: one which "engenders blame, hence guilt, in its recipient" (Barthes 1982, 428). The object of interrogation as confessor and monster face up to one another proves to be neither of the two participants.

7

Supercops and Superkillers

He who fights with monsters might take care lest he thereby become a monster. And if you gaze for long into an abyss, the abyss gazes into you. (Nietzsche, *Beyond Good and Evil*)

I was real close to Sheriff Boutwell: we were like father and son. Me and [Texas Ranger] Prince were like brothers. We'd go places, we'd do things, we'd do anything, anytime. It didn't matter what time it was, day or night. (Henry Lee Lucas, *Confessions of a Serial Killer*)

The FBI is not shy in telling us that serial killers often identify with instead of against the law enforcement community. (For police officer Gerald Schaefer, the killer of twenty or so men and women, such identification evidently proved relatively easy). In the House of Representatives hearing on serial killing, an FBI officer notes that when the FBI interviewed convicted serial killers in order to construct personality profiles, "a majority of offenders viewed us as associates who had interests (crime) but only from different perspectives" (26). It is also noted that "they look like you and me. They are gregarious, they are outgoing. Almost without exception they are always police buffs. They never could make the grade, so they do the next best thing. They may seek an occupation close to the periphery of law enforcement. It could be as a security guard, a private detective, or as a volunteer in a hospital where they would drive an ambulance" (20). Apparently, "the next best thing" after that periphery is violent crime.

We have grown accustomed to stories of the pursuit of justice, of the arrest of the criminal and of his crimes, that take the form of conflicts between rivals, conflicts involving mimetic gesture, conflicts which correspond to manly rivalry mythologized in the cinema and the novel, conflicts, in other words, which do not threaten the underlying bond between combatants. And in our stories of serial killers, of their crimes, and of the chase involved in their capture, the identification of the person doing the chasing, the controlling, and using the weapon may lose relevance. As Leyton notes, "The Son of Sam was not so very wrong when he thought the public was urging him on during his killing spree, for the media chronicled his every deed in a state of mounting excitement" (Leyton 24). In fictional representations, problems of narrative are solved invariably through the use of violence. The story becomes a perpetual cycle of the shifting of power, and what we seem to find thrilling are these expressions of power for their own sake. Before Dahmer's death, Larry King asks attorney Gerald Boyle whether his client will write a book as a way of raising funds for his victims' families (*Larry King Live*, 17 February 1992). If a movie had been made based on Dahmer's own version of events, how strange would it appear to us for the drama to depend on Dahmer's pursuit of victims as well as the police's pursuit of Dahmer? The continuum between law enforcement and violent crime evidently identified by serial killers is commonly translated in our representation of cops and killers as a rivalry for the same kind of power, a rivalry which transgresses boundaries between "civilization" and its others.

Ironically, by supplying information about the psychology of unconvicted serial killers, the police buff who becomes a serial killer after failing to join the FBI—or in Dahmer's case, after failing to become a military policeman—sometimes assumes a position of power within law enforcement once he is convicted. Hannibal Lecter's promotion to official expert repeated Ted Bundy's in 1986: "We just interviewed Theodore Bundy approximately two weeks ago. He wants to assist the FBI in our research project. He doesn't want to talk to anyone else. He has read some of our research. He likes what we came up with, and he wants to help us, he says, on the Green River case" (House 20). After Dahmer is convicted, he is similarly praised for cooperating with police with regard to his own crimes, for solving "unsolvable crimes" (*Larry King Live*, 17 February 1992). Meanwhile Westley Allan Dodd, convicted of murdering three boys, two of whom he raped, writes articles from jail offering advice for children on how to escape sex attacks (*Murder by Number*). The FBI's pride in the fact that Bundy respected their research and that they alone would be in communication with him is symptomatic of a reverence we have for the Bundys, Dahmers, and Lecters of this world, a reverence which is related perhaps to the particular type of knowledge they are perceived to possess, the knowledge of (and therefore power over) the unspeakable.

We ascribe such knowledge and power to some of our police heroes too. Together, the serial killer and his pursuer seem to be united by a special bond of knowledge and mutual respect. We are told that, like most serial killers—and, presumably, *unlike* other types of criminals—

Dahmer "behaved graciously" in his interviews, that his interviewer was "used to having defendants in jail or prison who curse at [him], spit at [him], take a punch at [him], threaten [him]," and that the interview felt like a "joint search" (*Day One*, 18 April 1993). Police and criminal monsters, existing together in their asocial world, have supervision; they are able to see into each other's minds as well as ours. Like the all-seeing Lecter, agents of the FBI's Behavioral Science Unit, from their desks in Quantico, Virginia, are able to view a murder scene in any part of the country (a scene at which the regular murder squad detectives are floundering) and all but name the murderer. Or so the story goes. In their chapter called "The Profilers," Wilson and Seaman describe New York cops getting nowhere with the murder of schoolteacher Francine Elveson in 1979. The appearance of the FBI—"Enter special agent John Douglas" (92)—is reminiscent of a scene from either Hollywood's or Nietzsche's version of Superman.

Omniscience, among other things, elevates the serial killer to a transcendent being "above the law": having broken one or more of society's most precious laws, having witnessed at first hand a dream of omnipotence fulfilled, the killer, physically imprisoned, is figured by society as a seer, able to transcend physical barriers and look deep into the soul of fellow monsters and police alike, and consequently perceived, like Lecter, as a potential defender of society from further violence. Those who so obviously disregard the law, those who are figured as existing in a world beyond the reach of the law, exist on the same plain as the lawmakers, those who disregard previous laws and establish new ones, those in authority. Ascribing authority to the convicted serial killer might appear strange if we didn't regard transcending the law as being *in* power. The figure of the serial killer is both outside of society (out of the law) and in authority (*beyond* the law). Because he transcends the law in both cases, there is no contradiction.

Foucault argues that "it's the characteristic of our Western societies that the language of power is law, not magic, religion, or anything else" (Foucault 1980, 201), but the language of what might be called "the law transcended" can be equally powerful, equally evocative in the West, and especially in America. And it is spoken by police and criminals alike. Discussing British police crime, Stephen Box notes that in the context of the criminal justice system being "presented as a slow bureaucratic machine which possibly provides too many protective civil rights to criminals," police crime is generally justified as "good and necessary police work" because it "effectively administers and achieves justice (albeit rough)" (Box 85). In the mythology surrounding the elevated world of the supercop and supercriminal, the breaking of the law by the police is justified by that which it seeks: the serial killer is, as the description goes, someone who manipulates and transcends the law to escape capture and punishment.

Our representations of the police imply that their increased powers of vigilance should be allowed, when necessary, to become the powers of the vigilante, powers unconstrained by law or by society's interference, powers justified on the premise that the end justifies the means. Richard Maxwell Brown argues that a profound respect for vigilantism characterizes Americans' relationship with the law: "The key to the apparent contradiction between our genuine lawfulness and the disregard for law emphasized by Lincoln lies in the selectivity with which Americans have approached the law . . . Perhaps in the long run the most important result of vigilantism has been the subtle way in which it has persistently undermined our respect for law by its repeated theme that the law may be arbitrarily disregarded—that there are times when we may choose to obey the law or not" (Brown [2] 178). Our acceptance of an arbitrary disregard for the law might explain the popularity of movies such as Clint Eastwood's *Dirty Harry*. Joan Mellen says, "Neofascist to the core, these films would substitute for the Bill of Rights a strong leader with absolute authority, making it clear that rights consist in allowing the strong leader to work his will against the unruly. It is thus for us to choose—and our survival is at stake. Nor is there ever any ambiguity about criminality. Guilt is instantly apparent to all; hence legal rights are but a pretext for tying the hands of the defenders of the good" (Mellen 307). The mythology of the supercop and superkiller is constructed with reference to the tradition of the vigilante, to the familiar figure of the detective who defeats not only the criminal but the legal system, who fights for a higher justice that is founded on the principle of an individual's right to assert power in the face of tainted society. For the authors of *Milwaukee Massacre*, Dahmer's story is disturbing because of "the absence of an heroic figure" (Dvorchak and Holewa xi), because of the unheroic society in which he lived, made up of neighbors not complaining loud enough about the smells from his apartment and of policemen not doing, or rather not being able to do, their jobs. The story of Dahmer lacks a lonely, "heroic" detective to rival the lonely Dahmer, and the absence of such a figure is the fault of the law and not the police: "What emerges is a shocking portrait of a justice system that failed to stop Dahmer from killing again and again" reads the cover of *Milwaukee Massacre*. The language spoken by the FBI belongs to the world of the serial killer—to capture him, it needs to speak his language—and conversely, he belongs to its language. It is a language infused with a distinctively American respect for lawlessness.

112

Superkillers and supercops need each other. Jane Caputi notes that "one of the components of the Ripper formula is the creation of a felt state of siege, a reign of terror in which the 'monster' is felt to be the 'master' " (Caputi 39). Such a construction necessitates a rival, and what is at stake is a power beyond the law: the war will never be won—the possibility of evil is always present—but the battles bring fame and good television. And it is a drama in which the police themselves seem only too willing to act. Joan Smith, describing the police conference held to give journalists details of the crimes committed by London's "gay killer," Colin Ireland, notes how Chief Superintendent Ken John appealed directly to the murderer to give himself up "in the classic Hollywood tradition of sheriff-versus-outlaw" (Smith 2). It was a reenactment of the appeal made fourteen years earlier by the head of the "Yorkshire Ripper" Squad, George Oldfield, to meet the killer "on his own terms." For Oldfield, as his book on his involvement in the case testifies, Peter Sutcliffe (the killer) had become a personal rival, and the rivalry evolved into a conflict between two men apparently existing on a different plane and speaking a different language from the rest of us. It is a scene evoked by Wilson and Seaman, who describe FBI officers from Quantico waging "their unique, solitary war against serial offenders either from a desk sixty feet underground . . . or from a plane or car seat" (111). "I don't march to the same drummer you do," Douglas Clark, killer of prostitutes in California, tells the jury (quoted in Wilson and Seaman 260), that so-called representative sample of society. But he might well find himself marching to the same beat as his "adversary." The mythology of the serial killer and the FBI is the story of individualized male figures whose rivalry exists in a heroic world transcending society and all things domestic.

It is a world made up of *loners*, unable to live within society's rules but able to identify and sometimes confront the forces which threaten that society. Constructing the serial killer involves empowering the lonely by turning them into loners. The common view of Dahmer as someone who kills to transcend society, as a killer on a quest, contrasts with Dennis Nilsen's view of him as someone whose killings are a means of creating the illusion of *having* a social existence. Dahmer, says Nilsen, needs "a totally unresisting, passive model of a human being in order to 'cross the bridge' temporarily into 'society.' (Being human he needs 'fulfillment' in the human, three-dimensional world of real flesh and blood)" (quoted in Masters 1991, 186). Instead of seeing Dahmer as a powerless and lonely figure who is, to employ the phrase Masters used as a title to his book on Nilsen, "killing for company," we prefer to see Dahmer as a loner who succeeds in dislocating himself from society. Distancing himself from society, able to see and not be seen, the loner possesses the power of the voyeur.[1]

The authors of *Habits of the Heart* allude to the more conventional embodiment of the loner in describing "the hero who must leave society, alone or with one or a few others, in order to realize the moral good in the wilderness, at sea, or on the margins of settled society" (Bellah et al 144). And yet "this obligation to aloneness," the authors note, "is part of the profound ambiguity of the mythology of American individualism, that its moral heroism is always just a step away from despair. For an Ahab, and occasionally for a cowboy or a detective, there is no return to society, no moral redemption. The hero's lonely quest for moral excellence ends in absolute nihilism" (146). For us, the detective, one step away from despair, can belong to the same world as the destructive lonely figure of the monster. Our story of the serial killer is often about the meeting of loners, those who hunt and those who are hunted. When detective and criminal combine in the figure of a Bundy or a Lecter, the idea of the loner has its most disturbing (and fascinating) embodiment.

The construction of the violent loner as the epitome of power can take various forms. Jack Henry Abbot says, "Dangerous killers who act alone and *without* emotion, who act with calculation and principles, to avenge themselves, establish and defend their principles with acts of murder that usually evade prosecution by law: this is the state-raised convicts' conception of manhood, in the highest sense" (author's italics; Abbot 13). We may find it easy to dismiss a prisoner's conception of manhood, but how distant is the emotionless vigilantism described by Abbot from the manhood expressed by the characters of Steven Segal, or of Chuck Norris, or Michael Douglas's character in *Falling Down?* This language pertaining to the space above the law is familiar to us. It is the language of heroes, of John Wayne and Sam Spade. It is the language of *Top Gun's* fighter-pilots, who find an untainted and transcendent existence in the skies and only frustration in the petty world below. It is the language of the valorized male vigilante. A *National Review* editorial on Dahmer's insanity defense wonders about the random violence that seems to be on the increase: "Each atrocity seems uniquely evil; but why are there so many of them? We don't know, except that what we call 'society' is less inclusive than we thought. A disturbing number of people are spiritually outside it and willing to do whatever

1. The relationship between radical selfhood and voyeurism is discussed by Sartre. Murray S. Davis notes that Sartre demonstrates in *Being and Nothingness* "how voyeurism heightens an individual's feeling of selfhood. By expanding one's distance from others, it increases one's experience of differentiation from them" (Davis 1983, 128). See Sartre on "the look" in *Being and Nothingness*, 252–302.

they can get away with" (2 March 1992: 18). To be spiritually outside of society can be a culturally valorized position, and it finds expression in the characters or themes of some of our most popular movies and television shows. Characterizing the ideologies that dominated America and Britain in the eighties is the idea that *society* is a dirty word, or a "myth" as Margaret Thatcher so (in)famously put it. Rugged (manly) individualism is valorized over (effeminate) society. Leyton regards the killings of the serial killer as "a kind of sub-political and conservative protest" (Leyton 26). However, he who Leyton sees as making "a substantial profit of revenge, celebrity [and] identity" (26), should perhaps be regarded less as a protester and more as the embodiment of a particular form of conservatism taken to its logical conclusion.

According to an FBI agent, one of the questions that convicted serial rapists are asked to help the FBI to construct personality profiles is, "What role, if any, do pornography and/or detectives magazines have in crimes?" (House 36). Rather than being placed antithetically and giving each other meaning by that placing, certain popular representations of "policing" discourse are indistinguishable from "monstrous" discourse, and both find meaning instead in opposition to the powerless. The coupling of pornography with detective stories in the mind of the personality profiler is indicative of the way the detection of crime is often presented. Pornography and the representation of crime and its detection can be two different but related forms of fantasy. The distinction between the two is blurred in the increasing number of "true crime" periodicals whose focus is violent or "sexual" crime. Advertisements for "female attractants" and other means of improving male sexual prowess in the pages of *Headquarters Detective, Detective Digest, Inside Detective,* and *Official Detective* are complemented by the magazines' covers, which frequently include young, seminaked women, often bound, gagged, and being threatened with a gun or a knife by a male aggressor. Park Dietz notes that "when we are able to search the possessions of sexually sadistic serial killers we find that many of them have collections of detective magazines or at least their covers" (*To Kill and Kill Again*). While the female victim's face shows terror, the attacker's face is usually hidden from view. Faceless, unidentifiable, he can be any man. (Dietz notes that when convicted killers speak of the appeal of such magazines, they invariably remark that when the male aggressor is identifiable, the image becomes much less of a turn-on). An obvious common factor in recognized pornography and detective magazines is that they both involve fantasies of power and control. Often in the true/fantasy crime magazine, the reenactments of crimes—especially crimes involving the subordination of women—from the perspective of the criminal are followed by the detection, capture, and subordination of the criminal from the perspective of the detective. Absent are possible causal factors, character issues, emotional consequences, and context related to the crime. Absent are stories from the perspective of those killed or raped. In the representation of detection as pornographic fantasy, detection becomes indistinguishable from the construction of and oppression of "the weak."

In the House of Representatives hearing, Chair English asks the FBI, "Do you think it possible to put together some kind of crime manual; things to look for, helpful hints?" (House 85). This follows a response by the FBI to a question about how a particular serial killer managed to escape detection: "It is a lot of luck on his part. A lot of expertise in the art, if you will, of crime. We have recovered items that indicate that he studied crime, even to the extent of appearing to study criminal psychology. He researched stories that are printed in magazines that deal in publishing criminal stories. These magazines appear to have been used as almost how-to manuals by this subject" (*House* 73). And apparently there are how-to movies: "*Henry: Portrait of a Serial Killer*, tells you how to select victims, how to kill them, how to enjoy killing them, how to dispose of the body" (Dr. Radecki on *Oprah Winfrey*, 4 September 1991). It seems we are all reading and writing the same books, watching and making the same films and television shows, and using them differently and sometimes not so differently. One person's detective manual can be another's how-to commit-a-crime manual. Ted Bundy, however, manages to dismiss altogether this *other*, this other person, by writing a pamphlet on rape prevention before raping and murdering scores of women. One person's detective fantasy is not always easily distinguishable from another's criminal fantasy, and the art of crime is not always distinct from the science of policing. In a photograph accompanying a *People Weekly* article (1 April 1991: 64) on the "real-life models" used in the making of *The Silence of the Lambs*, one of the special agents invited to the House of Representatives hearing, John Douglas, does little to help us distinguish the terms of the article's headline, "Cops, Killers & Cannibals," and does little to discredit the idea that FBI agents fulfill phallic fantasies, by pointing his high-caliber gun straight at the camera. The caption, previously quoted, is, "You try to understand what makes a person a murder victim."

Might the popularity of Thomas Harris's Lecter novels and their movie representations be related to our desire to blur the distinction between criminal fantasy and detection, to our respect for a particular form of power? We are more than willing to accompany the FBI as they enter "the mind of the serial killer"—the topic of an edition of *Geraldo* (29 March 1993)—and very willing to forget the fancifulness

116

of our flight of fancy. If we become at all uncomfortable, the presence of the police can help us explain our being there. In our representation of violent crime, detective, monster, and audience may lose their distinctiveness, conflate into a single figure. And, as I suggest in the next chapter, the apparent inability of our cops and killers to distinguish fact from fantasy goes along with our inability or lack of desire to do the same. Together we allow ourselves to dream the dream of omnipotence.

8

The Monstrous Self
Dreaming Up Reality

I made another world, and real men would enter it and they would never really get hurt at all in the vivid unreal laws of the dream. I caused dreams which caused death. This is my crime.
(Dennis Nilsen, quoted in Masters 1991, 265)

See you in Disneyland!
(Richard Ramirez to court journalists after the jury had recommended that he should die in the gas chamber, quoted in Wilson and Seaman 116)

Reality hasn't been real for a long time. With "real-life" television and especially "true-life" police shows increasingly filling prime-time television slots, reality in the nineties functions more as style than as an ultimate reference point. CBS's *Real Patrol* and *Top Cops*, NBC's *Law and Order* and *Prime Suspect*, Fox's *Code 3*, *America's Most Wanted*, and their nightly *Cops* might all be categorized as "infotainment." The more we stress the reality of our television—*Real Patrol* presumably exists in the same realm as KCOP's *Real News*—the more the meaning of *reality* shifts toward a parody of its former meaning.

People Weekly, remarking on the connection between *The Silence of the Lambs* and its story on Dahmer, headlines an article with the phrase "Fiction Pales" (12 August 1991: 36). But in comparison to what? Frequently Dahmer is not represented as being *like* Lecter or Buffalo Bill; in the world of infotainment the relationship between reality and fantasy is less that of simile than of metaphor. Reality does not reenact fantasy; it assumes fantasy's identity and renders it unidentifiable. Of course fiction and reality have rarely been distinguished without a struggle, but whether we are less concerned about maintaining the distinction or the *illusion* of the distinction, 1992 was a year in which we witnessed a series of events which questioned more than ever the sense of placing fiction and reality antithetically. Following Dan Quayle's attack on television's *Murphy Brown* (because the show's heroine decides to have a child out of wedlock), Murphy Brown, played by Candice Bergen, responded to Quayle on the show's season premiere, a movie which was considered front-page news. Raymond Williams, among others, has noted that the television experience is characterized by "flow," and it seems that such an experience has allowed for a greater sense of fluidity between the "real" and what is considered "unreal." Nineties television is characterized by shows like *Hard Copy* and *A Current Affair*, in which "real" characters are involved in the dramatizations of real events, by docudramas, by movies inspired by reality, by reality as the focus of sitcoms and dramas.

Arguing that "the only definition" of realism is that it "intends to avoid the question of reality implicated in that of art," Jean-François Lyotard remarks: "Those who refuse to re-examine the rules of art pursue successful careers in mass conformism by communicating, by means of the 'correct rules,' the endemic desire for reality with objects and situations capable of gratifying it. Pornography is the use of photography and film to such an end. It is becoming a general model for the visual or narrative arts which have not met the challenge of the mass media" (Lyotard 75). Similar to the experience of reading Capote's "non-fiction novel," our experience of "real" television is unimpeded by the conspicuous presence of a narrator. And it is sometimes easy to lose our sense of the situation from which we gain our perspective, to forget that observation can alter the observed, to lose awareness of our history and the history of the construction of that reality, and finally to allow reality's quotation marks to fade away. Infotainment manages to commoditize reality without questioning its own existence, and it might just meet Lyotard's requirements for being an example of realism if it weren't for its continual advertising of its "realness." If it fails to examine its own construction, we can't help but fail to do so ourselves.

All this can influence the debate about how to frame the relationship between "real-life" behavior and the media. We can no longer talk unproblematically of "the media" as a phenomenon that is separate from the "information" it "transmits," and separate from the "public" to which the "information" is "transmitted." And as my quotation marks might suggest, the terms *information, transmit,* and *public* are no longer free from interrogation. Remarking on previous studies on the relationship between media and society, Joshua Meyrowitz notes that

> people looked at how media affected real behavior and how real behavior related to the content of the media, but there were few models that dealt with both systems of communicating as part of a continuum

119

rather than a dichotomy. Most of the concerns were about people *imitating* behavior they saw on television, or about the inaccurate *reflection* of reality as portrayed in television content—real life as opposed to the media. Few studies examined both media and interpersonal interaction as part of the same system of "behaving" or responding to the behavior of others. Few people seemed to be studying the ways in which new patterns of access to information about social behavior might be affecting people's ability to play old forms of roles.[1] (author's italics, ix–x)

The inability to distinguish between the reality and fictionality of a role affects attempts to provide a "cultural context" for the serial killer. Attempts to provide such a context are usually criticized for helping to absolve the criminal of the crime. To make sense of such a criticism is to isolate culture from the individual and to isolate the media from the viewer/potential criminal. However, just as I could no longer suggest with a clear conscience that culture in the form of prime-time television and popular movies "produces" serial killers, hypothetical critics (for they cannot *really* exist) of such a suggestion cannot wholly individualize the crime. The serial killer and his representation are functions of each other to such an extent that ideas of a "relationship" (implying two or more agents) existing between the two begin to sound questionable.

One commentator suggests that the Marquis de Sade "attached greater importance to the stories he wove around the act of pleasure than to the contingent happenings" (Beauvoir 18). Dahmer, similarly attempting to overcome contingency, to relive, reinvent the moment, similarly attempting perhaps to achieve an intensification of the original feeling, photographs his victims in various stages of dismemberment or retains body parts. But what of the stories we weave—the reconstructions, the dramas whose structures lead us to familiar, conventional conclusions, the representations which maximize suspense and climax?

"They were in awe of him. They parted to let him through and stared at him like he was some kind of celebrity" (quoted in Schwartz 34), observed one policeman about the response of Dahmer's fellow prisoners in jail before the trial. Speculating on serial killers' motives, Leyton says, "What they are all orchestrating is a kind of social

---

1. In the days when we weren't encumbered by words like *infotainment*, T. S. Eliot was saying much the same about literature and "life" as Meyrowitz says about the media and reality. Among the functions of a literary review, Eliot wrote in the inaugural edition of *The Criterion*, is "to exhibit the relations of literature—not to 'life,' as something contrasted to literature, but to all the other activities, which, together with literature, are the components of life."

levelling, in which they re-write the universe to incorporate them-selves" (Leyton 295). If, fed up with being nobody, they kill in order to become somebody, their success depends on us. Schwartz remembers Dahmer's trial as having "the air of a movie premiere, complete with local celebrities, groupies who hounded for autographs, and a full-scale media onslaught—of which I was a part" (Schwartz 186). Those "groupies" included journalists and policemen. Her fellow reporters, she says, admitted to thinking about "getting Dahmer to scribble his name next to [their] bylines," and "several [police] officers decided to ask Dahmer to autograph a newspaper with the headlines blaring about death and dismemberment" (Schwartz 137). She quotes one of the officers: "I saw *Silence of the Lambs*, so I knew enough not to give him the whole pen. So I took it apart and stuck just the ink cartridge through the bars" (137). Dahmer is one of the biggest celebrities of the nineties. As Richard Roth notes, "Dahmer, or rather his likeness, is doing big business," and "The serial killer is packaged and sold in maga-zines, books, even trading-cards" (*Murder by Number*).

Our construction of Dahmer is a product we consume with great glee. If Dahmer kills to star in his version of *The Silence of the Lambs*, we ensure he has his fun. *People Weekly* reports him "confined to a cell with a glass front much like the fictional madman Hannibal Lecter in the film *The Silence of the Lambs*" (3 February 1992: 78). Geraldo Rivera intro-duces a show entitled "Jeffrey Dahmer: Diary of a Monster" (*Geraldo*, 12 September 1991) with "It's a real-life *Silence of the Lambs*, they say . . . It's unbelievable," and a *New York Times* editorial notes that "it's as though *The Silence of the Lambs* has suddenly burst from flat-screen fic-tion into inescapable 3-D reality" (6 August 1991: A16).

Serial killers have a penchant for role-playing. The troupe can in-clude John Wayne Gacy as a clown, the "Zodiac Killer" dressed as an executioner, and Dennis Nilsen (in *Le Grand Guignol?*) pretending to be dead while propping his dead victims alongside him. And now there is the new boy Dahmer, who, before accepting work in our recreation of Demme's movie, plays the emperor in *Return of the Jedi* (buying yellow contact lenses in order to increase the resemblance, his defense attor-ney tells us) and runs through the trance-routine from *Exorcist III*, "like he was wanting to be the character in the movie," as Tracey Edwards, who witnessed the performance before escaping from the set, put it. Henry Lee Lucas sees the serial killer as "being like a movie-star . . . you're just playing the part . . . I started staying on television twenty-four hours a day . . . I got so that I thought I was the biggest movie-star in this country . . . I think I even beat Elvis Presley . . . I think I even beat . . . what's his name? . . . Adolf Hitler" (*Confessions of a Serial Killer*). For Lucas, being bigger than Elvis and what's-his-name was

121

worth confessing to 360 murders, most of which, it now seems, he didn't commit.

While the killers are responsible for the script's details regarding the crime (except, perhaps, in the case of Lucas), we are the ones who help to create the roles that guarantee fame, who guarantee the drama of the story's "conclusion." As Wendy Lesser argues, we allow murderers to transcend our realities and fantasies and occupy a central role in our perception of the world: "[Murderers] are our truth and our fiction; they are our truth as fiction, and vice versa" (Lesser 2). While Dahmer says, "I made my fantasy life more powerful than my real one" (*Day One*, 18 April 1993), we struggle to make any distinction between our fantasies of crime and its realities, and struggle perhaps to keep our dreams from becoming reality. The questions asked during Dahmer's trial about his ability to distinguish dreams from reality seem just as applicable to his representers. Although the blurring of fiction and reality is not restricted to the discourse of serial murder, why should we *especially* want to represent serial killers in a manner which obscures the distinction between fact and fiction?

Lesser suggests that in fiction "the certainty that a murder will take place . . . is what fuels the artful murder plot," and that "the dramatic quality is initially produced by our expectation, by our foreknowledge of the murder itself, . . . whereas murder in real life . . . is almost always unexpected, and its dramatic possibilities are therefore limited" (Lesser 16). However, the drama is not so limited with real life *serial* murder. When we have been told of a serial killer on the loose, the expectation of murder and the dramatic possibilities that we bring to the story can be as strong as when we begin to watch a murder movie: this real-life genre contains a promise that is often fulfilled. A lack of closure of the case can help events become story, news become art, and can make the fictionalizing of real-life serial murder seem appropriate.

The serial killer seems made for television, especially the miniseries, which Michael Sworkin says is "predicated on the explicitness of a relationship between seriality and finitude." Television, he adds, "is always signalling an interruption and an ending" (Sworkin 180). One of those who claim to have first used the term *serial killer* is former personality profiler at Quantico, Robert Ressler, who saw the behavior of such criminals as "distinctly episodic, like the movie-house serials he enjoyed as a boy" (Michaud 41). However, Judith Halberstam identifies serial killings as having the characteristics of literature and arousing the expectations that we associate with it rather than television or the movies: "Serial murders have something of a literary quality to them: they happen regularly over time and each new one creates an expectation; they involve plot, a consummate villain and an absolutely pure (because randomly picked) victim; they demand explanation; they demand that a pattern be forced onto what appears to be 'desperately random' " (Halberstam 46).

The comments of Sworkin, Ressler, and Halberstam might lead one to suggest that the serial killer figure is a nightmarish reality constructed by a crime-obsessed culture seeking the ultimate mystery to solve; in other words, the serial killer is a reality satisfying the demands of fiction (a suggestion which, after literary and film theory had apparently removed reality without quotation marks from discussions about the nature of fiction, signals some kind of comeback by that troublesome idea). According to John Liccione, a psychologist at the Milwaukee County Mental Health Complex, Dahmer's confessions sounded "like a third-rate playwright script in Hollywood" (*Los Angeles Times*, 4 August 1991: A22). It was a script taken up by ABC's *Day One*, with actors playing the parts of Dahmer and the police officers who interrogated him (18 April 1993). The show, produced by ABC News, includes a gay bar scene in which a female impersonator (dressed as Annie Lennox's character in her video for "Why?") provides musical context for a Jeffrey Dahmer look-alike (consciously impersonating or coincidentally resembling, we're not sure) who lights a cigarette while eyeing potential pickups. If Dahmer sought to get to Hollywood by writing and starring in his own movie, given the fictionalized treatment of his actions, he more or less succeeded. If a serial killer tells his story to a psychologist using the discourse of entertainment, perhaps we should not be too surprised when real-life horror resembles our "entertaining" violent fantasies. If we confuse reality and fiction in the discourse of serial murder—if we experience/create a seamless entity of fantasy merged with reality, of dreams instantaneously realized—are we not in danger of inadvertently "dreaming up" real-life killers? When fictitious serial killers are our heroes, our fantasy figures, should we be surprised when real men and women "stray" into our fantasies?

The possibility that the serial killer construction is a fantasy figure of dominant culture is perhaps best illustrated by the speculative attributing of motive. Discussing the British press coverage of Colin Ireland, Joan Smith remarks that "one of the many myths about serial killers is that they are in some way motivated by revenge: the *Daily Mail* trotted out the theory that the man 'is targeting gays after contracting Aids.' *Today*, by contrast, quoted a criminal psychologist who suggested the killer may believe he has 'a divine mission to rid the world of homosexuals.' . . . Similar motives—a 'divine mission' against prostitutes and contracting a venereal disease from one of them—were attributed to [Peter] Sutcliffe" (Smith 3). As she notes, "in fact Sutcliffe selected prostitutes as some of his early victims because they were willing to accompany him to a secluded spot. In the [Colin Ireland] case, the readiness of some gay men to return home with a stranger may have influenced the killer. He may not be homosexual; even the fact that some of the victims were prepared to take part in sadomasochistic activities may simply have played into his hands" (Smith 3). The nature of the quests and missions which we give our serial killers may illustrate our underlying dreams. Might Dahmer be our dream as well as our nightmare?

According to Schwartz, the district attorney in Dahmer's trial suggested that "we should recognize the danger of fantasy and that thinking about anything is a definite precursor to doing it" (Schwartz 216). An (internal) eye for an "I"? Perhaps the D.A. dreams of being on/in *I Witness Video*, dreams of a world in which the hum of our minds running and of our video recorders is indistinguishable. The characters in such a world may experience the same kind of uncertainty as Perry in Truman Capote's *In Cold Blood:* "And just then it was like I was outside myself. Watching myself in some nutty movie. . . . And I thought, Why don't I walk off? Walk to the highway, hitch a ride. I sure Jesus didn't want to go back in that house. And yet—How can I explain this? It was like I wasn't part of it. More as though I was reading a story. And I had to know what was going to happen. The end. So I went back upstairs" (Capote 272). Alvin Kernan has argued that television is gaining cultural influence and that "more and more people derive, quite unconsciously, their sense of reality and their existential situation in it from television" (Kernan 147–48). If we agree with Kernan, and if by *culture* we mean the patterns of meaning with which we attempt to evaluate ourselves, our television culture is akin to Capote's genre, with our lives becoming indistinguishable from nonfiction entertainments.

Television's involvement in the creation of such a world is described by Sworkin, who argues that "the erasure of the difference between broadcasting the news and being the news . . . between adjudicating and narrating . . . is what must be accomplished" by television (Sworkin 194). For Sworkin, television is a process of simulation, often involved with, as Jean Baudrillard put it, "substituting signs of the real for the real itself" (quoted in Sworkin 164). Its "simulations serve primarily as an implement for the creation of continuities across the range of broadcast quanta, to further establish the principle of equality among images. Simulation is presently absorbed not with a structure of certainties but with a radical agenda of destabilization. It establishes the tenacious problematic of Memorex (is it real or is it . . .) as a useful, binding constant" (Sworkin 172). Sworkin uses *The People's Court*—a show made up of "real" people who, having filed complaints in a "real" small claims court, decide to drop their suits there and have them heard instead on television before a "real" judge—as an example of television's scrambling of fiction and reality. The scramble produces a mixture characterized by its smoothness, by plots which have been rehearsed repeatedly and lack any of those awkward, unsuspected moments with which *real life* and *real fiction* abound:

> Nobody really loses in *The People's Court*. Judge Wapner's awards are paid by the producers of the show; the only punishment is humiliation. This delimiting of penalty engenders an interesting slippage. Justice assumes the character of a game show, a format in which the worst outcome is loss of face and a failure to win. On *The People's Court*, infraction carries no real risk beyond this. By restricting justice to the parameters of entertainment, *The People's Court* becomes a show trial. It's lip-synch justice, however exemplary, because a way has been found to remove risk from uncertainty. The litigants (all of whom receive scale) become no more than actors in an ersatz real-life drama. (Sworkin 173)

Jeffrey Dahmer's show trial, the first serial killer trial televised live, was not heard before Judge Wapner, but it was a big-budget version of *The People's Court*. As fiction enters the business of the law, it seems the law is happy to enter the business of drama and play by its rules. Criticized for placing himself in a situation in which he might be seen to "view his or her docket as material for future popular exploitation," Dahmer's judge, Laurence Gram, writes a book *The Jeffrey Dahmer Case: A Judge's Perspective* which, according to *Time* (18 May 1992: 17), is to be the basis for a film script entitled *The Jeffrey Dahmer Confessions*. Agent Lew Breyer is quoted as saying, "The judge doesn't want a horror picture per se. But I have written in one or two horror scenes that are horrific in describing one of the murders." "Faction" with the backing of the law? Infotainment inscribed by the law with a kind of truth whose authority can come only from the law? That the serial killer is a product designed to serve the entertainment industry is the conclusion we can draw from Nick Broomfield's film *Aileen Wuornos: The Selling of a Serial Killer*. Unlike most convicted serial killers, Wuornos, a former prostitute awaiting the death sentence for the murder of seven men, rejects her serial killer identity, claiming she never stalked her victims and that she killed the men in self-defense after they had raped or attempted to rape her. Suggesting that it was in the best interests of the police (as well as the entertainment industry) to have Wuornos convicted and sentenced to death as "a serial killer," the film tells of two Florida policemen who were transferred from the Criminal Investigation Department and one who resigned after they were found to have been involved in discussions with Hollywood about movie rights to the Wuornos case.

With the usually entertainment-minded HBO setting a precedent with a show on serial killing, the producers of television's *Entertainment Tonight* obviously thought the Dahmer trial satisfied the show's directive and covered the media representation of the trial. One commentator describes the mood of Milwaukee County Courthouse: "As befits a courtroom which had been set up as a TV studio, Judge Gram's speech owes much to the Academy Awards ceremony: he thanks his secretary Vikki, and his stenographer Mary ("How many years have we been together now Mary? Fourteen?"), but first of all he thanks the media coordinator who has arranged matters so that Judge Gram gets more airtime than any judge before him" (Diamond 45). Back in real life, Dahmer's victims and their families have lost everything, but "Showtime with a Serial Killer" becomes a game in which, while the outcome of the insanity verdict is uncertain, everybody knows their parts, and nobody loses. Dahmer, described by his attorney as "the most unique man in the history of the world" (Diamond 44), wins a chapter devoted exclusively to him in the history of crime. The trial is attended by seventy news organizations, televised on cable, and carried live on WDJT, a Milwaukee radio station, which obtains record ratings. The *New York Times* tells of a transparent plastic shield placed between what it describes as the "spectators" and the "participants" (27 January 1992: A11). As Paramount Pictures hastily cancels advertisements in Milwaukee for its new movie *Body Parts*, outside of Dahmer's apartment building "people climb out of their vehicles, cameras dangling from their neck, and take pictures like tourists at Mount Rushmore. Indeed, a macabre sort of cottage industry has sprung up in the neighborhood. Everything is for sale, from information about encounters with Mr. Dahmer, whom most people in the building call Jeff, to tours of the inside, for the right price" (*New York Times*, 29 July 1991: A13). Dahmer has put Milwaukee on the map, a point not lost on Mary Ladish, vice president of Metro Milwaukee, Inc., the city's tourism promoters, who notes that "No one in the U.S. or the world can disagree that this is a catastrophic tragedy. But I don't think anyone is holding it against Milwaukee" (Diamond 45).

The trial is one of the last episodes of this latest serial killer serial. On *Hard Copy* and on *A Current Affair* excerpts from the trial are intercut with revelations from other stories, some scandalous and some not, and as Sworkin puts it, "Nothing fashioned from the field of bits is finally any different from any other selection. The uncertainties are merely formal, not substantial. By such deprivations of meaning, the medium renders itself purely aesthetic" (Sworkin 182). Similarly, Joel Black—suggesting that "our post-transgressive age marks the fulfillment of McLuhan's dictum about the medium becoming the message, the final phase of what Christopher Lasch calls the transformation of 'horrible events into images' " (Black 137)—argues that the "social norm in postindustrial society and in postmodern culture is no longer the ethical world of the real, but the aesthetic realm of the hyperreal" (138).

What happens to the idea of perversion in such a world? When we knew or thought we knew the difference between reality and fantasy, we also thought we could recognize the difference between self and other. A self was real, natural. We deprived our others of identity, cultural presence, a place in our/the reality. They were of another world which could impinge on ours but which we could only dream about. Freud told us they might be deep within us, but that they could only be reached once we left the reality of our conscious selves. Stallybrass and White, among others, tell us we need perversion in order to sustain the idea of civilization. But as fact and fantasy lose the meaning given by their antithetical relation, as they become *mis-placed* (both out of position and lost) so too perhaps do self and other, civilized and perverse. As our fantasies enter our realities, perhaps our notions of self become more permeable to our notions of other. And, as Judith Halberstam notes, we also lose our ability to judge: "It seems to me that *The Silence of the Lambs* emphasizes that we are at a peculiar time in history, a time when it is becoming impossible to tell the difference between prejudice and its representations, between homophobia and the representation of homophobia" (Halberstam 41). In the same essay she says, "We wear modern monsters like skin, they are us, they are on us and in us. Monstrosity no longer coagulates into a specific body, a single face, a unique feature, it is replaced with a banality that fractures resistance because the enemy becomes harder and harder to locate, and looks more and more like the hero" (38). And locating the enemy becomes that much more difficult when you are unsure whether what you are seeing is real or not, whether he wears a mask or not, whether it matters if the mask is real or not.

Our infotainment existence is subject to the same pressure suffered by our movie industry: the pressure of going one better, of finding new things to excite curiosity or shock a culture which can turn sensation into boredom with amazing ease. Like Sworkin, Joshua Meyrowitz has argued that as the electronic age has taken hold, we are finding it increasingly difficult to identify extremes: "The electronic combination of many different styles of interaction from distinct regions leads to new 'middle region' behaviors that, while containing elements of formerly distinct roles, are themselves new behavior patterns with new expectations and emotions" (311). Meyrowitz connects these middle-region behaviors with our inability to be shocked: "The act of exposure itself now seems to excite us more than the content of the secrets exposed. The steady stripping away of layers of social behavior has made the 'scandal' and the revelation of the 'deep dark secret' everyday occurrences" (311). But then a Jeffrey Dahmer comes along and manages to up the stakes: his crimes, as social psychologist Carol Tavris writes, "are a kind that put him in his own lunatic league" (*Los Angeles Times*, 9 August 1991: B7). But even he, she suggests, will soon be subsumed by a media of "one-minute political commercials, advertisements that posture as news stories, and the blurring of troubling news reports with amusing tales" which commits "the real violence to our minds." The following excerpt from an edition of *The Maury Povich Show* (whose subject was the alleged glorification of Dahmer by the media) illustrates Tavris's point:

Povich:	What do you think of this media circus that's going on here? In fact, why don't you hold that. We'll be back. We'll talk about how the media is treating Jeffrey Dahmer. Whether he is indeed being given celebrity status and much more right after this.
Voice-over:	Still to come, her addiction to Bingo has put her marriage on the line. [Commercial break] [video clip of Jeffrey Dahmer] (*Maury Povich*, 4 February 1992)

As previously noted, in *Civilization and Its Discontents* Freud suggests that "many systems of civilization" have become neurotic "under the pressure of the civilizing trends" (Freud 1953b, 141–142), but he concedes that such a diagnosis can be problematic without the presence of an environment functioning as normality. Such a diagnosis might be further complicated today. Instead of comparing individuals to the norms of society, we compare ourselves every so often to ever-more-extreme individuals, while simultaneously living out as a fantasy the reality of those individuals (and negating the realities of their victims). In *The Novel and the Police*, Miller argues that the "novel's critical relation to society . . . masks the extent to which modern social organization has made even 'scandal' a systematic function of its routine self-maintenance" (xii). Like the newspaper and television tabloids which in part constitute it, our modern social organization—which entertains while naturalizing a policing mentality—is one which needs to be ever-more scandalous, requires its monsters to be increasingly monstrous in order to win a place in the great tradition of crime, and one which (incidentally?) simultaneously justifies ever-more policing and surveillance. Perversion has become less that which civilization defines itself against and more of an event at which civilization cheers and feigns horror.

Carol Tavris is concerned "not only that violence permeates our entertainment media—our contemporary fairy tales; violence has always been a part of story-telling" (Tavris 7), but that it is rarely explained, given meaning. For David Edgar, it is this giving of meaning which can stop representation from becoming promotion: "One doesn't have to go all the way with Aristotelian catharsis to accept that Shakespeare and Brenton and Bond do not represent violence in order to encourage it, but rather to understand and confront it, and that one of the things that fiction allows you to confront about wickedness is how attractive it is" (Edgar 8). For Edgar, Lecter's attractiveness is no more "propaganda for cannibalism" than *Paradise Lost* is "propaganda for Satanism" (8). However, while Shakespeare, Brenton, and Bond may represent violence in an "understanding" manner, it's the meaning the audience gives which matters. We can take intention and context or leave them. In the debate about the portrayal of sex and violence and its relation to behavior, the divide between what Edgar calls "superior artists" and "the grimier end of the market" can be misleading. The understanding and confrontation of the "attractiveness" of wickedness depends not so much on the medium in which the wickedness is presented or the "seriousness" of the artist as on our questioning of our consumption of that presentation. (We might also question the assumed "attraction" of wickedness.) As I argue later, we should not be blaming technology, but questioning our use of it.

So what kind of consumers are we? What is the unspoken meaning of our infotainment existence? In his discussion of serial killing in the postmodern detective story, David Richter argues that "the foregrounding of the synthetic function usually is subordinated to the thematic function": in other words, "calling attention to the fictionality of a story not only undermines its mimetic function and its effect, it correspondingly serves to make it illustrative of a theme or thesis" (108). With our infotainments not only representing real murderers in fictional forms but parodying those forms, what are the themes we like to play out night after night?

For Sworkin, television's eclecticism limits meaning rather than increases it, tends toward homogeneity rather than difference, tends toward a single meaning, a single reality. For Lyotard, eclecticism "is the degree zero of contemporary general culture," and the "realism of the anything goes' culture is in fact that of money; in the absence of aesthetic criteria, it remains possible and useful to assess the value of works of art according to the profits they yield" (Lyotard 76). Lyotard's comments on contemporary art might just as well apply to television—barriers between art and mass culture are surely dissolved in the "anything goes" reality—and we might say that television's realism, or the only reality of television, is money, dependent as it is on ratings. However tempting it would be to lay dominant constructions of monstrosity at capitalism's door, perhaps we should look toward another, more dominant, all-embracing reality for which money might function as a disguise, a reality of which capitalism has only been a manifestation: power. Power comes in many guises, but sometimes it isn't so shy, knowing it can safely flaunt its charms without condemnation. The mythology of the serial killer is, I suggest, securely fixed by such a reality; ours is an age in which our fantasies of power, or what we think of as power, can safely surface as realities without fear of disapproval. And where particular forms of power are taken for granted, their manifestations can assume the aura of being "aesthetic." Sworkin argues that by its "deprivations of meaning" television renders itself "purely aesthetic" (182). But the history of aesthetics can be read as the history of dominant ideologies constructing the nature of aesthetical value, and the "purely aesthetic" medium is not *without* meaning. It is the medium through which the presence of particular forms of power can appear natural. Television's aesthetic quality allows fantasies of power to appear irreducible.

In 1987 Cameron and Frazer, noting that "horror today belongs to the domain of the aesthetic," wrote that "people who rush to the scene of a disaster for the pleasure of witnessing actual death and destruction are deemed to have acted inappropriately precisely because they have derived from reality a thrill which we think should be confined to the realms of fiction" (52). However, now we can rush live, without leaving our homes, to a scene of a crime or a disaster via a television camera strapped to an ambulance or police car. The sense of inappropriateness has disappeared. The pleasure of horror, that which was deemed appropriate only in a recognizable world of fiction, is now something one can experience (without fear of condemnation) on television framed as reality. In our creation and consumption of infotainment we have sprung the aesthetics of horror from fiction. We are able to appreciate the "natural beauty" of horror and violence by constructing their aesthetic value—by locating them, that is, on an amoral plain beyond the reach of condemnation—and erasing the memory of its construction. And similarly, our modern manifestations of horror and violence are constructed as aesthetic. Robert Ressler, president of the Forensic Behavioral Services, says that "the media, the news, and entertainment media have created the idea of what a serial killer is, and believe me, he is not Hannibal Lecter" (*Murder by Number*). Our perception of serial killers as being like or just plain *being* Hannibal Lecter—powerful, eloquent, member of a cultural elite—is, however, relatively clear and untroubled, and we, like Ressler, have difficulty in naming what it is that naturalizes that perception. One sign of his mythological status is that the serial killer is void of the meaning central to his construction. He is a figure whose derivation is unclear, but who is the product of dominant ideology nonetheless.

As I mentioned at the beginning of this chapter, the suggestion that our violent fantasies of power are indistinguishable from our violent realities should not be confused with the suggestion that violent fantasies *cause* murder. Such an argument, as well as its counterargument, relies on the assumption that fantasy and the reality in which we locate action or behavior (such as murder) are recognizably separate. Like Buffalo Bill "posing in front of his own video camera . . . making love to his own image" (Tharp 107)—an image which, as Julie Tharp notes, evokes the movie, *Sex, Lies and Videotape* (113, n9)—the serial killer who is familiar to us is unable to test his internal world with reference to a world "beyond," unable to identify where the barrier between (individual) fantasy and (social) reality starts. As I suggest in chapter 2, while we are increasingly perceiving the world in individualistic and asocial terms, radical individualism is also perceived as a characteristic of our monsters, something which makes them monstrous.

Our radically individual serial killers resemble the young Frankenstein. Reflecting on his education, Frankenstein says, "I confess that neither the structure of languages, nor the code of governments, nor the politics of various states, possessed attractions for me. It was the secrets of heaven and earth that I desired to learn; and whether it was the outward substance of things or the inner spirit of nature and the mysterious soul of man that occupied me, still my inquiries were directed to the metaphysical, or, in its highest sense, the physical secrets of the world" (Shelley 37). Kenneth Graham notes that

the category which is omitted in Frankenstein's education is the category which embraces encounters with the real world in its social organization. It is this category which seems to Frankenstein to hold no interest; to supplant it he turns to the two extremes, to the so-called "metaphysical" and to chronic introspection. In Kleinian terms, we could speak of problems of introjection. The young Frankenstein is given to us as a name for a syndrome which abandons reality-testing, for one reason or another, and which prefers to work on a direct link between the inner world and the untested fantasy. But this is a mask for destructiveness; that ignorance of the real world is also a need to wish it away, to place it under prohibition, to deal only in the inner world and the gigantic shadows which that inner world throws on the screen of experience if we choose to ignore the checks and balances of external constraint. (Graham 18)

Related to such a figure—the ultimate loner who has no social existence—the question of whether the pornography which putatively informs our serial killer's fantasy world causes the murders he commits has no meaning, for his fantasy and his behavior belong to the same, seamless existence. Without a sense of "social reality," there is only "fantasy." To construct such an asocial figure, one whose existence in large and busy cities bringing regular personal contact is not perceived as a contradiction to that construction, is to evoke the modern nightmare of individuals retreating to homes coolly lit by television and computer screens, individuals whose only sense of interaction comes from "participating" in chat-shows or playing virtual reality games. The abandonment of what Graham calls "reality-testing" might also describe our apparent lack of desire/ability to distinguish our fantasies from our realities, or our movie-characters from real-life serial killers, and lead to our becoming one gigantic self lacking a context to underscore the illusionariness of our fantasies, to our avoiding the contingency of life, the risk of disappointment. How real, so to speak, is that nightmare?

Clearly, our definition of our selves must take into account our relationship with, or how we make use of, technology. We might talk of our "media selves," our selves which participate in (or have the illusion of participating in) what is commonly referred to as "the media." In conversation with Stephen Heath and Gillian Skirrow, Raymond Williams notes that "they say on television now, 'and next week you will have a chance to take part.' We won't conceivably, if there are millions of us. But it means, this and this one we'll select: all you. This is a way of thinking" (Heath and Skirrow 11–12). Heath replies "That's the creation of the instantaneous mass in relation to which television clearly works at the moment" (12). Our sense of belonging to a "mass" audience to which television works is, I suggest, becoming increasingly important to the way we perceive our selves as a social body and as individuals within it. And yet what kind of a social existence is it? Though television promotes itself as being "discursive,"[2] what is the value of the presumed dialogue between itself and the viewer? As Williams notes, while a presenter will invite "us" to participate, only a tiny minority can actually do so. And when he or she addresses "us" as, for example, "the nation," this idea of all-inclusiveness, "of people whom we 'recognize,' excludes the majority of people of the world whom we don't recognize and watch on television" (11). Williams adds, "If the broadcaster believes that he is addressing the nation he starts talking in certain ways which are bad for him, bad for us. Even if people get used to it. Because they're false ways in that all he's really looking at is a camera and people in a studio and all he's otherwise learned is a convention, usually a false one, in its most developed form" (11). The lack of interaction that television engenders and the consequential lack of a sense of other is also described by Alvin Kernan in *The Death of Literature*: "Television viewers do not interact with others as they would in a localized oral situation of the small town or village. Their situation as viewers re-enacts the isolation of the members of 'the loner crowd,' the mass society of the urbanized West" (149). The sense of belonging that we feel from watching television may be false, but as Williams notes, this is not necessarily the "fault" of the technology: "I think these false images have only been developed because of certain specific problems in this society, problems of people knowing where they belong and how they relate" (quoted in Heath and Skirrow 11). In the "modern nightmare" we rely on the image of ourselves as belonging to a mass audience for our sense of social belonging and we are consequently prone to having only our selves for company, to having no meaningful social reality against which to gauge the boundaries of our internal world. While fantasy cannot be described as "internal" and the act as "external" because the internal/external opposition has no meaning, the other (to the self) has no meaning, no reality, and can therefore be treated as an object in a fantasy. The confusion of reality and fantasy in the "content" of what is transmitted is reenacted by an inability or unwillingness to differentiate the self from its surroundings. The "content" of those transmitted fantasies, the erasure of the other, reoccurs as a consequence of that failure to differentiate. And of course in such a nightmare we are unable to identify the nonreality of that nightmare.

Graham's assessment of the young Frankenstein and Kernan's and

2. In using the term here I have in mind Emile Benveniste remarking that "discourse" is "every utterance assuming a speaker and a hearer, and in the speaker, the intention of influencing the other in some way. [It comprises] all the genres in which someone proclaims himself as the speaker and organizes what he says in the category of person" (Benveniste 209).

Williams' view of the television age all correspond with the figure of Jeffrey Dahmer, who, like Frankenstein experimenting with body parts, is someone we insist is lost in his own fantasy world, whose outer limits are those of the self, a self unable to consider the reality of the other for fear of its own destruction. It is the world of Caligula, in which an inability to sense others brings a nonsensical self, a world of limitless boundaries in which one is both emperor and magician. Also corresponding to familiar representations of Dahmer is Simone de Beauvoir's assessment of Sade: "It is . . . a combination of passionate sexual appetites with a basic emotional 'apartness' which seems to me to be the key to his eroticism" (32). While Dahmer is rarely perceived as sadistic, the following from Sade are words we can imagine Dahmer speaking: "If the objects who serve us feel ecstasy, they are then much more concerned with themselves than with us, and our own enjoyment is consequently impaired. The idea of seeing another person experience the same pleasure reduces one to a kind of equality which spoils the unutterable charms that come from despotism" (quoted in Beauvoir 33–34).

Dahmer is often represented as a figure who is radically *selfish*, who knows only his self (and who consequently has no sense of what that self means)—he is figured as both someone who is self-obsessed and someone who dangerously forgets himself—and this representation is offered by a medium which knows only itself (and which consequently has no sense of what that self means). In representing the serial killer in this way, we see something of ourselves: the subject fades, is not only unspeakable, but grows invisible, indistinguishable from that which represents it. Not surprising, then, the Gothic forms of representation: the monster there and here, without and within, something which is both content and form, something which monstrously unsettles such oppositions. For Nietzsche, the man of *ressentiment* "loves hiding places, secret paths and back doors, everything covert entices him as *his* world, *his* security, *his* refreshment" (Nietzsche 1969, 38). Such a man, explains Mark Seem, "needs very much to believe in some neutral, independent 'subject'—the ego—for he is prompted by an instinct of *self*-affirmation and *self*-preservation that cares little about preserving or affirming life" (author's italics; in Deleuze and Guattari xvii), an instinct "in which every lie is sanctified" (Nietzsche 1969, 46). Our representation of Dahmer is like the closet the man of *ressentiment* constructs for himself, only he doubts if there is anything out there, any place to which he can come out. Like a double-agent who has crossed the border so many times he has lost any sense of where he is—where he is in relation to the concept of truth, of lies—we construct secrets and keep them from ourselves. In Dahmer's representation, Milwaukee is a Gothic castle into which heroes and heroines go on quests for knowledge, peering into crypts, bringing back confessions, a place where sex is secret, where murders are secret; but that representation itself is a Gothic castle, from which not only is there no way out, but "no way out" has no meaning, a castle whose walls are lined with mirrors.

9

Sanity, Satan, and
Sanitized Evil

[There is] no doubt at this time that he is a Schizoid Personality Disorder who may show marked paranoid tendencies. He is definitely SPOOKY!
(From the prognosis of clinical psychologist Dr. Evelyn Rosen, following Dahmer's conviction for disorderly conduct in 1987 after two boys had reported him to the police for masturbating by the side of the Kinnickinnic River; quoted in Masters 1993, 107.)

In chapter 1, I described our construction of the sane but evil serial killer. His sanity reassures us of his culpability, allows us to legally condemn. His evil allows us to differentiate his sanity from our own. Our modern monsters arise from a nostalgia for an era preceding the science of psychiatry, an era when Satan was the essence of otherness. But when the serial killer's evil is represented more in terms of cartoon mischief than Biblical notions of wickedness, our estrangement becomes uncertain, half-hearted, and the serial killer who emerges is one closer to the center of society than to its fringes.

Lecter ridicules the fear of confronting evil: "Nothing happened to me, Officer Starling. *I* happened. You can't reduce me to a set of influences. You've given up good and evil for behaviorism, Officer Starling. You've got everybody in moral dignity pants—nothing is ever anybody's fault. Look at me, Officer Starling. Can you stand to say I am evil?" (Harris 1991, 20). It is a speech remade by Dahmer: "The person to blame is the person sitting across from you. Not parents, not society, not pornography. Those are just excuses," he tells an *Inside Edition* interviewer (cited in *People Weekly*, 12 December 1994: 129). For Lecter, to name and confront evil is a heroic act. Likewise, we contrast the discourse of good and evil to the equivocation and moral weakness which are considered characteristic of the discourse of psychiatry, and it is a contrast made more stark by the perception of evil as something which can be identified in the individual, and insanity "as a set of influences"—something dispersed socially.

Lecter feels the need to assert his individuality in the face of behaviorism, but the reception Dahmer receives would have been much more to his liking. Dahmer is given his moment of glory, is allowed to be seen as an individualized manifestation of evil, is allowed to be *some body*. The story of a shy, eighteen-year-old Jeffrey being asked to the prom is turned a decade later into an article headlined HIGH SCHOOL BEAUTY'S CHILLING PROM DATE WITH THE DEVIL (quoted in Schwartz 41). And the manner in which he dies is an opportunity to end this story of personified evil with a dramatic and final scene. Like *Newsweek, People Weekly* begins its article on the killing with Dahmer reading the Book of Revelation—"pages brimming with prophecies of hellfire, damnation and apocalyptic fury" (12 December 1994: 128)—five days before his journey to hell. Rather than seeing his death as the result of a prison attack in which *two* men died, we figure the murder as Satan claiming his man, a version in which the death of a fellow inmate, Jesse Anderson, has to be edited out. In contrast to the forceful figure of evil—he who "happens" alone, he *to* which nothing happens—is the confusing figure drawn by the psychiatry profession, the product of childhood experiences, familial relationships, and encounters with that fuzzy entity, "society."

As a figure of estrangement, the sane and evil monster personifies power which only those who "can stand" to recognize it can share. In our rejection of "mental illness"—in our deriding of psychopathology and of attempts to discover "the mechanisms of hatred and loneliness that warp the human soul" as Carol Tavris puts it (Tavris 7)—we bring Dahmer into our sane world. But how far do we simultaneously eject him as representative of the forces of evil? Dahmer's uneasy straddling of sanity and evil is an image in which we invest much curiosity and which keeps him central to our culture. Foucault, describing the segregation of the mentally ill in the nineteenth century, says, "As for a common language, there is no such thing any longer; the constitution of madness as a mental illness at the end of the eighteenth century, affords the evidence of a broken dialogue, posits the separation as already effected, and thrusts into oblivion all those stammered, imperfect words without fixed syntax in which the exchange between madness and reason was made. The language of psychiatry, which is a monologue of reason *about* madness, has been established only on the basis *of* such a silence" (Foucault 1988, x–xi). The current redundancy of the notion of mental illness, however, the making sane and Satan of individuals we once might have called mad, forces us to confront the possibility that there never was much of a linguistic divide between us and them, and also forces us to construct a common language which removes any doubt. In order to regard our monsters as sane we have to build bridges: "I, too, have struggled with sexual impulses," confesses State Attorney McCann during Dahmer's trial (quoted in Masters 1993, 228). The common language is the language of sanity, and the nature of that language is suggested by our ideas of what makes sense and what does not, what is insane and what is not. McCann, apparently appealing to the shared norms of our culture, argues that "Dahmer's drugging men at the gay bathhouses was calculated and no more insane than men using alcohol to convince women to have sex with them" (quoted in Schwartz 195). Doctor George Palermo, supporting McCann's judgment of Dahmer's sanity, declares in court that Dahmer "is an organized, nonsocial, lust murderer, who killed in a methodical and shrewd manner. He is driven by obsessive fantasies of power over others" (quoted in Schwartz 207). And according to a *National Review* editorial one month after the completion of the trial, Dahmer, compared to New York's "senseless killers," has already been relegated to the realm of normality: "Some murders have a pointless fiendishness about them that makes one doubt the very humanity of the killers . . . Maybe the murderers in these cases killed for fun. We have no reason to believe the only serial killers are those like Jeffrey Dahmer who obligingly keep the corpses in refrigerators for easy checking" (2 March 1992). Dahmer and normal people like us evidently share the same language—a language which naturalizes the use of alcohol to take sexual advantage of women, naturalizes power over others, and naturalizes murder as a form of acquisition, as a sign of one's consumerism.

And not only do we now share a common language with our monsters, we allow them to come out of the dark and into our homes. Those that we estrange now—if that is what we are doing—are much more visible. No longer do we delegate medical intermediaries to communicate with our monsters. While access to mental institutions is still limited, we allow individuals on trial for their insanity to speak directly to us on televised trials, convicted serial killers like Dahmer to speak to us on *Inside Edition*, and others to speak via movies like *Confessions of a Serial Killer*. Monstrosity has once again become spectacle, and while capital punishment has not (yet) become a regular television event,[1]

1. For a discussion of the legal case, *KQED v. Daniel B. Vasquez*, in which a public television station argued its right to record and broadcast the execution of a condemned man in a San Quentin gas chamber, as well as a discussion of our response to murder as spectacle, see Lesser, Wendy, *Pictures at an Execution* (Cambridge, MA: Harvard University Press, 1993).

the visibility of criminals on death row has increased sufficiently to suggest that matters have changed since "only the reading of the sentence on the scaffold announced the crime—and that crime must be faceless . . . The more monstrous a criminal was, the more he must be deprived of light: he must not see, or be seen" (Foucault 1979, 14–15). Although "theatrical elements" of punishment were "downgraded" in early-nineteenth-century France "as if this rite that 'concluded the crime' was suspected of being in some undesirable way linked with it" (Foucault 1979, 9), we do not seem to fear that our ritualization of the conclusion of particular crimes could be somehow linked to the crimes themselves. Theatrical elements of execution are upgraded zealously. Television represented the executions at San Quentin in the summer of 1992 with actors playing an execution's audience. The actual audience included a large proportion of television journalists who themselves recreated the scene in their respective shows. Fear of revealing a connection between crime and punishment was also absent in the execution of Ted Bundy; many newspapers published pictures of Bundy's corpse. The presenter of television's *American Justice*, Bill Curtis, argued that "the public welcomed [Bundy's] death with the kind of glee he himself might have felt when his victims gave up their lives."

Noting that although the insanity of William Edward Hickman was "beyond doubt," Wilson and Seaman suggest that "the horror of the crime demanded the ritual exorcism in the death chamber" (Wilson and Seaman 174). Repositioning "the eye for an eye" argument, they figure execution as a repaying of irrationality with irrationality: "The serial killer has no monopoly on irrationality" (174). For Wilson and Seaman, society has the right to exercise *its* powers of unspeakableness, a belief shared, it seems, by many of those we may wish to *see* die. Westley Alan Dodd, serial child murderer, also uses television to promote the justice of retribution, a spectacle for a spectacle: "Hang me . . . because that's the way Lee Iseli [one of his victims] died . . . I don't think I deserve any clean, painless little death" (*Murder by Number*). Rather than being deterred by the risk of death, serial killers, according to Jack Henry Abbot, are aware of the growing spectacle of capital punishment, are motivated by the opportunity of a ritualized execution. He suggests that "Men like Son of San are consciously motivated by capital punishment," and then asks, "what else do you call their now-standard manner of toying with the police by leaving clues in the form of riddles and notes to mock the hangman?" (Abbot 126). Such goading, suggests psychiatrists, is coupled with an eventual desire to be caught (*Times*, 28 July 1986: 10), to have the true identity of the Night Stalker, or the Thrill Killer, or the Hillside Strangler revealed, to have the name connected to a body. The execution of a monstrous criminal is a power trip in which many of us want to be involved, albeit in varying degrees.

Foucault contrasts the historical period about which he writes with Greek culture, and notes that "the Greek Logos had no contrary" (Foucault 1988, xi). With the ubiquity of the monster's voice and of his image, and with his voice and his image being sometimes indistinguishable from our own, identifying a contrary to our own Logos can also prove difficult. Echoes of endeavors to distinguish reason from madness are barely audible in an age in which the Word of our others is our Word. Even the powers of evil "they" represent seem to have been appropriated, commoditized. Hannibal Lecter—his emotional attachment to Clarice at odds with the apparent reality of most serial killers' failure to bond emotionally with others—represents a sanitized version of the serial killer. But the way we read Lecter is the way we like to perceive most of our real-life serial killers, and the sanitized version assumes the nature of truthfulness, authenticity. The notion of evil is tailor-made for our world of infotainment, and we, having been brought up on a diet of adventure cartoons and monster movies, have grown familiar and even quite fond of it. Anthony Hopkins, explaining his decision not to be involved in a possible sequel to *The Silence of the Lambs*, describes being asked by twelve-year-old children "to do the 'fava bean' scene." Lecter as cuddly? as a marketable soft-toy?

Increasing serial killer marketability is the fact that they come in a variety of recognizeable *types:* "typically—the typical serial killer, as opposed to the stereotypical serial killer, the typical serial killer is very much in control" explains James Fox, Criminal Justice Professor, on *Oprah* (4 September 1991). And the types are suitable for entertainment. Describing television's wrestler/personality/cartoon character Hulk Hogan, Sworkin says, "The image of the Hulk as himself dissolves into the image of Hulk as cartoon. Higher 'reality' (or lower-degree simulation) dissolves into higher simulation (or lower reality). The implication is of simulation established not as reality's mirror but as its microscope. As the power of resolution is adjusted up and down, the subject becomes, variously, man as cartoon, cartoon as man, man as robot, etc. Hulk is not so much dehumanized as he is conceptualized, rendered isomorphic with his aura" (Sworkin 170). Our construction of serial killers resembles Sworkin's description of the Hulk as "good concept." The crossover between serial killing and the world of cartoons was explicit in the case of Dahmer. Hart Fisher, publisher of the Boneyard Press, represented the story of Dahmer as a comic strip and declared, "It's something you can't get anywhere else—if you like the truth, if you like something a little bit more fresh, a little bit more bloody, we've got the meat" (*Murder by Number*). A complicity between

Fisher and Dahmer, an active relationship between crime and its representation, is hinted at in the show's introduction of Fisher: "In the underground layer of an upstart publisher the saga of Jeffrey Dahmer unfolds in the pages of a not-so-comic book." It is a relationship whose existence we find increasingly difficult to deny or one whose existence we are not sure we want to deny.

Perhaps, like the pre-Renaissance period, before the conceptualisation of madness became scientific, ours is an age in which dialogue with monstrosity takes the form of a "debate in which [we confront] the secret powers of the world; the experience of madness [is] clouded by images of the Fall and the Will of God, of the Beast and the Metamorphosism, and of all the marvelous secrets of Knowledge" (Foucault 1988, xii). As we enter an age in which the scientific categorizing of mental illness is being questioned, the Dahmers of our culture are likewise inscribed with secret powers, with superintelligence, and special knowledge and vision. And according to Philip Jenkins, Christianity supplies the stories of power which serial killers fantasize about and attempt to reenact: "The single book which has probably had the greatest impact on stimulating serial killers, or what they have used to justify their crimes has undoubtedly been the Christian Bible and especially the Book of Revelations, the imagery of which has an enormous appeal" (*To Kill and Kill Again*). But with images of the Fall and the Beast now having as their reference point Saturday morning television instead of the Old or New Testament, we're not sure whether we should take those images seriously. However "appealing" imagery from Revelations may be, a return to a theocracy does not seem to be in the cards. What we have is a world divided neatly, or rather too neatly, between good and evil, the Goody and the Baddy; the extremity of the polarization parodies the polarizing procedures. Dennis Nilsen's assertion that Dahmer's "contrition after his conviction for molesting a child was genuine enough" (quoted in Masters 1991, 266) (an implication being that monsters are not evil *all* of the time) contrasts with Schwartz's interpretation of his contrition and of the belief on the part of his defense attorney that Dahmer was sincere: "It is a testament to the cunning and manipulativeness of Jeffrey Dahmer that he was able to con people like Gerry Boyle" (Schwartz 67).

Our cartoonlike representation of good and evil is reflected in a letter to *The Los Angeles Times* (9 August 1991: B6) which complains of demonstrations of forgiveness for Paul Rubens, the actor who plays the television and movie character Pee-Wee Herman, who was arrested for masturbating in an X-rated movie-house: "It is the casual acceptance of this type of porno-house prowling that enabled Dahmer to kill as many men as he did. Evil is still evil, no matter how much we enjoy it." The association of Reubens' actions with multiple murder is also made in an article on Dahmer in the *Washington Post*: "Look at the picture of Pee-Wee Herman wearing a beard in the Style section of the *Washington Post* yesterday. Suddenly, Paul Rubens looks more like a Charles Manson than a Pee-Wee" (1 August 1991: C3). That we sometimes choose not to differentiate between masturbation and mass or serial murder (or, considering the connection of Pee-Wee with Dahmer, between emasculation, homosexuality, and serial murder), that we prefer to leave intact our all-embracing concept of evil and then like to sit back and "enjoy it," makes us ideal consumers of violent crime framed as entertainment.

And inscribing real-life horror with the discourse of Disney enables us more easily to tell jokes about it. Our explanation for the desire to tell such jokes usually resembles that of Schwartz, who remembers that many of her colleagues at the Dahmer trial told jokes in order to keep their "sanity" (Schwartz 211). Similarly, a *New York Times* editorial (6 August 1991: A16) on serial killer jokes notes that "there is a need for people to distance themselves from the horror." But how distant do we really like to be? Desensitized not only from too much exposure to violence but from a mixing of news and entertainment and a consequential inability to identify extremes, we cannot help existing as we commonly perceive Lear's Fool to exist, laughing both at horror and at those horrified, laughing both at and with our monsters. (How can we claim to be distanced from our uncaught killers when our speculative stories about them seem to be designed to strike even greater terror in the minds of the "types" of victims we imagine to be the killer's targets?) Or perhaps we cannot help existing in the way Foucault tells us the eighteenth-century madman was perceived, as "Different only in so far as he is unaware of Difference" (Foucault 1973, 49), loading "all signs with a resemblance that ultimately erases them" (50).

Perhaps we can afford to exist in this way because infotainment monsters have only infotainment victims. Meyrowitz describes the homogenizing effect of the new electronic media as they deconstruct all oppositions—he offers adult/child and masculine/feminine as examples—in their wake. But the particular use we are making of technology is characterized by our doing all we can to realize fantasy in an age in which fantasies are mostly fantasies of power. In such fantasies, oppositions and the violent hierarchies they engender are strengthened not deconstructed. While traditional forms of monstrosity and normality rediscover a common language, and while we excite ourselves by watching violent crime and its victims through the eyes of a serial killer, the self/other opposition is alive and well.

10

Fantasies of Power

Every age needs its heroes—and for the nineties, it's the Serial Killer. (Television
reviewer of *Confessions of a Serial Killer. The Daily Mail,* 29 January 1993)

Beliefs which attribute spiritual power to individuals are never neutral or free of the
dominant patterns of social structure. (Douglas 112)

My introduction includes a quotation from Dennis Nilsen in which he
says the portrayal of Hannibal Lecter as a powerful figure is "pure
myth" and that his own offenses arise "from a feeling of inadequacy,
not potency." In this chapter I want to explore more fully the ascription
of power to the serial killer, which is one way we can distance ourselves
from the serial killer and in the process figure ourselves as (innocent)
victims. As I hope to have demonstrated in these later chapters, however, our desire to estrange sometimes seems to dissipate, and our behavior can be mistaken for awe-struck reverence. Speculating about
the serial killer's motivation, Gregg McCrary of the FBI's Investigative
Support Unit says, "It's this God-like rush of power over life and death,
it's playing God with these victims, and it's that thrill, and it's that
same thing that all of these offenders enjoy. It's that discretion that they
have, this control over life and death" (*Murder by Number*). The idea
that serial killers are "playing God" is common in attempts to explain
their behavior (a fact which presumably reveals as much about how we
perceive God as how we regard the serial killer). Absent in such com-
parisons is a questioning of the "rush," the "thrill," the "enjoyment" of
causing arbitrary destruction.

The cultural need for the spectacle of power has been discussed by
George Bataille, and Jane Gallop notes that " 'a thought of the crowd' is
precisely how Bataille describes the function of the sovereign in ancient
times when the ancient games would have it that the *spectacle* of royal
privileges compensated the poverty of common life" (author's italics;

Gallop 27). "A thought of the crowd" can also, I suggest, describe the function of our monsters. Ian Brady calls the part of him which tortured and murdered children the "higher" self (Masters 1993, 198). How far does our own construction of the serial killer go in similarly figuring him as a transcendent, elevated being? The serial killer can appear less as something against which we define ourselves, and more as the embodiment of dominant themes in our cultures, the fulfillment of dreams of omnipotence. Possessor of power over life and death, superintelligent, transcender of barriers between sanity and madness, ultimate loner, sanctifier of violence—he is deserving of eternal fame, of media attention on a massive scale, of groupies. We may question Doreen Lioy's desire to marry Richard Ramirez, the killer and torturer of thirteen people, or think it strange that Sandra London would want to become Mrs. Gainesville Killer. But if power is an aphrodisiac, no wonder our omnipotent serial killers get the girls. What is the function of these superhuman characters whom we can't get enough people (fictional or otherwise) to play? Roy Norris, murderer of at least six women in California, suggests that "the rape wasn't really the important part, it was the dominance" (quoted in Levin and Fox 68). How much effort do we spend estranging the association of rape and murder with power? If the serial killer representation has the characteristics of a dreamed-up reality, whose dream is he?

Reading Kenneth Lynn we might suggest that he is as much the dream of those who feel their power slipping away as the dream of the powerful. In "Violence in American Literature and Folklore," Lynn says, "When we consider the humorists of the region between the Alleghenies and the Mississippi River, which in the 1830s and 1840s was known as the American Southwest, we are immediately struck by the theoretical possibility that the literature of violence in America has been written by losers—by citizens who have found their political, social, or cultural position threatened by the upward surge of another, and very different, group of Americans" (Lynn 134). We can make sense of the serial killer myth by providing the context of a *changing* social scene. We can suggest that, in a culture which glorifies violence and aggression, it is not surprising that a violent white male should be represented as powerful by media still dominated by white males, and that the representation is the result of their fear of the precariousness of their dominant position. While Lynn suggests that the humorists of the old Southwest wrote to exaggerate the crudity and the cruelty of the "enemy," the serial killer myth can be read as an exaggeration of the power of those threatened, as a sign of revenge upon a changing society.

144

THE SERIAL KILLER AND THE POWERS OF INTELLIGENCE

When I read that with money sent to him by a "young British woman" the imprisoned Dahmer ordered "books on art and cassette recordings of Bach, Schubert and Gregorian chants" (*Times*, 12 March 1994: 3), I find myself interpreting his shopping as another attempt to play the role of the serial killer with as much authenticity as possible. As I have discussed earlier, the figure who has perhaps done most in recent times to define what is authentic when it comes to serial killing is the intellectual/connoisseur, Hannibal Lecter, whose last name suggests the imparting of valuable knowledge, who quotes Marcus Aurelius before butchering his guards (Harris 1991, 217). As we watch Lecter and Senator Martin stare at each other on the tarmac at the Baltimore airport, we are told that one of them is "extremely bright" while the other is "not measurable by any means known to man" (190). Someone on a par with Lecter is *Seven's* monster, who kills with reference to Dante and Chaucer and is described by *Time's* film reviewer as "a high-concept kind of guy" (25 September 1995: 68).

Whether we are portraying a fictional or a real-life serial killer, we commonly represent him as being not only of above-average intelligence but superintelligent, philosophical, able to see the world in strikingly original ways. Sometimes it is his powers of speech which are remarkable: a *New York Times* article on psychopaths—which gives Ted Bundy and Angelo Bueno Jr. as examples—refers to "the slippery ease with which psychopaths lie, twist language and manipulate and destroy people" (7 July 1987: C1). The higher-class killers/intellectuals like Lecter, Nilsen, and Bundy—Lecter is a psychoanalyst, Nilsen a civil servant, Bundy a former law student "who once seemed destined for a promising career in Republican politics in Washington State" (*People Weekly*, 1 April 1991: 68) and whose self-defense and demonstration of intelligence in court wins commendation from the judge[1]—stand in contrast to the killers from (or destined to belong to) society's "underclass." While *their* intelligence is of a much more sneaky kind, not the kind which makes them deserving of sympathy or allows them to be perceived as "one of us" who merely went off the rails, they are supersmart nevertheless. Dahmer—whose father was a Ph.D. and who was enrolled at Ohio State but ended up, at least as far as the

---

1. "Take care of yourself, young man. I say that to you sincerely. It's a tragedy to this court to see such a total waste of humanity. You're a bright young man. You'd have made a good lawyer. I'd [have] loved to have you practice in front of me. I bear you no animosity, believe me. You went the wrong way partner. Take care of yourself" (quoted in Wilson and Seaman 282).

collective class-consciousness is concerned, in one of Milwaukee's dodgier areas—is described by Don Davis as a "near-genius" (1991, 56). Presumably in support of his assessment, Davis notes that Dahmer's former army colleagues were so impressed by his ability to "devour" books (some of his favorites being "children's classic fairy tales of trolls and goblins") that they estimated his IQ at 145. Why should we insist time after time that serial killers are often much more intelligent than the rest of us? Is it just to defend the failure of the police in catching these people?

Of course it is in the interests of the police to exaggerate the intellect of an elusive criminal. Jane Caputi remarks on the tendency to justify the representation of the "all-powerful, ubiquitous, even supernatural" killer by referring to his ability to avoid detection. She quotes a reporter covering the Ted Bundy case who describes Bundy as having a "preternatural ability to manipulate, a capacity whose effect was akin to magic." "It was this power," the reporter continues, "that made him such an effective killer and so impossible to track down" (Caputi 38). Arguing that "such assertions only glamorize and mystify the sex killer while distracting from a realistic assessment of the actual conditions of sex crime," Caputi brings matters down to earth by noting that "logic suggests that a lone man moving from place to place and killing only strangers would leave few clues to his identity and remain well beyond the scope of traditional detection" (38).

The presupposition of the serial killer's intelligence indicates, I suggest, elements of both estrangement and celebration. Officer Dewey, rejecting the apparent motivelessness of the crimes in *In Cold Blood*, reasons thus: "The expert execution of the crimes was proof enough that at least one of the pair commanded an immoderate amount of cool-headed slyness, and was—*must* be—a person too clever to have done such a deed without calculated motive" (Capote 103). Dewey's reasoning points to a possible motive for this particular form of representation, namely, that we identify them as intelligent in order to reassure ourselves that there must be a motive. Because we often associate intelligence with rationality, the inscription of serial killers with intelligence can shield us from meaninglessness, from a disruption of our models of cause and effect, from the behavioral non sequitur.

But if we are comforted by the existence of motive, we don't necessarily want to try to explain it. The serial killer replete with monstrous nerdiness allows us to believe that his motive must be incomprehensible, nothing to which we, who do not read Dante or Marcus Aurelius, could relate. We are reassured that there is meaning at the same time as we are reassured that we wouldn't be able to get it. If our inscription of serial killers as intelligent provides us with a comforting rationale for their actions (and in the process allows them to be imprisoned rather than hospitalized, on the grounds that they are sane), we also estrange them by that inscription, by that mark of "wise guy" (a term the FBI used to describe Bundy), by the implicit celebration of America's B− grade-point average. As Harriet Hawkins notes, the decision to offer the part of Hannibal Lecter in the movie version of Thomas Harris's *Manhunter* to a Scot (Brian Cox), and of Lecter in *The Silence of the Lambs* to a Welsh actor (Anthony Hopkins), "follows the rigid Hollywood convention whereby a cultivated, sophisticated, intellectual male villain of the type so often played by James Mason is traditionally *un-American* as well as traditionally wicked" (author's italics; Hawkins 262).

And sometimes the un-American mind can corrupt the body, persuade it to perform abnormal and unpatriotic acts. As Hawkins points out, "If cultural sophistication, book-learning and intellectuality are deemed by Hollywood to be fundamentally foreign, they are also deemed unmanly and sissified, in so far as virility and sex-appeal are equated in American literature and films with frontier virtues as opposed to the effete urbanity of the city slicker" (Hawkins 263). The association of a corrupting homosexuality with intellectual sophistication has a long history. Jonathan Dollimore identifies the suspicion of Wilde's commentators as stemming from the belief that intellectuals have always been weird and prone to do strange, uncivilized things:

> Something informing these descriptions of Wilde and his art is a fear of degeneration as conceived by writers of the time. It was not just that degenerates were thought to be intelligent and gifted; their intelligence manifested one of the most disturbing paradoxes of the perverse: a vitiating regression to the primitive *from within an* advanced cultural sophistication. For these commentators Wilde represents both a cultural 'decay' and a resurrection of 'pagan viciousness' and 'primal errors.' . . . What is simultaneously acknowledged and denied is that 'wholesomeness' is not invaded from without so much as corrupted from within. (author's italics; Dollimore 241)

The gesture of elevating serial killers into the realm of cultural and intellectual sophistication—into a contemporary version of the aristocracy to which the wicked Marquis belonged—replays the gesture of the nineteenth-century novel identified by Guy Le Gaufey, namely, the figuring of vampires as aristocrats, as social parasites, as impurities which need to be expelled. In other words, it is estrangement built on the valorization of the wholesome middle: civilization is proud of that grade-point average and suspicious of those *unnaturally* gifted guys of sometimes dubious sexuality. Serial killers are either aristocrats or peasants, but not from that wide band of mediocrity in between.

However, as I have suggested earlier, from that world of mediocrity we like to dream of its transcendence. Wilson and Seaman note that "crime—particularly murder—produces the feeling of being 'beyond the pale.' Case after case demonstrates that the 'self-esteem killer' copes with this problem in a manner reminiscent of the Marquis de Sade; by telling himself that, in the war against society, he is right and society is in the wrong" (Wilson and Seaman 187). In their discussion of the case of Melvin Rees, who was executed in 1961, they suggest that "Rees was an 'intellectual' who, like the Moors murderer Ian Brady in the following decade, made the decision to rape and kill on the grounds that 'everything is lawful.' He may therefore be regarded as one of the first examples of the curious modern phenomenon, the 'high-IQ killer' " (188). With the Marquis de Sade or Nietzsche in mind, we are prone to see the desire to set oneself apart from society, to confront society with one's individuality, to justify one's lawlessness, as a sign of high intelligence. Deprived of "familiar" criminal motives to give our serial killers—sex or money—we assume they must be on some kind of crusade, waging war on society for the sake of an idea. "The creepy, brainy, religious fanatic," the "high-concept killer [who] prowls the murk" (*Time*, 25 September 1995: 68) is *Seven*'s version of the moral crusader. When we construct the serial killer as someone who struggles violently with society in order to assert his individuality, intelligence is presumed. Our construction of the "high-IQ killer" is a sign of our desire to figure the serial killer as being above and beyond society, as someone who attempts to assert his freedom. It makes him Byronic or, more exactly, makes him related to the hero of every Bildungsroman taught to every child, from Huck Finn to Holden Caulfield.

A card in the cab of the "Yorkshire Ripper," Peter Sutcliffe, read, "In this truck is a man whose latent genius, if unleashed, would rock the nation" (quoted in Wilson and Seaman 283). For Sutcliffe, it seems, freedom meant the expression of his "genius": a natural force dissipated by the material demands of everyday life. To ascribe genius is to ascribe extraordinary *natural* ability, exalted *power*. It is a major factor in the construction of a figure whose power is to be regarded as naturally ordained. The ascription of superintelligence is instrumental in figuring the serial killer as someone of transcendental power in possession of the world's wondrous secrets. It is a quality which helps to construct him as someone to be feared and revered. Lecter's particular genius, his ability to see into the lives and histories of others, amounts to a transcendence of his material surroundings. This special power of hav-

ing insight not only into their own crimes but those of other superkillers whom they have never met is one which we seem particularly keen to confer upon the serial killer. Brian Masters's interview of
Dennis Nilsen for *Vanity Fair*, in which he who has a "penetrating gaze"
(184) is asked to take the reader on a journey into Dahmer's mind,
seems to reenact *The Silence of the Lambs*. Two years later, the English
newspaper, the *Daily Express*, describes police intentions to interview
Michael Lupo and Nilsen with the hope of providing a unique perspective on the killer of five gay men in London (17 June 1993:5). (The police
discounted the newspaper's version of events.) Once caught, though
physically imprisoned, the serial killer we like to dream up has a mind
that enables him to remain free as long as he has others (or rather their
stories) to feed on; his *pure intellect* contrasts with the weak and fuzzy
thinking of the masses.

The need to free oneself from the speciousness of modern society
strikes R. J. Hollingdale, in his introduction to Penguin's edition of
Twilight of the Idols and *The Anti-Christ*, as a reason to read Nietzsche:
"Everywhere in the active world today intelligence is on the defensive;
it has to fight to survive. For what characterizes the present age, the
present decade? An excess of emotion, a constant stimulation of the
emotions and a desire to have them stimulated more." (in Nietzsche
1988, 7). For Hollingdale, intelligence opposes emotion and is an anti-
dote to the decadence of the sixties that surrounds him.[2] This opposition, which is alive and well in the nineties, can explain our ascription
of power to he who brings the lifestyle and politics of the soft, sharing
sixties to a violent halt—he who is hard, impervious, above feeling.
And when one considers that traditionally this is a gendered opposition, it can appear even more natural to presuppose that the male transcender of emotion, the male victimizer of female "weakness," is of
high intelligence, someone who feels that his manhood/intelligence is
threatened by the chaos and shapelessness of emotion, someone who
has "to fight to survive." In the same way that we may attempt to
describe highbrow serial killer movies as art, we describe highbrow
serial killers as the practitioners of an art, as artists of crime, as think-
ers, philosophers. And since aesthetics is that discipline which confers
the *natural* right of power on the powerful (the political activity, in
other words, of conferring apoliticality), it just so happens that the
serial killers we inscribe most often with the powers of the aesthete are
white, middle-class men. And if it is true, as Joel Black claims, that our
"experience of murder and other forms of violence is primarily aes-

2. Hollingdale complains that "there has never in all history been so much *music*; it
sometimes seems as if intelligence were being dissolved in rhythm" (author's italics, 8).

thetic" (3), that experience can speak of our desire to be in dialogue with the powerful.

With the ascription of intelligence, we ascribe a sense of freedom that comes from the expression of power over the female, over that which is figured in female terms. Our serial killer desires to free himself from social constraints, and especially those pertaining to sex, and one way for him, for us, to justify that freedom is to intellectualize it. Ascribing powers of intelligence to the serial killer has the effect that Gallop sees in Sade's conflation of pornography and philosophy: "The result of this mixture is that each undercuts the other. The brute impact of sex and violence is softened, for they can be taken seriously, can be studied and interpreted, as acting out certain philosophical questions (for example, the reality of the existence of others, the arbitrary nature of morality)" (Gallop 2–3). Intellectualized as a demonstration of one's disregard for social norms, as a radical gesture, that which is figured as sexual freedom can be a sign of the intellectual elite, a sign of power. Fidelity is for the conforming masses. The high-IQ serial killer is constructed in the context of the myth which associates intellectual elitism with a freedom which can be confused with or take the form of sexual conquering. Haunting our serial killer construction is a Sadean dream in which images of violence and sex are layered upon each other, a layering justified by the assumed complexity of the mind behind it.

THE SERIAL KILLER AS WARRIOR KNIGHT

Perhaps it is to be expected that a culture which celebrates the beauty and nobility of violence should have among its popular heroes those who satisfy a nostalgia for a particular version of the warrior knight: motivated by a higher goal, courteous yet unconstrained by the court, the perpetrator of extreme violence when he feels his dignity and rights threatened. The dream of transcendence is often expressed by the discourse of chivalry, and it is a discourse which is spoken with equal ease by society's "defenders" and its "others."

For Davis, Dahmer's victims were not only murdered but "conquered" (Davis 1991, 210). Leyton remarks that "with varying degrees of explicitness multiple murderers see themselves as soldiers: small wonder then that they feel neither remorse for their victims, nor regret for launching their bloody crusades" (Leyton 23). Wilson and Seaman, speculating on Robert Bilden's motive for raping "the innocent and prudish" Tina Schuster, suggest that the "ultimate pleasure was to rape a shy virgin" (Wilson and Seaman 156). They add, "It must be recognized that this element of 'conquest' is present in all male sexuality" (156). If serial killers see themselves as crusading warriors, it is an

150

image we help to construct. References to the warrior knight, or the use of language that we usually associate with him and his world, may be examples of history "innocently" being used to describe a modern phenomenon, but, like the use of "man the hunter" in our stories of the violent pursuit of what popular jargon constructs as female "prey," such language can have the effect of naturalizing and normalizing the serial killer's acts. And in a world full of role models for the male loner—the gunslinger, the road-movie transient hero, the vigilante cop—the warrior knight represents a transcendence of all that American vulgarity: a male loner with class.

Elizabeth Young points out that in a movie in which names resonate with meaning, Hannibal Lecter's first name invokes the figure of the male warrior, the male invader (Young 28 n.6), and it is also easy to make sense of him by seeing him more specifically as a contemporary manifestation of the figure of the knight described above. What separates his violence from that of others, and what separates his relation with Starling from those of other men—police officers especially—is his courtliness. His violence occurs in the name of "courtesy." He is the "killer connoisseur," as *People Weekly* describes him (12 August 1991: 36). In his world, sophisticated murderers and cannibals are distinguished from their sleazy counterparts. Our "sleek and serene" (*People Weekly*, 1 April 1991: 64) Lecter is the defender of all that he and we value against "discourtesy," that which is constructed as vulgar, low-down. Before encouraging Miggs, a fellow prisoner, to commit suicide after this prime example of Mailer's category of "punks and snitches"[3] had thrown semen on Starling, he tells her, "I would not have that happen to you. Discourtesy is unspeakably ugly to me" (24). Like Ed Gein, supposedly one of the "real-life" killers used as models for the killers in Demme's movie and about whom a neighbor remembers, "I never heard him tell a dirty joke or use a dirty word" (*People Weekly*, 1 April 1991: 66), Lecter answers discourtesy with his own unspeakableness, but returns, unaffected, to the serenity of his civilized world and its ordered, well-chosen words.

When Starling first meets Lecter, "Courtesy was implicit in her distance and her tone" (Harris 1991, 14). Later, when her style of questioning causes her to lose standing in his eyes, he tells her: "You were doing fine, you'd been courteous and receptive to courtesy" (18). But despite Lecter's portrayal of her as a bourgeois aspirant of sophistication, she regains his respect by treating him as a gentleman, and when he escapes, we and Clarice are assured that she will not be one of his future victims: "I have no plans to call on you Clarice, the world being more

3. A category defined in opposition to the "brave" (see Dollimore 15).

151

interesting with you in it. Be sure to extend me the same courtesy" (351). In terms of class, Lecter sees himself as one of life's gentlefolk, superior to the provincialism of much of the police force. In the movie's final scene, as he strolls down a busy Caribbean street and towards his next meal, we see that he has dressed for dinner, and his appearance resembles that of a shabby but elegantly attired English aristocrat. Clarice hovers between Lecter's world of courtesy and being a distinctly (nouvelle) bourgeois heroine who responds positively to Crawford's middle-class concerns: "He wanted her to do well. For Starling, that beat courtesy every time" (31). What emerges is a partnership between Lecter's "nobility" and Starling's version of the bourgeois, and *The Silence of the Lambs* seems to represent a shift in the construction of beast and saviour in class terms from the model Le Gaufey identifies (see p. 48). In Demme's movie the partnership between bourgeois and aristocrat (a partnership cemented by hints of a heterosexual attraction) is defined against the "lower classes" (represented by Buffalo's Bill's "sexual perversion," by Chiltern's lasciviousness, by Miggs' unspeakable behavior).

Watching *The Silence of the Lambs*, we have difficulty in conflating the opposition of courtesy and discourtesy with that of self and other, at least the opposition in which self stands (up) for the law. There are courteous serial killers and discourteous policemen. There are courteous and discourteous serial killers. Similarly, beyond the movies, Joan Ullman identifies a particular representation of Dahmer which distinguishes his courtesy from the discourtesy of his victims. Referring to the emphasis placed by expert trial witnesses on Dahmer's lack of sadism or hatred directed against gays, she notes that "Milwaukee's mass murderer appeared to be a squeamish, picky—and gentlemanly—homosexual: a reluctant practitioner with refined sensibilities (as shown by his preference for predominantly one-way, nonreciprocal, 'light sex'). This made Dahmer sound considerably superior to the brutish, mostly black bathhouse and gay-bar pick-ups and/or victims" (Ullman 30).

The same distinction between those who are courteous and those who are not, irrespective of their criminality, is made at the House of Representatives hearing. An FBI officer, comparing two rapists, says of the second, "In the twelve years that he raped, he never physically struck or beat a victim. If he encountered resistance, he would flee. In police parlance, he would be referred to as a 'gentleman rapist.' He was not profane or derogatory in his verbal behavior. He relied on his presence rather than physical force to subdue and control his victims, and engaged in vaginal assault only" (*House* 41). The "rapist in case number one," he continues, "enjoyed hurting his victims, while the second rapist had no motivation to physically harm them. Investigation determined that their personalities were as opposite as their intent and method of operation" (42). The second rapist, then, is described as "gentlemanly" for committing "vaginal assault only," and he is to be considered at odds with someone who enjoys "physically harming" his victims. "Physical harm," it seems, is to be distinguished from "vaginal assault": a distinction which presumably makes sense in a society of gentlemen who know it is discourteous to strike or beat the fairer sex. Discussing the stereotype of the "sex beast," Cameron and Frazer suggest that "the sex beast is either someone outwardly repulsive . . . or else he is a latter-day Jekyll and Hyde, concealing his depravity beneath a facade of respectability and even charm" (35). At first glance the references to gentlemanliness and chivalry in regard to rapists and serial killers can appear to be examples of this second kind of stereotyping. But the "gentleman rapist" of "police parlance" is not concealing depravity by gentlemanliness, but is presumably gentlemanly during the rape. For the FBI officer who describes the second rapist as committing "vaginal assault only," what matters in his distinction between the two rapists is the level of harm *beyond* or *gratuitous to* the "sexual" attack. It is a distinction which can help to play down the abnormality of "vaginal assault," to normalize the idea of the female body as something which gentlemen are free to conquer.

The link between male violence and imagery of the chivalric knight and of the courteous gentleman is explored in Klaus Theweleit's *Male Fantasies*. The book's visual material often presents the Nazi male in chivalric garb and functions as an ironic commentary on the text, which is largely a psychoanalytical attempt to understand the "Nazi mind." With Freud's notion of the ego (as a mental projection of the surface of the body) apparently in mind, Theweleit argues that references in Nazi literature to "body-armor" (his metaphor) can provide a literary context to the iconographical representation of the SS or *Freikorps* (private armies of former imperial soldiers, anti-Communist youth, and drifters) wearing suits of armor. The references he is mostly concerned about describe the German soldier as a "figure of steel," in possession of a body so hard that he is impermeable to external threats whether they be in the form of bolshevism, the bourgeoisie, or women. Anson Rabinbach and Jessica Benjamin, in their foreword to the second volume, discuss this chivalric imagery: "In this volume the armored organization provides the key to understanding the emotional underpinnings of fascist militarism. The self is mechanized through a variety of mental and physical procedures: military drill, countenance, training, operations which Foucault identified as 'techniques of the self' " (in Theweleit 1989, xvii). And in her foreword to the first volume, Barbara

Ehrenreich notes the relevance of Theweleit's work to our contemporary world: "As Theweleit says, the point of understanding fascism is not only 'because it might "return again," ' but because it is already implicit in the daily relationships of men and women . . . I think here of the man who feels a 'normal' level of violence towards women" (in Theweleit 1987, xv).

Theweleit's work is especially useful, I suggest, in shedding light on our dressing some our monsters in chivalric attire. Contemporary versions of the warrior knight are given meaning by their opposites, and the serial killer's victims can be naturalized as such by the warrior knight construction. In *The Serial Killers* Wilson and Seaman suggest that "in spite of enormous changes in our sexual attitudes, modern man's reaction to a pretty girl is in most respects exactly like that of the troubadours or the knights of the Round Table: she is an unknown country, a sovereign state, that he would love to be allowed to explore" (Wilson and Seaman 298). To figure the serial killer as on a crusade is also to figure his victims as entities to be conquered. The armored self of the serial killer indicates a dream related to the dreams of Theweleit's fascists, indicates a culture in which the normality of violence against women or the idea of women is questioned infrequently. It is an image which stands for the "strength" of the past against the "weakness" of modernity. Against the chaos, impurity, and monstrosity of a culture of mass communication—a culture made up of individuals who experience what Baudrillard suggests is the "state of terror proper to the schizophrenic: too great a proximity of everything, the unclean promiscuity of everything which touches, invests, and penetrates without resistance, with no halo of private protection, not even his own body, to protect him anymore . . . bereft of every scene, open to everything in spite of himself, living in the greatest confusion" (Baudrillard 132–33)—the serial killer violently asserts *his* individuality and physical presence in a world gone soft.

A MAN'S MAN: JEFFREY DAHMER AND THE DREAM OF MASCULINITY

I was always haunted by the idea of a murder which would cut me off irremediably from your world. (Jean Genet, *The Thief's Journal*)

The prison society described by Jack Henry Abbot in *In The Belly of the Beast*—a collection of letters to Norman Mailer about Abbot's experiences in prison and the justice system—is a hierarchy structured by the power to subordinate "sexually." Once power relations have been settled, the dominated are figured as female: "In prison, if I take a punk, *she is mine.* He is like a slave, a chattel slave. It is the custom that no one addresses her directly. He cleans my cell, my clothing and runs errands for me. Anything I tell him to do, he must do—exactly the way a wife is perceived in some marriages even today. But I can sell her or lend her out or give her away at any time. Another prisoner can take her from me if he can dominate me" (author's italics; Abbot 80). In a society in which there are no women, the idea of "woman" is very much alive. Abbot's mixing of pronouns displays a disregard for the sex of the prisoner he describes. It is the role the prisoner plays which is important, a role which stands for weakness and passivity, which represents the feminine: "One of the things that takes place in a prison riot is this: guards are sexually dominated, usually sodomized . . . what is clear is that when a man sodomizes another to express his *contempt,* it demonstrates only his contempt for woman, not man. The normal attitude among men in society is that it is a great shame and dishonor to have experienced what it feels like to be a woman" (author's italics, 78). According to Abbot, the state's purpose in imprisoning him was to inflict upon him such shame and dishonor: "I was even told by the pigs who transported me to the prison that I was being sent there to be reduced to a punk, to be shorn of my manhood" (79).

The assumption of male and female roles in man-to-man relationships is the subject of much critical debate, which often focuses on the question of whether such role-playing is subversive by denaturalizing gender. Leo Bersani argues that "the gay male parody of a certain femininity . . . is both a way of giving vent to the hostility toward women that probably afflicts every male (and which male heterosexuals have of course expressed in infinitely nastier and more effective ways) *and* could paradoxically be thought of as helping to deconstruct that image for women themselves . . . The gay male bitch desublimates and desexualizes a type of femininity glamorized by movie stars, whom he thus lovingly assassinates with his style" (author's italics; quoted in Dollimore 321). Jonathan Dollimore reads Bersani here as conceding "a potentially subversive dimension to camp, but one inseparable from a more problematic and ambivalent relation to both femininity and women" (321). He adds, "Of the subversive claims for gay machismo, Bersani is even more sceptical, since he regards it as involving not a parodic repudiation of straight machismo, but a profound respect for it" (321). According to Dollimore's reading of Bersani, ideas of masculinity and femininity do not necessarily lose much in translation from heterosexual to gay relationships: power is represented by the masculine (and vice versa), and weakness by the feminine (and vice versa).

For Dennis Nilsen, killer of men, Dahmer offers a brutal demonstration of masculinity and femininity transcending the homosexual/

heterosexual divide. Speculating that Dahmer is "buzzing with excitement and power (his heart rate pounding at maximum speed) as he 'lives out' his omnipotence," he says that "it is significant that a common view of the Stone Age depicts a potent male clubbing a sexually desirable female into unconsciousness and 'wedding' her by an act of copulation with her passive body. Here we have the ingredients of power/violence rendering the desired person into a state of extreme passivity followed by sexual release for the conqueror. It is the opposite poles of gross action and gross passivity that attract. This is the constant in the serial-killing conundrum whether the victim is male, female or child" (quoted in Masters 1991, 186). Despite the shock to the stereotype of masculinity as the preserve of male heterosexuals, the conflation of the oppositions powerful/weak and masculine/feminine is the same in the representation of the "homosexual" Dahmer's relationship with his victims as it is in the representation of "heterosexual" killers and their victims. While we, like Nilsen, can only speculate about what drove Dahmer, we assume masculinity's presence and femininity's absence in Dahmer's fantasy-world. In our attempt to make sense of Dahmer, he is given the male role: he kills to prove his manhood. Brian Masters speculates that Dahmer hates any male who is "more homosexual" (Masters 1991, 189) than he, a phrase we would commonly read as "more feminine." Abbot refers to this reading thus: "The majority of prisoners I have known—something like ninety percent—express sexual interest in their own sex. I hesitate to call this 'homosexual' because American society recognizes *only* the passive homosexual—the one who plays the female role—as being a 'homosexual' " (author's italics; Abbot 80). Masters also notes that "it has been suggested that [Dahmer] is a homosexual by default—that his sexual orientation was not a preference but a compensation for the impossibility of having a relationship with a woman." (Masters 1991, 189). From the perspective which sees Dahmer's victims as women-substitutes, Dahmer's behavior can be explained by the same paradigm that Abbot describes as relevant to all-male prison society: Whatever the sex of the player of the woman's role, masculinity is realized by that player's subordination.

The way we make sense of Dahmer's murders can indicate how accustomed we are to figure murder in terms of a masculine idealism; to ascribe the role of woman to the weak, the oppressed, the victim; to regard male-female politics in terms of a violent hierarchy. The ascription of power and weakness with reference to gender is perhaps most obvious in war. We have witnessed, for example, the expression of the domination of women *as* power in the rape and torture of women in the occupied territories of the former Yugoslavia. With victorious forces expressing their power by the rape and murder of women, how should we interpret war itself except as the conflict between competing masculinities? Identifying connections between war and the oppression of women, Klaus Theweleit sees fascism as "an extreme example of the political polarization of gender" (1989, xix). No doubt the example of warfare and Abbot's description of power in prison are extreme examples, and we can comfort ourselves by arguing that they occur when society as we know it has broken down, or does not exist. But power *as* masculinity, power as the domination of women or the idea of women, is a meaning we carry around with us, a meaning with which we make sense of our world, of our lives, of other people's lives. The silence which surrounds a male serial killer's sex may have less to do with a conspiratorial patriarchy and more to do with the received notion of what power is, a notion with which we are so familiar that we can forget the history of its construction.

Leaving intact the idea of masculinity as power is Buffalo Bill, who wants to be shorn of his manhood and appears repulsively weak in the process: "Their roles as protagonist and antagonist aside, Clarice Starling is attractive in her tough, self-controlled manner, whereas Bill is shocking and, I think intended to be, repugnant in his effeminacy" (Tharp 111). Part of his monstrosity is his vision of masculinity as mutable, vulnerable to fantasy and the knife. His crimes are not only the murder and torture of women but his questioning of the desire to be a man and his attempt to meddle with gender. However, Bill's demise is also the demise of the idea that gender identity may not be fixed in nature after all. The evil is defeated, the evil, that is, of those who have a "fluid notion" of the model of gender "outside the logic of the binary," in which gender "becomes a kind of costume or masquerade" (Young 14). Those like Ed Gein, who similarly used the flesh of his female victims as "sewing material, fashioning vests, belts, and even a face mask made from a real face" (Davis 1991, 163) and then proceeded to dance around his house wearing his made-to-measure outfit. Opposed to Buffalo Bill's and Ed Gein's unspeakableness is Lecter, a man whose identity transformations leave his gender, as well as his speech and social standing, relatively untroubled. We can love those who covet Clarice from a courteous distance (or who flirt with the idea of consuming her), but to want to *be* her is just plain sick.

While male serial killers are represented as having the aura of a neutral, engendered, asocial power, the acts of female serial killers like Christine Falling (who killed the children she was meant to baby-sit) represent a more perverse, strange, and especially evil form of power. The ascription of "male" power to the serial killer does not proceed unproblematically when the serial killer is female. While male victims can be given the female role, the role of the male aggressor cannot so easily be taken on by a female. For a society accustomed to perceiving murder as a form of male power, the presence of female serial killers is a paradox that is considered unnatural and threatening in a way that male serial killers are not. Leaving questions of gender unasked when considering the powers of male serial killers but overtly gendering the powers of female serial killers replays our selectivity in benign circumstances. While we talk of the powers of God our Father, God's power is represented as transcending earthly matters of gender, and the fact that we refer to His omnipotence in male terms still mostly goes without saying. But while His relation to masculinity remains mysterious, masculinity gains reverence from this unspoken association with the Almighty. In our patriarchal myths, some of the nature of His power is translated into the essence of maleness. God's power is figured as neutral and natural, and in stories told of he who is invisible, he who can strike whenever and wherever he likes, he who has the power to threaten society's very existence, so too is the power of the male serial killer.

Speculating, dreaming, imagining, we (we men), make up stories about serial killers, about what is natural about them. While somehow the monstrosity is not always ours, we are evidently content to make the monster one of us. Not always bothering to reinvent masculinity in a way which unambiguously distinguishes "masculine power" from the power of the serial killer, our monster is a man's man. Staring back at us from our portraits of monsters are men whose masculinity remains familiar. Might our automatic ascription of machismo to the serial killer be not only the result of habit but symptomatic of, to use Dollimore's words, "a profound respect for it," a profound respect, that is, for what machismo is meant to represent? Might our figuring Dahmer's male-to-male violence and murder in male-to-female terms be another indication of the way the serial killer figure functions as a kind of wish fulfillment, as a hero of male fantasy? In order to answer those questions, perhaps we should describe what it is that we see in our serial killers that gives them the "right" to take the male lead in our stories.

Serial killers, we say, achieve empowerment through transcendence, through reaching a condition defined as ideal because it is free of materiality. The dream of transcendence is both a dream of transcending materiality to omniscient spirituality and a dream of transcending society to untainted and liberated individuality. The two dreams merge in the figuration of society in material/corporeal terms. Mary Douglas says, "Any culture is a series of related structures which comprise social forms, values, cosmology, the whole knowledge, and through which all experience is mediated . . . The rituals enact the form of social relations, and in giving these relations visible expression they enable people to know their own society. The rituals work upon the body politic through the symbolic medium of the physical body" (Douglas 128). In the dream of transcendence, that physical body is female. The negation of the female body symbolizes the transcendence of society, and the transcendence of society symbolizes the transcendence of the female body. When the social body is figured as female, criminality is an affirmation of one's masculinity. Transcendence is hardness, imperviousness, and strength; sociability and tolerance are associated with softness and weakness. Former Milwaukee Police Chief Harold Breier—quoted as saying "You can take community policing and stick it in your ear . . . When I was chief, we were relating to the good people and we were relating to the other people too: we were throwing those people in the can" (*The Washington Post*, 16 October 1991: A3)—is described in a *Los Angeles Times* article on the police's handling of the Dahmer case as a "tough-as-nails administrator under whose term relations with the black community deteriorated badly" (27 January 1992: A10). Why this association of toughness with apparent intolerance, with a willingness to construct the idea of and condemn "the other people"?

In Capote's nonfiction novel we enter Perry's dream: "It was after one of these beatings . . . that the parrot appeared, arrived while he slept, a bird 'taller than Jesus, yellow like a sunflower,' a warrior-angel who blinded the nuns with its beak, fed upon their eyes, slaughtered them as they 'pleaded for mercy,' then so gently lifted him, enfolded him, winged him away to 'paradise' " (93). In this apparent reworking of Nietzsche's depiction of "we aeronauts of the spirit" (Nietzsche 1910, 575)—or this nightmarish vision of *Sesame Street*—the warrior-angel is an avenger of the evil women who made a hell of Perry's childhood, and may symbolize the romanticized (masculine) world running counter to the earthly (feminine) society of small-town America, a romanticized world to which Perry wishes to belong. Contrasting with this dream is the dream of Buffalo Bill in *The Silence of the Lambs*. Buffalo Bill, unlike Hannibal Lecter, manages to get the dream of transcendence confused in a way which alienates him from the movie's viewers. Near the movie's conclusion he gazes at Clarice through night-vision glasses and dreams of having hair like hers, dreams that his efforts to become a woman could result in an impression as beautiful. His final dreams are of becoming Clarice. Instead of transcending female corporeality and obtaining the omniscience of male spirituality, his dream is to transcend his male body and become a female version of the warrior-angel.

Elizabeth Young refers to "criticism that focuses on [*The Silence of the Lambs's*] formal status as the unique achievement of cult-auteur Jonathan Demme's attempts to differentiate it from those lowbrow serial films about serial murder known as 'slasher' movies" (6). "But this approach," she says, "rather than sealing off an aesthetic realm from the 'other' of mass culture, only succeeds in registering art's unstable affinity with that other." (6). Tania Modleski remarks on the "tendency of critics and theorists to make mass culture into the 'other' of whatever, at any given moment, they happen to be championing—and moreover, to denigrate that other primarily because it allegedly provides pleasure to the consumer" (Modleski 157). The other to the serial killer construction is also "mass culture," that culture to which the masses belong, the masses who seek merely "pleasure" and who are figured as female. And while Tharp argues that Hannibal "is the New Man as surely as Clarice is the New Woman"—Hannibal, she says, "befriends Clarice, talking to her about her feelings and paying attention to her perfume and handbag, unlike the Traditional Male"—he is a New Man who is also a "sociopathic murderer with respect for few boundaries," a figure who "penetrates male gender anxieties and offers an alternative to perceived loss of power" (112). The serial killer, new or traditional, represents a thrill compared to "mere" pleasure; he is the wrecker of safe "domesticity," the bad to the masses' "specious good."[4]

Without our particular meaning of male power, we would find it difficult to make sense of a large range of texts, both "academic" and "popular." In our crime stories, the romanticized world of the chosen and transcendent few includes not only those criminals whose higher goal is the defense of the "good" (those defenders of society who break society's rules in order to carry out their pledge), but also those criminals who seek a higher goal in itself. André Gide describes murder as "the culminating *act gratuite* that liberates man from the determinism of the material universe . . . the point at which—irremediably—man opts for his own freedom" (from *Les Caves du Vatican*, quoted in Coe 181). The noble warrior of Norman Mailer's *The Naked and the Dead*, seeking initiation into male adulthood through violence, corresponds with the violent criminal seeking escape from the constraints of society, described by Mailer in his preface to *In the Belly of the Beast*. Mailer divides the prison population into, on the one hand, those "juvenile delinquents who are drawn to crime as a positive experience—because it is more exciting, more meaningful, more mysterious, more transcen-

4. Lionel Trilling's term: see "The Fate of Pleasure: Wordsworth to Dostoevsky," *Partisan Review* (Summer 1963): 182.

dental, more religious than any other experience they have known" (xii–xiii) and, on the other, "those petty criminals who are not fundamentally attached to such existential tests of courage and violence, for whom crime is the wrong business, [for whom] prison is not a problem" (xiii). Mailer argues that "the social practice of mixing these two kinds of criminals together is a disaster, an explosion. The timid become punks and snitches, the brave turn cruel" (xiii). In the prison world described by Abbot, "punks and snitches" embody the idea of woman. But there is a divide between Mailer's preface and Abbot's letters: the latter depicts a world defined by male power, and the former comes close to prescribing one. The divide is noted by the prisoner (figured by Mailer as belonging to the "brave" category, those seeking religion and transcendence through crime) when he attempts to deflate Mailer's romanticism: "My life is not a 'saga' and I resent your using the term like that. I do not feel 'heroic' " (22). Our serial killers, our exciting, mysterious, transcendental monsters, our warring, questing monsters, resemble the hero Mailer constructs from Abbot's letters. In such cases their heroism and power depends on their transcendence of the law, society, weakness and impurity—concepts which are implicitly and sometimes explicitly gendered.

For the male loner figure, transcendence is also silence: the freedom and purity which come with an existence untainted by language. Like Dahmer, who, according to former classmates, remained tight-lipped about himself but was forever seeking attention, the valorized loner figure says, "Pay attention to what I do, not what I say." Figured as extratextual, and almost extraterrestrial, beyond the reach of normal man, the loner in all his forms exists in a world of unspeakableness, an immaterial world beyond the (female) body of language and the text. Above all, it is an idealized masculine world. The man's man is represented by risk-taking heroes such as Tom Cruise's character in *Top Gun*: reaching for the skies in one scene, simultaneously ignoring the laws of society and the presence of women in another by barging into the ladies' bathroom to speak to his prospective girlfriend. He is the hero of road movies which, according to Cameron and Frazer, celebrate "the vast spaces of the continent, being on the move without any ultimate goal" and "a masculine ethos of sexual conquest and random violence" (Cameron and Frazer 162). And he is represented by a common construction of the serial killer, he who flouts "the law with impunity," who exhibits "an antisocial trait," who needs "to seek thrills that make criminal risk-taking a high" (*New York Times*, 7 August 1991: 8).

Distinguishing the spiritual from the material and the ideal from the imperfect are metaphysical gestures that some Sade critics describe him as challenging. Gallop, for example, argues that "the move to contaminate philosophy, whether in Sade's mode of scandal and sensationalism or in the current critical mode of carefully considered questioning of philosophy's a priori ideology, is an attack on the hierarchical distinction, underlying Western metaphysics since Plato, between the ideal . . . and the material. Modern continental philosophy, typified by a current running through Friedrich Nietzsche, Martin Heidegger and Jacques Derrida, strives continually to undermine that entrenched hierarchy, to loosen its hold" (Gallop 3). Simone de Beauvoir, however, identifies in the writings of Sade a hedonism which "ends in ataraxia, which confirms the paradoxical relation between sadism and stoicism. The individual's promised happiness is reduced to indifference. . . . With a severity similar to Kant's, and which has its source in the same puritan tradition, Sade conceives the free act only as an act free of all feeling. If it were to obey emotional motives, it would make us Nature's slaves again and not autonomous subjects" (Beauvoir 72). Similar to Beauvoir's reading of the Sadean act, the acts of our heirs to Sade, our intellectual and philosophizing serial killers, are represented as seeking to strengthen the distinction between the ideal and the material, and they are celebrated as such. Their violence acts *against* the material, not in its name. It is violence which seeks to negate all that is considered impure, a violence, in other words, involving the destruction of "the feminine." It is depicted as the fulfillment of the dream of indifference, of the murder of a sex.

In addition to transcendence, another (related) characteristic of the serial killer which justifies giving them the masculine role is their putative desire for control, "sexual" or otherwise. "These people are the most controlled people you can imagine," says Park Dietz (*Newsweek*, 5 August 1991: 41). That we empower the serial killer may be due to the entrenched view of what power *is*, and while we associate many qualities with power, it is generally synonymous with the control of people, of our environment, and our lives. It is central to our definition of ourselves as sane, conscious beings. Control is the central factor in the judgment of legal sanity: Dietz, witness for the prosecution in the Dahmer trial, pointed to "Dahmer's capacity to exert control as an indicator of his sanity and premeditation" (Norris 1992, 9–10).[5] George Palermo, also giving expert witness at the trial, denied that Dahmer was psychotic or legally insane and suggested that Dahmer was an organized, nonsocial, lust murderer . . . [who was] driven by obsessive fantasies of power over others" (quoted in Schwartz 207). The court, emphasizing the *con* in control, finds Dahmer sane after he is

---

5. With Dahmer and his defense admitting he knew "right from wrong," the question of premeditation was the main factor under consideration in his insanity trial.

shown to be "a coldly calculating monster" (*Washington Post*, 31 January 92: A3), one who demonstrated "cold-blooded planning for sexual satisfaction" as Michael McCann, prosecuting attorney, described it (*ABC World News*, 15 February 1992). The court's verdict is contrary to the reasoning of a family member of one of Dahmer's victims—"This is how you act when you are out of control" (*Maury Povich*, 28 September 1992)—and to the opinion of Brian Masters, who argues that "one may make sane sequential moves towards an insane and inconsequential purpose" (205). With regard to sanity, the law is unconcerned with *what* one wants to do, only with whether one is responsible for what one does. Rejecting the idea that "hypervigilant premeditation is actually an integral part of the insanity" (author's italics; Norris 1992, 278), it neither questions the desire to be in control, nor questions the sanity of that desire.

When the trial is over and we hear Dahmer on *Dateline NBC* explain that he needed to live in a world in which "[he] could completely control a person—a person that [he] found physically attractive, and keep them with [him] as long as possible" (cited in *People Weekly*, 12 December 1994), we find it difficult to estrange his words from a world in which love is confused with possession. Masters notes that while Dahmer has "been consistent in admitting that control was his aim, he has never said that he enjoyed the act of killing, and the image with which he has left us is that of a lover choking his unconscious mate before wrapping him in his arms" (Masters 1993, 200). Regarding his victim's bodies as "mementos of conquest," as Dvorchak and Holewa put it, and literalizing the normative idea of love as conquest, Dahmer puts into practice the sexual politics of our shared, sane world.

Of the FBI's two categories of serial killers, "organized" and "disorganized," it is the positive category that has come to mean the "true" serial killer, the one inspiring the most interest. What makes the construction remarkable—what separates it from the descriptions of society's monsters offered by discourses previously in power—is its lack of estrangement: the serial killer is a sane, sober adult doing what he wants to do, in control of his actions. For our self-controlled serial killer, it is the desire for ultimate control over others which propels him towards another killing. For the serial killer, like a premodern caught up in a postmodern world, murder is closure without final closure, an ending which signals the end by directing him to new beginnings. His desire can never be fully satisfied; it apparently brings only the need to kill again in order to gain another fleeting sense of control.

Characteristic of our monsters and of our selves, control is something which assumes a neutral, unquestionable quality, assumes the aura of reality, something the victims of that control—those who are subsequently figured as without power—are denied. In Dahmer's trial, the denial of his victims' reality is performed by psychiatrists called to give expert testimony, whose discourse replicates rather than merely describes Dahmer's putative objectification of his victims:

> The killing was the unintended consequence of the drilling . . .
> The taking-of-life issue . . .
> Dismembering was a disposal problem . . .
> The drugging [was done] to satisfy his sexual need for a not-fully co-operative partner . . .
> Death was an unintended by-product of his efforts to create a zombie . . .
> The drilling enterprise . . . was not sadistic . . . it was a realistic attempt to disable, but not to kill . . .
> The disemboweling . . . [was] the most efficient way of handling all the remains, which only served an administration . . . (quoted in Ullman 28)

While Dahmer remains silent, his legal sanity, his power of self-control, is articulated by this sanitized language, this language of laudable self-control.

Control of the self evidently necessitates erasure of the other, and in stories of serial killers, the other is often the victim. The sister of Richard Guerrero, one of Dahmer's victims, notes that "[people] just have the impression that all these boys were gay and they came from dysfunctional families, [that] they were no good to society" (*Maury Povich*, 4 February 1992). As she suggests, when we hear about a victim we may be guilty of jumping to conclusions about his or her identity, of readily constructing victimhood out of those structures considered as weakening society. And we consider those structures weak because we position them opposite masculinity (the passive homosexual, the fatherless family) and associate them with being out of control (the promiscuous homosexual, giving in to sexual desires; the dysfunctional family, unable to operate).

In Dahmer's case, as I have suggested, erasure of the other is clearly represented in terms of gender. We see Dahmer seeking to maintain and control his "masculine" self, constructing and then seeking to erase a "female" other. And the Dahmer we then see is someone radically selfish, lost in his own world, in possession of a self with no other and therefore no meaning, someone who has destroyed his sense of difference and consequently destroyed his own sense of self. Literature offers numerous examples of violent loners who take radical individualism to its logical conclusion and who, in rejecting society and difference, can only turn on themselves. According to Jane Gallop, for

Bataille, "The sovereignty of Sade's character's marks them for a course leading to the 'definitive silence' (a solitary rigor, unmediated self-destruction, an heroic code)." (Gallop 24). In our books and movies the deaths of such characters represent a release from a troubled and often violent relationship with society and its laws, a release to omnipotence.

In the stories we tell of such characters and of those framed as their real-life counterparts, power (in terms of a freedom gained by the erasure of the other) and meaninglessness go together. For Hegel, "The sole and only work and deed accomplished by universal freedom is . . . death—a death that achieves nothing, embraces nothing within its grasp. . . . It is thus the most coldblooded and meaningless death of all, with no more significance than cleaving a head of cabbage or swallowing a draught of water" (from *Phenomenology of Mind*, quoted in Gallop 38). And for Jack Henry Abbot, the apparent freedom gained from a total escape from difference is similarly death, death for the other *and* for the self. He notes that solitary confinement leads to pure abstraction, that every stage in the confinement process removes the prisoner "from experience and narrows it down to only the experience of himself" (Abbot 50): "The *concept* of death is simple: it is when a living thing no longer entertains experience. . . . So when a man is taken farther away from experience, he is being taken to his death" (51). In the prison world described by Abbot, a world structured by competitive masculinity, the ultimate power—possessed by the state—is the power to enforce another to pursue to its end the narrative of masculinity.

Stephen Heath has argued that, given the cultural context of patriarchy, any act which fails to take difference into account, which seeks the certainty of its oneness, is implicitly gendered as masculine. Although Jacques Lacan is so often concerned with sexual difference, there is, says Heath, an assuredness, an indifference to the person he might be addressing, and it is this indifference which is "finally masculine, not because of some conception of theory as male but because in the last resort any discourse which fails to take account of the problem of sexual difference in its enunciation and address will be, within a patriarchal order, precisely indifferent, a reflection of male domination. It might be added, moreover . . . that where a discourse appeals directly to an image, to an immediacy of seeing, as a point of its argument or demonstration, one can be sure that all difference is being elided, that unity of some accepted vision is being reproduced" (Heath 1978, 55). Serial killer Charles Starkweather offers his own version of the "elision of difference": "Dead people are all on the same level" (quoted in Leyton 295). The elision of difference is a characteristic of the "psychopath," that mostly male phenomenon who has "one of the most perplexing of emotional defects, the apparent incapacity to feel compassion or the pangs of conscience" (*New York Times*, 7 July 1987: C1). And then there are all those other performers of so-called perplexing or meaningless acts. Jack Levin says, "We're seeing more people spraying bullets into crowds, innocent victims being targeted, all kinds of incredibly gross, heinous acts of homicide being committed as an end in itself, for the pleasure of it" (on *Geraldo*, 4 December 1991). Instead of describing the "pleasure" of killing people with whom one has no relation as an end "in itself," perhaps we should begin to demystify such pleasure by talking of an end in *his* self. As Heath suggests, in the context of patriarchy, indifference can be equated with masculinity. And because our meanings rely on difference, indifference assumes the mystique of meaninglessness. In the context of patriarchy, the perpetrator of unspeakable meaninglessness is also the expresser of masculinity taken to its logical extreme; his "inexplicable" behavior is masculinity's logical conclusion. He signifies the unspoken and unspeakable essence of patriarchal discourse.

In the preceding chapters I have suggested that the serial killer's meaninglessness has a familiar meaning, that his *insignificance* is a sign for something. In the context of the asymmetrical relation of masculine and feminine, so naturalized and often valorized that the destruction of women or the idea of woman is sufficient to invoke and celebrate the full presence of the male self, it is meaning which we give to the term *masculinity*. But it is also meaning which we give to the term *fascism*, or at least that which "waged an implacable war against anything tending to divide or differentiate, or which stood for diversity or pluralism" (Sternhell 347)—or that which stands for inexplicable instinct over ephemeral explication, the action of the transcendent few who will undertake the "reconquest." It is the meaning arrived at by "the total man in the total society, with no clashes, no prostration, no anarchy" (Marcel Deat in Sternhell 347)—in other words, that total society with no other: all manifestations of other having been destroyed. But if we are to attempt to disrupt the procedures by which we empower, perhaps it is better not to search for a single name, a defining origin. Perhaps we should instead regard the meaning of the serial killer's power as dependent upon a network of meaning and be always alert to and suspicious of constructions of meaninglessness. The "mindless," "meaningless," and "motiveless" acts of the serial killer are the acts of a figure who is also represented as achieving "ultimate" selfhood: a state without difference, a state defined as the dead end of a continuum of behavior which we in the twentieth century have experienced to horrifying degrees. For the most part history tells us that, just as attempts to control the text end in the figurative death of the text and of the reader, the desire to control the world by distancing oneself from it, by fixing it in time and place, ends in self-destruction, tells us that the erasure of difference brings an end to a sense of self. In the spectacle of the serial killer and of his capture and punishment, in the stories we write for him, those reproducing fantasies of misogynistic male culture, such a conclusion may variously assume the meaning of heroic sacrifice, of celebration, of a sacred rite of passage.

Conclusion

Following the discovery that Dahmer had illicitly joined his High
School Honors group for their yearbook photograph, his image was
blocked out with a marker pen before publication. That empty space
among smiling, well-groomed students is one which we have been
particularly keen to fill. Sometimes the blackness, the darkness, the
void within the ordinary is transformed into the distinctly unordinary.
We can imply and sometimes explicitly state that Dahmer did what he
did because that's what homosexuals are supposed to do. We can suggest that he did what he did because that's what people from dysfunctional families are supposed to do. But Dahmer, we are also told,
comes from a traditional, white, middle-class family, and any attempt
to block him out from normality usually proves unsuccessful. The
space becomes one *contextualized* by ordinariness, its mystery framed
by normality. Earlier in this study I talked of the ways we attempt nevertheless to protect that normality. Thus we read former FBI agent Robert Ressler remarking that "Jeffrey Dahmer falls into the subcategory of
the sadistic, sexually oriented serial killer who is inevitably a white
male loner" (*Newsweek*, 12 August 1991: 28), and instead of examining
what "maleness" or "whiteness" or "the loner" means in our culture,
we turn away, are content in our dumbfoundedness, and attempt to
close the interrogation with "but there are no real theories as to why
that is so." I later suggested, however, that we sometimes peer a little
more knowingly into that space and, off our guard, allow the unordinary to trickle into the ordinary. And sometimes we allow the space
and indeed the ordinariness that it touches to be invested with the
power of the unspeakable.

The connection between unspeakableness and power is one expressed by Nietzsche's Zarathustra: "You would do better to say: 'Unutterable and nameless is that which torments and delights my soul
and is also the hunger of my belly.' Let your virtue be too exalted for the

familiarity of names" (Nietzsche 1977, 63). We make this connection repeatedly in our serial killer stories. In chapter 10 I suggested that the serial killer's empowerment proceeds in part from our readiness to construct him as a symbol of the unspeakableness lying at the heart of masculinity, as a symbol, that is, of masculinity's mystical essence. At the same time as we reassure ourselves that the serial killer's acts "just happen," like bolts from the blue, we confer an authority on him by figuring his acts as natural, as acts which simply occur, that require no words to justify or explain them. He signifies the possibility of motivelessness that lies within our writing, the mystical and frightening possibility of the writing to which we are accustomed (the possibility that is essential to narrative: the gap, the space, the silence into which narrative propels itself, only to create more gaps, spaces, and silences). He becomes the conductor of an irreducible force of violent nature.

As a mystical essence of particular forms of familiar discourse, as unspeakable (that which cannot be spoken for fear of deconstructing that discourse), the serial killer is constructed by discourses whose involvement in that construction is shrouded in mystery. Patriarchal discourse cannot articulate fully his unspeakableness without beginning to unravel. His crimes are associated with the *breaking down* of valued social structures—the family, patriarchy—not with them. Like all essences, he can never be fully known through or as discourse. As an essence he must be protected: he is unspeakable and must remain so. As a result, our representation of the serial killer is repetitive: in an age which fervently demands explanation, the denial of explanation requires us to ask again and again. The repetitiveness of his representation echoes the repetitiveness of his performance. In the same way as the apparent randomness and motivelessness of his crimes make him largely undetectable, he evades capture by familiar language. Our *powers* of representation fail us. The construction of the serial killer is one which cannot be *controlled;* consequently, he is figured as more powerful than those powers of representation, than those who attempt to represent him.

J. Gerald Kennedy sees Poe as anticipating the ascendency of death as a metaphysical presence in the twentieth century, and identifies Saul Bellow's Herzog as a witness to that ascendency. "What is the philosophy of this generation? Not God is dead, that point was passed long ago. Perhaps it should be stated Death is God" (Bellow 353), says Herzog. One of Herzog's struggles, Kennedy reminds us, is to come to terms with the Holocaust's "impact on contemporary 'metaphysics' ": Herzog worries "that the sheer volume of modern death, especially in the form of genocidal projects, has stripped individual existence of dignity and meaning" and that "through this debasement of life, death has become an insatiable deity against whose ravages religion and ethics seem impotent." For Herzog, says Kennedy, "amid the contending beliefs and ideologies which define the horizon of philosophical relativism—that is, the locus of metaphysical uncertainty—death looms as an ineluctable presence, a virtual god" (Kennedy 178). A vital element of Poe's Gothic form was what Poe called this "universe of Vacancy," and the effect of the consequential uncertain status of words on writing. But in the twentieth century, as Bellow traces, that which potentially unsettles metaphysics has been turned into something of a metaphysical presence itself, a maneuver indicative of the seemingly ineluctable desire on the part of collective culture for the notion of metaphysical presence, whatever its identity.

The serial killer satisfies that ineluctable desire. He answers in the affirmative to Nietzsche's madman who, after proclaiming the death of God, asks, "Is not the greatness of [God's murder] too great for us? Must not we ourselves become gods simply to seem worthy of it?" (Nietzsche 1974, 125). The serial killer can also be seen as Foucault's fifteenth-century lunatic, he who scornfully contemplates "that nothing which is existence itself," he who "laughs with the laugh of death" (Foucault 1988, 15), who disarms death by his production of the macabre. In a culture in which death is taboo, he is the embodiment of that sacredness, that unspoken power. He is the contemporary bringer of meaningless death, an earthly Grim Reaper who strips existence of dignity and meaning. He is, as Dahmer said about himself in court, the creator of a holocaust. The serial killer, though potentially the great unsettler of metaphysical truth, is turned into the embodiment of a kind of truth, the truth of death.

Figured as extratextual, our manifestations of evil assume the aura of a deathly silence. The quiet ones are always the worst. Our silences resound deafeningly with the silences of the serial killers we find most scary. The screaming Mansons we can deal with. It's those who seem to do their business without a word whom we invest with the most authority. In a society which equates silences with closets, our unspeaking, unspeakable serial killers signify closets of mainstream culture. Their unspeakableness, literalizing everyday metaphors of aggression and domination, speaks of the violence, the misogyny concealed within benignity. The serial killer turns those closets inside out. As a potential destroyer of reassuring, benign meaning, his unspeakableness is either silenced or voiced, depending on one's relation to the safety of the middle, the "specious good."

For Wilson and Seaman, "Supreme power places one above the 'rat-race' " (226). We define power in terms of being "above"—above chaos, above shapelessness, above "low life," and often above that "specious good." Invariably, we define the powerful as such by referring to their ability to distance themselves and to objectify. We see them in the same way we see, or used to see, the artist: the artifacts of the powerful being the powerless. Eric Fromm's *Sane Society* exemplifies normative ways of figuring power as the ability to create, and creativity as the possession of power: "[Man] is driven by the urge to transcend the role of the creature, the accidentalness and passivity of his existence, by becoming a 'creator.' . . . In the act of creation man transcends himself as a creature . . . into the realm of purposefulness and freedom. In man's need for transcendence lies one of the roots for love, as well as for art, religion and material production. . . . There is another answer to this need for transcendence: if I cannot create life, I can destroy it. To destroy life makes me also transcend it. Indeed, that man can destroy life is just as miraculous a fear as that he can create it" (Fromm 37). For Sade, the suggestion that creativity and destruction are mutually interdependent is demonstrated by nature: "Who doubts that murder is one of nature's most precious laws? What is her purpose in creation? Is it not to see her work destroyed soon after? If destruction is one of nature's laws, the person who destroys is simply obeying her!" (quoted in Cameron and Frazer 57). The notions that power means transcendence and transcendence means power inform the mythology of the serial killer, that doyen of the art of crime. For Brian Masters, "the creative isolation of the artist" makes him the "antithetical twin of the murderer" (Masters 1993, 41), and for Wilson and Seaman, the ability to transcend social reality, to exist in a fantasy world, is a characteristic of serial killers and artists alike: "It is difficult to avoid the conclusion that what turned [Albert Fish, the "Brooklyn Vampire"] into a dangerous pervert was precisely the same tendency to morbid brooding and fantasy that turned Edgar Allen Poe into a writer of genius" (Wilson and Seaman 176). The serial killer, we hear, destroys to create. Like Franco Moretti's description of Dracula and of Frankenstein's monster as "dynamic, totalizing monsters . . . [who] . . . threaten to live forever, and to conquer the world" (Moretti 84–85) we represent our monsters, our serial killers, as supreme totalizers, consuming (sometimes literally) in order to rejuvenate themselves.

It may sound strange to talk about art at such a time, but then perhaps not according to Jeffrey Dahmer, who, "reducing what was once a vital living person to a piece of sculpture" (Norris 1992, 32–33), paints a victim's skull gold and places it atop the victim's hands, "cupped with the palms up" (32), and then photographs the result, and perhaps not to the magazine, *Art and Antiques,* which reports that "after a Wisconsin judge ruled that the estate of serial killer Jeffrey Dahmer (knives, a drill, a handsaw, a sponge, records, tapes, etc.) could be sold to raise money for his victims' families, queries poured into lawyer Robert Steuer, receiver of the estate" (Summer 1996: 18). As we naturalize the idea that power and creativity can imply deathly transcendence, Dennis Nilsen demonstrates the reversibility of that notion—that victimization can be art: "I just sat there and watched him. He looked really beautiful like one of those Michaelangelo sculptures. It seemed that for the first time in his life he was really feeling and looking the best he ever did in his whole life," he says of his last victim, Stephen Sinclair (Masters 1991, 267). "I remember being thrilled that I had full control and ownership of this beautiful body" (267), he says of another. For Nilsen, the art of crime is the appreciation of the sublime: "I think that in some cases I killed these men in order to create the best image of them. . . . It was not really a bad but a perfect and peaceful state for them to be in" (267). Fromm's universal man of creativity has, of course, a particular history, and Nilsen's comments can make one cry out that creativity need not presuppose objectification, idealization, a transcendence of the object created, that it need not suggest a dichotomy between the creator and the created, between the live artist and the dead object. We may be tempted to prescribe a dose of postmodernism, at least the postmodernism which sees creativity less as the demonstration of power and more as a mutual exchange between artist and artifact. But then Tania Modleski reminds us that Lyotard "insists that postmodernism is an 'aesthetic of the sublime,' " that the sublime has often struck commentators (she gives Kant as an example) as potentially terrifying, and that "there is certain evidence to suggest that the converse . . . has some truth as well, since a film like *The Texas Chainsaw Massacre* . . . strikes a critic like Robin Wood as sublime or at least as 'authentic art' " (Modleski 162).

There is always another postmodernism. As a figure representing the powers of deconstruction, the serial killer can find himself adjacent to particular postmodernist heroes, heroes of a postmodernism which locates itself in opposition to what Barthes calls the "regime of meaning," proclaims itself in the manner of Lyotard as adversarial to the harmony and comfort of bourgeois society. Arguing that many examples of the contemporary horror film "are engaged in an unprecedented assault on all that bourgeois culture is supposed to cherish— like the ideological apparatuses of the family and the school" (158), Modleski notes that "a few of the films, like *The Texas Chainsaw Massacre*, have actually been celebrated for their adversarial relation to contemporary culture and society" (158). "Just as the individual and the family are *dis*-membered in the most gruesomely literal ways in many of these films," she says, "so the novelistic as family romance is also in the process of being dismantled" (160). The means with which the dismantling takes place include open-endedness, "to allow for the possibility of countless sequels," a delight in "thwarting the audience's expectations of closure," and a tendency to "dispense with or drastically minimize the plot and character development that is thought to be essential to the construction of the novelistic" (160–161). The well-known "story" of the serial killer—all repetition and no plot, endings which only signal new beginnings, shadowy and undeveloped villains and victims—corresponds with, and is sometimes being told by, the horror movies Modleski describes. It is the story of a grand transgression. And sometimes it seems to ask, along with Nietzsche, "Whither does this mighty longing draw us, this longing that is worth more to us than any pleasure?" (Nietzsche 1910, 575).

The grandest transgression of all is perhaps that which makes us forget what it was that was transgressed. For Maurice Blanchot, "the disaster" is that which "seems to say to us: there is not, to begin with, law, prohibition, and then transgression, but rather there is transgression in the absence of any prohibition, which eventually freezes into Law, the Principle of Meaning" (Blanchot 75). How do we write "about" forms of monstrousness which appear not merely to transgress but seem to negate or make meaningless the oppositions law/transgression, meaning/meaningless? Perhaps Capote makes an attempt; he writes a book whose tension might be said to arise from its constant potential for what Blanchot calls "disaster," for that which "ruins books and wrecks language" (Smock, quoted in Blanchot ix). The monstrousness of our monsters is their wrecking of familiar language. Our serial killer is he who de-scribes, defies the logic of explanation, frustrates the desire for narrative by *just happening*, by entering randomly the stories of our lives, breaking their flow, bringing premature closure. While narrative anticipates closure, our serial killer is the bringer of random closure. Evading narrative representations, the meaning of the serial killer's acts comes from their repetition, not their place in a narrative. Sometimes we attempt to regain control of the figure, to reassure ourselves, by placing it as the conclusion to a story of evil or of child abuse. But mostly this representation seems to disrupt itself (or the serial killer, in the manner of Lecter, will directly ridicule such attempts to explain him, will enjoy evading attempts at representational capture), and then we see him simply doing what he wants to do with no reference to time or place, no reference to the structures of meaning with which we are accustomed to evaluate ourselves, no regard for the principles upon which we believe our language and our lives are founded.

Whether we attempt to preserve the "middle" by constructing the idea of the serial killer's unspeakableness, or whether his unspeakableness, his ability to silence familiar discourse, is celebrated (as an antibourgeois gesture), his unspeakableness represents power: the power of the suppressed, exotic, mystical other on the one hand, and the power of the rebel, the transgressor, he who manages to express his individuality in the face of sanitized, harmonious, mass culture on the other. And, as I suggested in the last chapter, that power and its opposite are gendered: thrill-seeking ("masculine") individuals are different from the pleasure-seeking ("feminine") masses, and according to the the *Oxford English Dictionary,* as Lionel Trilling reminds us in "The Fate of Pleasure," "pleasure in the pejorative sense is sometimes personified as a female deity" (Trilling 168).

Constructed with reference to various familiar genres of fiction and cultural paradigms, the serial killer is a continuation of the male heroes and antiheroes of, say, the Western, of the road movie, of the Gothic, of chivalry. A common theme in all the various manifestations is that of radical selfhood. Mark Seltzer has commented on the possible connection between ideas of maleness and the logic of selfhood in relation to the serial killer's motivation. Referring to the idea that there might be an "urgent transformation of the egoistic into the erotic—the instant translation of the uncertain difference between self and other into the 'basic' difference between male and female" (Seltzer 96), Seltzer suggests that the value of the idea is to "intimate the violence that proceeds from the subject's logic of singularity" (97). He also quotes Leo Bersani on the violent sexualization of the egoistic: "The sacrosanct value of selfhood [appears as] a value that accounts for human beings' extraordinary willingness to kill in order to protect the seriousness of their statements" (Bersani 222; quoted in Seltzer 97). We might make use of Seltzer's and Bersani's comments in the context of cultural criticism by seeking the wording of those "statements." In America, I suggest, the wording is especially vociferous in its sanctioning of violence to protect the self, and especially the male self. When we construct the serial killer as the latest hero/antihero (the distinction, in this case, being noticeably vague) in the tradition of the male loner *on a quest,* the quest is one whose wording might be ambiguous, but whose effect is invariably violence against the "unmale other."

How to dispel the fear, the mystery, the fetishization of the power which we ascribe to the serial killer? How best to avoid conferring upon him the power of the unspeakable? In part 1 I described the policing discourses which seek closure, which thrive on cause and effect, on sequence, clues, and the tying up of loose ends. Those discourses anticipate capture (of the criminal and of his image, that is, a representation which fixes the origins of the criminal and his crime). For such a discourse, closure can only be an illusion: there are always other crimes to solve, and as Barthes reminds us, the discourse which purports to be wholly instrumental is a "stubbornly polysemant space" (Barthes 1988, 147). To such discourses the serial killer is a powerful symbol of evasion. He represents unattainable closure; his capture means the end of untidily polysemous language. He functions as the unattainable dream of our language of totality, of authority. Perhaps we can begin to demystify him by representing him in a way which does not seek his representational capture, which does not figure him as something that *can* be captured, that is, as something different from his captors. Perhaps we write too much "about" the serial killer, and not enough in a manner which demonstrates that the figure is inseparable from the language with which it is constructed. Perhaps to write without implicit reference to a world beyond, without assuming the opposition within/ without, without assuming the reality of closure, of purity, is to dispense with the fetishization of all that is extratextual, to dispense with the notion that language is a medium of power, the idea that all that *cannot* be controlled is intrinsically powerful. Perhaps we should attempt to disorient our absolutes, to write "disastrously."

What this might mean in our everyday lives is an attempt to denaturalize the existence of power. In his preface to Deleuze and Guatarri's *Anti-Oedipus*, Foucault describes "the fascism in all of us, in our heads and in our every behavior, the fascism that causes us to love power, to desire the very thing that dominates and exploits us" (in Deleuze and Guattari 10). Even after questioning our definition of power, after foregrounding, for example, our equation of masculinity with power, there is still another more firmly fixed idea to estrange: the assumption of the existence of power itself, of power's eternal and natural presence, of its "truth."

Where do we look to find the origins of power, of its naturalness? In much of our representation of Dahmer, that which sets up a binary between him and the rest of society, that which figures the latter as the innocent victim of the former, power is located within the individual. We take this idea, rightly or wrongly, from Nietzsche. R. J. Hollingdale, in his explication of *Thus Spoke Zarathustra*, says, "What determines the nature of 'truth'? The nature of the I which asserts '*I* am the truth.' *Why* truth, and not rather untruth or indifference to truth? Because each particular life and being needs a fortress within which to preserve and protect itself and from which to reach out in search of aggrandizement and more power, and truth is this fortress" (in Nietzsche 1977, 26). Hollingdale's reading of Nietzsche's vision of identity—that is, as something whose expression depends on gaining power, which itself depends on the existence of truth—corresponds with widely held notions that the need for power is intrinsic to the idea of self. We talk of the nature of our selves, of essence, that which is essential to personal empowerment, that which is the truth from which the power of the individual proceeds. One way that the naturalness of power is expressed is by the binary I have sought to question in this book: the truth of the individual as distinct from society, of society opposed to the individual. And with our insistence on framing all that we see in terms of power and hierarchy, we perceive crime in one of two ways. Generally, society is perceived as the victim of individuals (an idea which, as I have suggested, can result in the empowerment of those individuals). Any questioning of this idea is translated as promoting the contrary idea that criminals are "victims of society" (an idea which ascribes power to society and powerlessness to the individual). To denaturalize the idea of power is to unsettle this misleading binary.

Foucault says "power in the substantive sense, *le pouvoir*, doesn't exist. What I mean is this. The idea that there is either located at—or emanating from—a given point something which is a 'power' seems to me to be based on a misguided analysis. . . . In reality power means relations, a more-or-less organized, hierarchical, co-ordinated cluster of relations" (Foucault 1980, 198). But even Foucauldians are sometimes guilty of mythologizing power by assuming its presence to be inevitable. The editors of *Feminism and Foucault*, Irene Diamond and Lee Quinby, warn against the often indiscernible presence of power in sexual relations and suggest that "perhaps the most obvious example of . . . feminist involvement [in the deployment of sexuality] is the assumption that sexuality exists outside of and untainted by power. To claim, as [Linda] Gordon and [Allen] Hunter have, for instance, that 'we can be in principle unequivocally pro-sex because sex itself is a human activity that has its own worth and which can be separated from those oppressive power relations that invade it' is to ignore both the historicity of sexuality and the interplay between power and sexuality" (Diamond and Quinby 198). To say, as Gordon and Hunter do, that sex *can* exist without power is not the same as saying that it does exist or has existed without it, nor is it the same as saying it can exist without reference to culture or history. Gordon and Hunter's "assumption," if that's what it is, is matched by Diamond and Quinby's assumption of "the interplay between power and sexuality."

Of course Eve Sedgwick is correct in reminding us that figuring nature as an illusion does not mean that the power structures it engenders will instantaneously disappear: "I remember the buoyant enthusiasm with which feminist scholars used to greet the finding that one or another brutal form of oppression was not biological but 'only' cultural! I have often wondered what the basis was for our optimism about the malleability of culture by any one group or program" (Sedgwick 1990, 41). The assumption of power's existence—expressed, per-haps, by our obsession with conspiracy theories—is so great that power still lingers, is still *experienced* in a substantive sense long after the sets of hierarchical relations have theoretically fallen. But perhaps the unmalleability of culture is related to our not going far enough; while we attempt to estrange forms of masculinity or patriarchy, for instance, we fail to estrange the idea of power itself, and as power relations fall, we allow others to take their place. Is it not possible to imagine sex and culture without power? Is it possible to perceive the form power takes today as something other than the sublimated form of primitive drives? Would not our futures be more hopeful if we dis-pensed with the idea of sublimation?

Presumably among those replying in the negative would be Pat Califia, proponent of sadomasochism. Diamond and Quinby quote her as recalling "a private world of dominance, submission, punish-ment and pain . . . [since] . . . the age of two." Califia is implying, they say, that "people are born into sadomasochism" (Diamond and Quinby 200), that power, in other words, is natural and therefore good. To prescribe the desexualizing of violence as a means of laying bare the naturalized power relations in our culture is to run headlong into critical debate over issues surrounding sadomasochism, debate which has value here for bringing into focus the dramatic interplay of concepts such as "power," "selfhood," "nature," and "society." Resist-ing arguments made by proponents of sadomasochism that it is a consensual activity, Diamond and Quinby note that "given the current mechanisms of normalization in our society, sexual consent is often a function of disciplinary power, and the highly ritualized directives for engaging in sadomasochistic practices testify to just how prescriptive these activities are" (200). On the other hand, Eve Sedgwick asks whether the sexual drama of sadomasochism may actually "stand in some more oblique, or even oppositional, relation to [a woman's] rela-tion to her political experience of oppression" (Sedgwick 1985, 6). While Diamond's and Quinby's remarks perhaps deny subjecthood to sadomasochists, implying that they don't know what they're doing, that they are playing someone or something else's ("power's"?) game and not their own, Sedgwick's suggestion assumes an ability to differ-entiate between the drama of sadomasochism and the reality of politi-cal oppression. The ability to destabilize or critique that reality is ham-pered when the drama and the reality fuse, when play and nonplay are blurred, when one's ability to give consent to play—play at dominat-ing or being subordinate, or playing at not playing—loses meaning. In an age in which fantasies of violent domination are seemingly realized with increasing frequency, the danger of becoming involved in someone else's masochistic "reality" increases. Critical gestures can be subsumed in a world in which power is fetishized, in which games of domination and submission are indistinguishable from the reality of violent domination.

In this study I have suggested that the myth of the serial killer is maintained with the help of fantasies that we ascribe to the serial killer being inextricably implicated in and interpenetrated by the dreams of "normal" society. I have suggested that it is a myth whose attraction lies in the power with which the figure of the serial killer is constructed, power whose meaning corresponds with seemingly benign powers which structures that "normal" society. The presence of the power of masculinity within both our constructions of the contemporary monster and of normality helps to explain why we find the idea of female serial killers strange, or perverse, or threatening.

Violence helps to shape the normal society in which our normal monsters live anonymously and, as Seltzer suggests, helps to demarcate our selves from our others. Richard Maxwell Brown suggests that part of America's distinctiveness is its ingenuity in connecting violence with achievement, with value: "By now it is evident that, historically, American life has been characterized by continuous and often intense violence. It is not merely that violence has accompanied such negative aspects of our history as criminal activity, political assassination, and racial conflict. On the contrary, violence has formed a seamless web with some of the most positive events of U.S. history. . . . The patriot, the humanitarian, the nationalist, the pioneer, the landholder, the farmer, and the laborer (and the capitalist) have used violence as a means to a higher end" (Brown [1], 40–41). If we are puzzled as to why serial killing seems to be such an *American* problem, perhaps we should consider America's willingness to believe unquestioningly that violence is a justifiable means to a "higher" end, especially when we live in an age in which representations of violence as a means to a higher end fail to define rigorously what a "higher" end might be, or in which the ends defined by dominant culture as "higher" turn out to be forms of empowerment at the expense of particular sections of society. Thrilled by watching the world through the eyes of our monsters, watching and enjoying movies like *Halloween* and *Friday the Thirteenth*, which "adopt the point of view of the slasher, placing the spectator in the position of an unseen nameless presence" (Modleski 161), we fail invariably to avoid sitting in judgment upon their victims, fail to avoid helping to naturalize victimhood, a victimhood gendered female.

This is a meaning of victimhood which our policing discourses do little to disrupt. The language we use to describe serial killers and their crimes, language sanctioned by state and social norms, naturalizes the existence of power and its masculine forms. Helping to locate the source of that power in eternity, in nature (beyond society), and giving policing an aura of priestly intervention, contemporary criminal monstrosity is constructed with reference to evil instead of insanity, and in a manner which negates notions of prevention or cure. Just as we begin to hear that imprisonment had changed Dahmer for the better, that he was truly contrite and had become a practicing Christian—just as we begin, in other words, to think about modifying parts of our story—he is bludgeoned to death, and the original story can reassert itself: Goodness has finally triumphed over Evil, the only true response to wickedness has been made. The sane but evil monster is constructed in a manner which assumes self to be the only form of reality, which justifies increased policing of the individual as opposed to the questioning of social norms and values. Helping to justify the individualization of crime (which leads to the mystification of links between "benign" social forms and the empowerment of the serial killer), the myth figures the detection of the crime as an individualized confrontation between cop and killer. As a figure of monstrosity, the serial killer is that which gives meaning to much of our policing discourse. In this respect, it is a figure of mystery; at the same time, however, signs of the serial killer are all around us. In the moment when our surveillance locates or constructs a serial killer, we encounter what amounts to pure spectacle, content without form, a figure shining with the brilliancy reserved for that which functions as an ultimate referent to the language of power.

The serial killer is a paradoxical figure: one who must not be fully represented and one who is made in our own image. The myth of the serial killer is one whose single meaning is unclear but which can serve us by validating particular ways of evaluating ourselves, of policing ourselves. It can serve to explain how and why our society is put together the way it is, to illustrate its preoccupations, anxieties, and fantasies. It is a myth which figures society as a battlefield and individuals as warriors, either victorious or defeated, either natural oppressors or natural victims. It is a myth in which victims are represented in contrast to the glamour, mystery, and power of those who brought their lives to an end.

Bibliography
Index

Bibliography

Abbot, Jack Henry. *In the Belly of the Beast*. New York: Vintage Books, 1991.

Altman, Dennis. *Homosexual Oppression and Liberation*. London: Allen Lane, 1974.

Altman, Dennis. *The Homosexualization of America, the Americanization of Homosexuality*. New York: St. Martin's Press, 1982.

Andreano, Ralph, and John Siegfried. *The Economics of Crime*. Cambridge, Mass.: Schenkman, 1980.

Arendt, Hannah. *Eichmann in Jerusalem*. New York: Penguin, 1963.

Arens, W. *The Man-Eating Myth*. Oxford: Oxford University Press, 1979.

Barthes, Roland. *The Pleasure of the Text*. Trans. Richard Miller. New York: Hill and Wang, 1975.

Barthes, Roland. *Selected Writings*. Ed. Susan Sontag. 1982.

Barthes, Roland. *Roland Barthes by Roland Barthes*. Trans. Richard Howard. London: Macmillan Press, 1988.

Baudrillard, Jean. "The Ecstasy of Communication." Trans. John Johnston. In *The Anti-Aesthetic: Essays on Postmodern Culture*, ed. Hal Foster. Port Townsend, Wash.: Bay Press, 1983.

Beattie, John. *The Yorkshire Ripper Story*. London: Quartet Books, 1981.

Beauvoir, Simone de. "Must We Burn Sade?" In *Selections from His Writings and a Study by Simone de Beauvoir*, Marquis de Sade. New York: Grove Press, 1953.

Bellah, Robert N., et al. *Habits of the Heart*. New York: Harper and Row, 1986.

Bellow, Saul. *Herzog*. New York: Fawcett Crest, 1970.

Benveniste, Emile. *Problems in General Linguistics*. Coral Gables, Fla.: University of Miami Press, 1971.

Bersani, Leo. "Is the Rectum a Grave?" *October* 43 (1989): 194–222.

Black, Joel. *The Aesthetics of Murder: A Study in Romantic Literature and Contemporary Culture*. Baltimore: John Hopkins University Press, 1991.

Blanchot, Maurice. *The Writing of the Disaster*. Trans. Ann Smock. London, Nebraska: University of Nebraska Press, 1986.

Box, Stephen. *Power, Crime, and Mystification*. New York: Tavistock Publications, 1983.

Bibliography

Brown, Richard Maxwell (1). "Historical Patterns of American Violence." In Graham and Gurr, eds. (1979, 19–48).

Brown, Richard Maxwell (2). "The American Vigilante Tradition." In Graham and Gurr, eds. (1979, 153–86).

Butler, Judith. *Gender Trouble: Feminism and the Subversion of Identity.* London: Routledge, 1990.

Cameron, Deborah, and Elizabeth Frazer. *The Lust to Kill: A Feminist Investigation of Sexual Murder.* New York: New York University Press, 1987.

Capote, Truman. *In Cold Blood: A True Account of Multiple Murder and its Consequences.* London: Hamish Hamilton, 1966.

Caputi, Jane. *The Age of Sex-Crime.* Bowling Green, Ohio: Bowling Green State University Popular Press, 1987.

Coe, R. *The Vision of Jean Genet.* London: Peter Owen, 1986.

Conrad, Joseph. *The Secret Agent.* Harmondsworth: Penguin, 1988.

Dahmer, Lionel. *A Father's Story.* New York: William Morrow, 1994.

Davis, Don. *The Milwaukee Murders.* New York: St. Martin's Press, 1991.

Davis, Murray S. *Smut: Erotic Reality/Obscene Ideology.* Chicago: University of Chicago Press, 1983.

Deleuze, Gilles. "Postscript on the Societies of Control." *October* 59 (1992): 3–7.

Deleuze, Gilles, and Felix Guattari. *Anti-Oedipus: Capitalism and Schizophrenia.* Preface by Michel Foucault. Introduction by Mark Seem. Trans. Robert Hurley, Mark Seem, and Helen R. Lane. New York: Viking, 1977.

Diamond, Irene, and Lee Quinby. "American Feminism and the Language of Control." In *Feminism and Foucault,* ed. Irene Diamond and Lee Quinby. Boston: Northeastern University Press, 1988: 193–206.

Diamond, John. "Roll Up for the Great Trial Show." *The Mail on Sunday* (magazine section), 12 April 1992: 42–46.

Dollimore, Jonathan. *Sexual Dissidence.* Oxford: Clarendon Press, 1991.

Douglas, Mary. *Purity and Danger.* London: Routledge, 1966.

Dvorchak, Robert J., and Lisa Holewa. *Milwaukee Massacre.* New York: Dell, 1991.

Edgar, David. "Seeing Isn't Believing." *The Sunday Times,* 22 August 1993. Section 9: 8–10.

Fasteau, Mark Feigen. *The Male Machine.* New York: McGraw-Hill, 1974.

Foucault, Michel. *The Order of Things: An Archaeology of the Human Sciences.* New York: Vintage Books, 1973.

Foucault, Michel. "About the Concept of the 'Dangerous Individual' in Nineteenth-Century Legal Psychiatry." Trans. Alain Baudot and Jane Couchman. *International Journal of the Law and Psychiatry* 1 (1978): 1–18.

Foucault, Michel. *Discipline and Punish.* Trans. Alan Sheridan. New York: Vintage Books, 1979.

Foucault, Michel. *Power/Knowledge: Selected Interviews and Other Writings, 1972–1977.* Ed. Colin Gordon. Brighton: Harvester, 1980.

Foucault, Michel. *Madness and Civilization: A History of Insanity in the Age of Reason.* Trans. Richard Howard. New York: Vintage Books, 1988.

Freud, Sigmund. "The Uncanny," in *Standard Edition of the Complete Psychological Works.* Trans. under the general editorship of James Strachey, in collabo-

Bibliography

ration with Anna Freud, assisted by Alex Strachey and Alan Tyson. Vol. 17. London: Hogarth Press, 1953a.

Freud, Sigmund. *Civilization and Its Discontents.* Trans. J. Riviere. London: Hogarth Press, 1953b.

Fromm, Erich. *The Sane Society.* New York: Rinehart, 1955.

Fuss, Diana. *Essentially Speaking.* London: Routledge, 1989.

Gallop, Jane. *Intersections: A Reading of Sade with Bataille, Blanchot, and Klossowski.* Lincoln and London, Nebraska: University of Nebraska Press, 1981.

Graham, Hugh Davis, and Ted Robert Gurr, eds. *Violence in America: Historical and Comparative Perspectives.* Preface by Milton S. Eisenhower. Beverly Hills and London: Sage Publications, 1979.

Graham, Kenneth, ed. *Gothic Fictions: Prohibition/Transgression.* New York: AMS Press, 1989.

Gross, Louis S. *Redefining the American Gothic.* Ann Arbor, Mich.: UMI Research Press, 1989.

Halberstam, Judith. "Skinflick: Posthuman Gender in Jonathan Demme's *The Silence of the Lambs.*" *Camera Obscura* 27 (Sept. 1991): 37–52.

Harris, Thomas. *Red Dragon.* New York: Dell, 1990.

Harris, Thomas. *The Silence of the Lambs.* London: Mandarin, 1991.

Hawkins, Harriet. "Maidens and Monsters in Modern Popular Culture." *Textual Practice* 7, no. 2 (1993) : 258–66.

Hazelwood, Robert D., and John E. Douglas. "The Lust Murderer." Federal Bureau of Investigation Law Enforcement Bulletin 49 (April 1980): 18–22.

Heath, Stephen. "Difference." *Screen* 19, no. 3 (1978): 51–112.

Heath, Stephen, and Gillian Skirrow, "An Interview with Raymond Williams." Modleski (1986): 3–18.

Hickey, Eric W. *Serial Murderers and Their Victims.* Pacific Grove, Calif. Brooks/Cole, 1991.

Holmes, R. M., and J. DeBurger. *Serial Murder.* Newbury Park, Calif.: Sage, 1988.

House of Representatives Hearings before a Subcommittee of the Committee on Government Operations. *The Federal Role in Investigation of Serial Violent Crime.* 99th Cong., 2nd sess. April 9 and May 21 1986.

Huyssen, Andreas. "Mass Culture as Woman: Modernism's Other." In *Studies in Entertainment,* ed. Tania Modleski. Bloomington and Indianapolis: Indiana University Press, 1986: 188–207.

Jefford, Andrew. "Dr. Jekyll and Professor Nabakov: Reading a Reading." In *Robert Louis Stevenson,* ed. Andrew Noble. London: Vision Press, 1983.

Jenkins, Philip. *Using Murder: The Social Construction of Serial Homicide.* New York: Aldine de Gruyter, 1994.

Jenkins, Philip. "Sharing Murder: Understanding Group Serial Homicide." *Journal of Crime and Justice* 13, no. 2 (1990): 125–47.

Kennedy, J. Gerald. *Poe, Death, and the Life of Writing.* New Haven, Conn.: Yale University Press, 1987.

Kernan, Alvin. *The Death of Literature.* New Haven and London: Yale University Press, 1990.

Lasch, Christopher. *The Culture of Narcissism.* New York: Norton, 1978.

Bibliography

Lesser, Wendy, *Pictures at an Execution*. Cambridge, Mass.: Harvard University Press, 1993.

Levin, Jack, and James Alan Fox. *Mass Murder: America's Growing Menace*. New York: Washington Mews Books, 1986.

Leyton, Elliott. *Compulsive Killers: The Story of Modern Multiple Murder*. New York: New York University Press, 1986.

Lynn, Kenneth. "Violence in American Literature and Folklore." In Graham and Gurr, eds. (1979, 19–48).

Lyotard, Jean-François. *The Postmodern Condition: A Report on Knowledge*. Trans. Geoff Bennington and Brian Massumi. Foreword by Frederic Jameson. Minneapolis: University of Minnesota Press, 1989.

Mailer, Norman. "The Homosexual Villain" and "Advertisement for 'The Homosexual Villain.'" In *Advertisements for Myself*. London: André Deutsch, 1961: 197–205.

Masters, Brian. "Dahmer's Inferno." *Vanity Fair* (November 1991): 183–269.

Masters, Brian. *The Shrine of Jeffrey Dahmer*. London: Coronet Books, 1993.

Mellen, Joan. *Big Bad Wolves: Masculinity in the American Film*. New York: Pantheon, 1979.

Meyrowitz, Joshua. *No Sense of Place: The Impact of the Electronic Media on Social Behavior*. New York: Oxford University Press, 1985.

Michaud, Stephen G. "The FBI's New Psyche Squad." *New York Times* (magazine section), 26 October 1986: 40.

Miller, D. A. *The Novel and the Police*. Berkeley, Calif.: University of California Press, 1988.

Modleski, Tania. "The Terror of Pleasure: The Contemporary Horror Film and Postmodern Theory." In *Studies in Entertainment*, ed. Modleski, Tania, Bloomington and Indianapolis: Indiana University Press, 1986: 155–66.

Moretti, Franco. *Signs Taken for Wonder: Essays in the Sociology of Literary Forms*. Trans. Susan Fischer, David Forgacs, and David Miller. London: Verso, 1983.

Morse, Margaret. "The Television News Personality and Credibility: Reflections on the News in Transition." In Modleski (1986, 55–79).

Nietzsche, Friedrich. *The Dawn of the Day*. Trans. Johanna Volz. London: T. F. Unwin, 1910.

Nietzsche, Friedrich. *Beyond Good and Evil*. Trans. Helen Zimmern. Introduction by Willard Huntington Wright. New York: Boni and Liveright, 1917.

Nietzsche, Friedrich. *On the Genealogy of Morals*. Trans. Walter Kaufman. New York: Random House, 1969.

Nietzsche, Friedrich. *The Gay Science*. Trans. Walter Kaufman. New York: Vintage Books, 1974.

Nietzsche, Friedrich. *Thus Spoke Zarathustra*. Trans. and introduction by R. J. Hollingdale. Harmondsworth: Penguin Books, 1977.

Nietzsche, Friedrich. *Twilight of the Idols* and *The Anti-Christ*. Trans., introduction, and commentary by R. J. Hollingdale. Harmondsworth: Penguin Books, 1988.

Norris, Joel. *Serial Killers: The Growing Menace*. New York: Doubleday, 1988.

Bibliography

Norris, Joel. *Jeffrey Dahmer*. New York: Pinnacle Books, 1992.

Pfohl, Stephen J. "Ethnomethodology and Criminology: The Social Production of Crime and the Criminal." In *The Mad, the Bad, and the Different*, eds. Israel L. Barak-Glantz, and C. Ronald Huffs. Lexington, Mass.: Lexington Books, 1981.

Porter, Bruce. "Mind Hunters." *Psychology Today* (April 1983): 44–52.

Postman, Neil. *Amusing Ourselves to Death*. New York: Viking, 1985.

Ressler, R. K., A. W. Burgess, and J. E. Douglas. *Sexual Homicide*. Lexington, Mass.: Lexington Books, 1988.

Richter, David. "Murder in Jest: Serial Killing in the Post-Modern Detective Story." *Journal of Narrative Technique* 19, no. 1 (1989): 106–15.

Sagan, Eli. *Cannibalism: Human Aggression and Cultural Form*. Foreword by Robert N. Bellah. New York: Harper and Row, 1974.

Sartre, Jean-Paul. *Being and Nothingness*. Trans. and introduction by Hazel E. Barnes. New York: Washington Swaure Press/Pocket Books, 1956.

Schwartz, Anne E. *The Man Who Could Not Kill Enough*. New York: Birch Lane Press, 1992.

Sears, Donald J. *To Kill Again: The Motivation and Development of Serial Murder*. Wilmington, Del.: A Scholarly Resources Imprint, 1991.

Sedgwick, Eve Kosofsky. *Between Men: English Literature and Male Homosocial Desire*. New York: Columbia University Press, 1985.

Sedgwick, Eve Kosofsky. *Epistemology of the Closet*. Berkeley, Calif.: University of California Press, 1990.

Seltzer, Mark. "Serial Killers (1)." *Differences* 5 (Spring 1993): 92–128.

Shelley, Mary. *Frankenstein*. Afterword by Harold Bloom. Harmondsworth: Signet Classic, Penguin, 1983.

Smith, Joan. "The Fear and the Fantasy." *The Guardian* (section 2), 18 June 1993: 2–3.

Stallybrass, Peter, and Allon White. *The Politics and Poetics of Transgression*. London: Methuen, 1986.

Sternhell, Zeev. "Fascist Ideology." In *Fascism: A Reader's Guide*, ed. Walter Laqueur. Berkeley, Calif.: University of California Press, 1976: 315–76.

Sworkin, Michael. "Faking It." In *Watching Television*, ed. Todd Gitlin. New York: Pantheon, 1987: 162–82.

Tanner, Tony. "Death in Kansas." In *Truman Capote's In Cold Blood: A Critical Handbook*, ed. Irving Malin. Belmont, Calif.: Wadsworth Publishing, 1968: 98–102.

Tavris, Carol. "America Is Still Shockable—Barely." *Los Angeles Times* (section B), 9 August 1991: 7.

Tharp, Julie. "The Transvestite as Monster." *Journal of Popular Film and Television* 19 (1991): 106–13.

Theweleit, Klaus. *Male Fantasies*. Vol. 1. *Women, Floods, Bodies, History*. Foreword by Barbara Ehrenreich. Trans. Stephen Conway in collaboration with Erica Carter and Chris Turner. Minneapolis: University of Minnesota Press, 1987. Vol. 2. *Male Bodies: Psychoanalyzing the White Terror*. Foreword by Jessica Benjamin and Anson Rabinbach. Trans. Erica Carter and Chris Turner in collaboration with Stephen Conway. Minneapolis: University of Minnesota Press, 1989.

Trilling, Lionel. "The Fate of Pleasure: Wordsworth to Dostoevsky." *Partisan Review* (Summer 1963): 167–191.

Tropp, Martin. *Images of Fear: How Horror Stories Helped Shape Modern Culture, 1818–1918.* Jefferson, N.C.: McFarland, 1990.

Ullman, Joan. " 'I carried it too far, that's for sure': A First-Person Report from the Insanity Trial of Jeffrey Dahmer." *Psychology Today* (May–June 1992): 28–31.

Van Leer, David. *The Queening of America.* London: Routledge, 1995.

Vernado, S. L. "The Idea of the Numinous in Gothic Literature." In *Literature of the Occult*, ed. Peter B. Messent. Englewood Cliffs, N.J.: Prentice-Hall, 1981; 51–66.

Weeks, Jeffrey. *Sex, Politics, and Society: The Regulation of Sexuality Since 1800.* London: Longman, 1981.

Wilson, Colin, and Donald Seaman. *The Serial Killers.* London: W. H. Allen, 1990.

Woodhull, Winifred. "Sexuality, Power, and the Question of Rape." In *Feminism and Foucault*, eds. Irene Diamond and Lee Quinby. Boston: Northeastern University Press, 1988: 167–77.

Young, Elizabeth. *"The Silence of the Lambs* and the Flaying of Feminist Theory." *Camera Obscura* 27 (September 1991): 5–35.

Yurick, Sol. "Sob-Sister Gothic." In *Truman Capote's* In Cold Blood: *A Critical Handbook*, ed. Irving Malin. Belmont, Calif.: Wadsworth Publishing, 1968: 76–81.

TELEVISION

To Kill and Kill Again. Directed by Patrick Fleming. Ottoman Television for Channel Four, 1992.

Aileen Wuornos: The Selling of a Serial Killer. Directed by Nick Broomfield. Lafayette Films for Channel Four. Strand Releasing, 1992.

Confessions of a Serial Killer. Twenty Twenty Television for Carlton Television, 1993.

Murder by Number Cable News Network, Inc., January 3 1993.

Geraldo. Investigative News Group, Inc.

The Maury Povich Show. Paramount, Inc.

The Oprah Winfrey Show. Harpo Productions, Inc.

Donahue. Multimedia Entertainment, Inc.

Crossfire. Cable News Network, Inc.

Larry King Live. Cable News Network, Inc.

Sonya Live. Cable News Network, Inc.

Nightline. American Broadcasting Companies, Inc.

Day One. American Broadcasting Companies, Inc.

Index

Index